S0-CFE-651

LIBRARY

Gift of

The Bush
Foundation

RESTORING THE IMAGE

Lincoln Studies in Religion & Society, 3

RESTORING
THE
IMAGE

ESSAYS ON RELIGION AND SOCIETY IN HONOUR OF DAVID MARTIN

edited by
Andrew Walker & Martyn Percy

www.SheffieldAcademicPress.com

Copyright © 2001 Sheffield Academic Press

Published by Sheffield Academic Press Ltd
Mansion House
19 Kingfield Road
Sheffield, S11 9AS
England

www.SheffieldAcademicPress.com

Printed on acid-free paper in Great Britain
by Antony Rowe Ltd,
Chippenham, Wiltshire

British Library Cataloguing-in-Publication Data

A catalogue record for this book is available
from the British Library

ISBN 1-84127-064-4

BL
60
.R484
2001

110101-396078

Contents

Foreword

Andrew Walker and Martyn Percy

This volume—the third in the Lincoln Studies in Religion and Society—takes the form of a festschrift.

The book is affectionately dedicated to Professor David Martin, a scholar with a national and international reputation in the field of the sociology of religion. The book is intended to mark his seventieth birthday, but all the contributors are really registering their appreciation for a scholar who has done more than most to shape an academic field for a generation and more.

David Martin's sociology of religion covers an enormous range of subjects and issues: secularization; South American Pentecostalism; religion in Eastern Europe; church–state relations; the state of the Church of England; and more besides. A significant number of his books have become seminal texts, and are still regarded as indispensable reading within their particular field. The authors in this volume are conscious of their own debt to David, not least for his friendship, encouragement and his desire to see the field and its proponents truly flourish.

David Martin's interest in and relationship with British churches has also meant that his sociology of religion has, at times, represented a new kind of practical theology. Scholars within the arena of ecclesiology, or commentators on the present state of the Church, will have trouble in studying and researching the field without reference to David's work. Correspondingly, his work has become widely known for its tenacity and depth in theological colleges and in parishes. Moreover, the tone of this work has been of a 'friendly/critical' type, generously offered, and never imposed.

Each of the authors in this volume has taken a different aspect of

David's work which he or she has personally found enriching or challenging. As Editors, we have followed the usual conventions of a Festschrift, and this book therefore represents a celebration and appraisal of a significant scholar and his output. It has been a privilege and a joy to put this work together, and in so doing we offer our thanks and appreciation to David Martin for all that he has given to sociology and theology.

List of Contributors

Editors

Andrew Walker is Professor of Theology, Religion and Culture in Education at King's College, University of London.

Martyn Percy is Director of the Lincoln Theological Institute for the Study of Religion and Society at the University of Sheffield.

Contributors

Steve Bruce has been Professor of Sociology at the University of Aberdeen since 1991.

Grace Davie is a Reader in the Sociology of Religion at the University of Exeter.

Christie Davies is Professor of Sociology at the University of Reading.

Karel Dobbelaere is Emeritus Professor of the Catholic University of Leuven, Belgium, and the University of Antwerp, where he taught Sociology, Sociology of Religion and Sociological Research.

David Docherty is Managing Director of Broadband at Telewest. Previously he worked at the BBC, where he was a member of the Board of Management, as Director of New Services and Deputy Director of Television.

Richard K. Fenn is Maxwell Upson Professor of Christianity and Society at Princeton Theological Seminary, New Jersey, USA.

Kieran Flanagan is a Reader in Sociology at the University of Bristol.

Paul Freston is Lecturer in Sociology at the Federal University of São Carlos, Brazil.

Robin Gill holds the Michael Ramsey Chair of Modern Theology at the University of Kent, Canterbury.

Graham Howes is Staff Fellow and Director of Studies in Social and Political Studies at Trinity Hall, Cambridge.

Bernice Martin is David Martin's wife. She is Emeritus Reader in Sociology at the University of London (Royal Holloway College).

Jessica Martin is Fellow and College Lecturer in English, Trinity College, Cambridge. She is also training for ordination.

Bryan Wilson FBA is Reader Emeritus in Sociology in the University of Oxford, and Emeritus Fellow of All Souls.

PART ONE: PERSPECTIVES ON SECULARIZATION AND SOCIAL THEORY

In Praise of the History Man

Steve Bruce

Introduction

It is often no easy matter to identify the sources of one's own ideas. God forbid that my early publications should be trawled to count citations but if they were, the names of Roy Wallis, Bryan Wilson and Peter Berger would top the poll. Wallis was a student of Wilson and I was a student of Wallis. My first sociological work, an undergraduate research project, was an ethnographic study of a branch of the Student Christian Movement (SCM) and it was heavily influenced by the work of Wilson and Wallis on sects and new religious movements. Although his writings did not bear directly on my research, I was also heavily influenced by Peter Berger's phenomenological sociology. Like many others of my generation, were I to name just one book that had a profound impact on my future thinking, it would be Berger and Luckmann's *The Social Construction of Reality* (1966).

My doctoral research followed on from my undergraduate work and broadened my interest in the SCM. I gradually became aware that the fate of the SCM could stand for the fate of liberal Protestantism in general. What had initially been an evangelistic conservative Protestant organization became increasingly liberal in the first quarter of the twentieth century and provoked a conservative schism that eventually became the Inter-Varsity Fellowship (IVF). The SCM and IVF shared a common history, recruited from the same field, and had almost identical structures; what distinguished them was theology. Hence their contest could be taken as a small-scale simulation of the battle between liberal and conservative varieties of Protestantism. Although I was only dimly aware of it at the time, Wallis clearly saw the extent to which I was being influenced by the work of David Martin and he invited Martin to examine my thesis.

I have to confess, for it is a sin, that it was not until almost a decade later, when I read one sentence in his *The Dilemmas of Contemporary Religion*, that I fully appreciated what I owed to Martin. He wrote: 'The logic of Protestantism is clearly in favour of voluntary principle, to a degree that eventually makes it sociologically unrealistic' (1978a: 9). That encapsulated what I had been blundering to articulate since my first encounter with the SCM and it became the motto of my first general sociology of religion work: *A House Divided* (1990). As my understanding of secularization matured I became better able to sort the contributions of others and by the time I wrote *Religion in the Modern World* (1996), I had clarified a two-lay model in which the 'deep structure' causes identified by Durkheim, Weber and Marx were articulated through the interpretations of Berger and Wilson and the 'surface structure' of a range of patterns were adapted from Martin's *A General Theory of Secularization* (1978b).

The Importance of History

Perhaps the most important lesson I learnt from Martin was that sociology could only operate in creative conjunction with history, political science, and geography. Although it remains one of his least accessible works, and would have benefited considerably from rigorous editing, *A General Theory of Secularization* was a powerful antidote to the naive positivism that informs much empirical sociology of religion. Rather than recite the virtues of that work, I would like to honour it by applying its approach and some of its conclusions to a contemporary debate in the sociology of religion.

It is commonplace to observe that religious pluralism is associated with secularization. Those societies that are the most religiously diverse are by and large the least religiously observant. The explanation is complex but it can be shoe-horned into two brief observations. In stable democratic and basically egalitarian societies, diversity breaks the links between a religious worldview, the life of the community and the operations of the state. Diversity also changes the way in which believers can hold their beliefs. Where circumstances allow people to see others of very different religions as decent, honourable people, believers tend to reconcile their divergences either by compartmentalizing their beliefs (and thus reducing their salience) or by becoming increasingly relativistic, or both. The result is that religious belief systems lose compulsion and most believers cease to strive to pass them on intact to the next generation. Hence religion becomes increasingly a matter of personal preference and leisure activity and pluralistic societies become increasingly secular.

There is a radically different reading of the consequences of diversity. Rodney Stark and his colleagues have argued that the greater religious vitality of the United States (compared with most European countries) is explained by it having a free market in religious goods and considerable competition between the providers of such goods. Diversity allows everyone to find a form of religion that suits their interests, keeps down costs and thus makes the creation of new religions easier, and provides the clergy with incentives to recruit and sustain a following (for a full bibliography, see Young 1997).

Although there is some evidence to support small parts of the rational choice or 'supply-side' model, only those studies produced by the model's small coterie of proponents find support for the general approach. Almost all attempts to replicate their work, either by comparing religious vitality and diversity for different areas within one society or by cross-cultural comparison, have failed to find any positive effects of diversity on religion. Across Europe, church attendance and membership is far higher in those countries where almost everyone belongs to the same religion (e.g. Poland and Ireland) than in places such as Britain where there is considerable pluralism. If we take a clutch of states that are in many respects similar (e.g. the Baltic countries of Lithuania, Latvia and Estonia), we find that overwhelmingly Catholic Lithuania has far higher rates of church attendance and adherence than the more mixed Latvia and Estonia. Iannaccone, one of the leading rational choice theorists, has admitted that while (to his mind) church attendance rates in Protestant societies are positively related to diversity, those in Catholic countries are not; which rather undermines the status of what is purported to be a universal theory of human behaviour (1991: 169).

Elsewhere I have offered a detailed critique of the supply-side approach (Bruce 1999). Here I will confine myself to commenting on only one side of the supply-side contrast: religion in state-regulated religious economies.

Nordic Religion

Denmark, Sweden, Finland and Norway can be grouped together as Protestant nations that differ importantly from England and Scotland in having state churches that were the product of the Lutheran strand of the Reformation rather than the more radical Calvinist wing.

In each country, the Lutheran church was initially the state church because it was the church of the royal family. In the second half of the nineteenth century, with increased democratization and national autonomy, Lutheranism was construed as the church of the folk. The requirement to belong was gradually reduced, usually by first permitting membership of another specified Christian organization and eventually by the dropping of all religious tests.

The Nordic countries can be used to challenge the supply-side model on two grounds. The first concerns change over time; the second cross-national comparison.

All the Nordic countries have relaxed their control over the religious economy and have become more diverse. According to the supply-side model this should have resulted in increased religious vitality. Instead there has been a marked decline in religious observance. The data is presented in detail elsewhere (Bruce 1999) but the following data illustrate the change. In Finland, the proportion of Lutherans taking communion once a year fell from 55 per cent in 1912 to 20 in 1962, and has since halved again. Between 1980 and 1985, the number of church attendants fell by more than a quarter. Fewer than 3 per cent of members now attend weekly. In Sweden average mass attendance fell from 17 per cent at the start of the century to 2.7 in 1965 and remained at that low level for the rest of the century. Denmark shows the same pattern of decline. In 1927 church attendance in rural areas was between 7 and 13 per cent; in 1967 it was 2 to 7 per cent. In 1964 only 1.7 per cent of Copenhagenners attended church. Different commentators use different measures but no one has suggested that church membership or church attendance has increased in the Nordic countries.

If comparisons of the Nordic states over time fail to support the supply-side case, comparisons between them also fail to support Stark and his colleagues. On most measures the Finns appear to be both more rigorous and more orthodox than their neighbours. The 1998 'Religion and Moral Pluralism' survey (RAMP) showed the remarkably consistent figure of 33, 34 and 32 for the proportion of Norwegians, Danes and Swedes who 'never' attended church; for Finns it was only 19 per cent.[1] Equally consistently, 9, 9 and 8 per cent of Norwegians, Danes and Swedes attend at least monthly while the figure for Finns is 13 per cent. Half of Finns pray at least once a month, as compared with a third of Norwegians and a quarter of Danes and Swedes. Finland also has the highest number of people who believe in God and who believe in a traditional Christian version of that God. Only 3 per cent of Swedes and 7 and 8 per cent respectively of Danes and Norwegians believe that the Bible is 'the literal word of God', but 18 per cent of Finns take that view. On the issue of how important were a variety of church activities the Finns consistently scored higher than the others. The averages for all items were 4.4 for Finns, 4.1 for Danes, 3.8 for Norwegians and 3.7 for Swedes. A very clear difference is visible in the answers to the question 'How important is God in your life?' used in the World Values Survey. Denmark and Sweden rank lowest with a score of 18 and 19, Norway scored 27 but the Finns scored 42 (Inglehart, Basanez and Moreno 1998).

Whatever distinguishes them it is not the structure of the religious economy, which in all four countries is very similar. Finland was only exceptional in that spending the nineteenth century under Russian rule delayed until after the Russian Revolution the liberalization that occurred elsewhere in the mid-nineteenth century, and that goes directly against the supply-side expectation.

Nor is diversity (in the sense of people being free to choose between a range of religions) relevant. Finland might be described as more pluralistic than its Western neighbours in that it had a dual establishment of recognizing both the Lutheran and the much smaller Orthodox Church, but membership of these was determined by geography and ethnicity: almost no one moved from one to the other. In terms of plausible choices, Finns were slightly more constrained than their Nordic neighbours because Finland was less influenced by the pietistic movements of the nineteenth century and suffered fewer breaks from the folk church than its neighbours.

---

1. These data were presented at the fourteenth Nordic Conference in Sociology of Religion in Helsinki, August 1998. I am grateful to the RAMP team of Professors Riis, Heino, Pettersson, Gustafsson, Holm and Sundback for access to their data and to Professor Eila Helander for inviting me to the conference.

A more promising line of explanation concerns economic development. All four countries are now similar in prosperity: the 1990 gross
domestic product of Norway was $23,830 per head, Finland's was
$24,540 and Sweden and Denmark fell in between. But this represents
a recent change. In 1957 Norway, Sweden and Denmark were all
between $1057 and $1380 but Finland was only at $794. Even in 1970
the Finnish GDP was only three-quarters of the average for the other
three. So we are looking at a country that for a long time lagged
behind the economic development of its neighbours. There is also a
significant difference in urbanization. In the 1990s, Denmark and
Sweden were the most urban of the four with 85 and 83 per cent of
their people in large towns and cities. Then came Norway at 73 per
cent and Finland was the least urban at 64 per cent. These data are
consistent with the conventional secularization view that economic
modernization is likely to be associated with a decline in religious
commitment.

However, there is another vital difference between Finland and its
neighbours that is hinted at in the RAMP data. Those surveyed were
asked to respond to ten versions of the statement 'the national church
should be present...' where the sentence was completed by such
options as 'at the celebration of the national day' and 'at festivities
among the royal family' (of course, phrased differently for the non-
regal Finns). All four countries are united in accepting the autonomy
of politics. On a scale from 1 to 7, 'at the national conventions of the
political parties' only scored between 1.5 for Denmark and 1.9 for
Finland. However, over all the possible items, the Finns averaged 3.2
against 2.0 for the Danes, 2.4 for the Norwegians and 2.5 for the
Swedes. While no other country scored more than 4 on any item,
Finland scored over 4 on three: the celebration of its national day, festivities among the royal family, and the end-of-school-year cere-
monies. And the greatest disagreement between the four countries
concerns the question of whether the church should be present at a
regiment's jubilee celebrations. The Danes scored only 1.7, the Norwegians 1.9 and the Swedes 2.1, but the Finns scored 3.7.

These results suggest that the greater religiosity of the Finns may be
related to issues of national integrity. Denmark and Sweden were
themselves imperial powers and since their demise and democratization they have been relatively free from external interference. Norway
has been relatively untroubled by predators since the introduction of

home rule in 1814 and full independence in 1905. But Finland was under Russian rule through the nineteenth century and, although it gained its freedom in 1917, it did not regain Karelia. Finland fought two wars against the Soviets and was forced to pay heavy war reparations after it made a truce in September 1944. For the rest of the twentieth century it had to maintain cautiously polite relationships with a threatening super-power neighbour.

The result was a strong desire to maintain a very clear national ethos. Although it is primarily carried by the Lutheran Church, it is also expressed by the Orthodox Church, which is not affiliated to the neighbouring Russian Orthodox Church but to the Greek Orthodox Church. For the vast majority of Finns, Lutheranism is what distinguishes them from the Slavs next door. That ethnicity has played a major part in Finnish religiosity is further suggested by an interesting internal difference. The west coast of the country shares the Gulf of Bothnia with Sweden and there is a significant population of Swedish-speaking Finns. The RAMP data suggest that, although this is the least urbanized and industrialized part of the country, its inhabitants are less religious than the average Finn. That, given their greater distance from Russia, is what we would expect if national autonomy was a major consideration.

However, Lutheranism did not distinguish the Finns from the Swedes on the west coast of their country and on the other side of the Bay of Bothnia or the Norwegians to the north. As the Swedish empire had been Lutheran, religion could only form an enduring part of national consciousness after Russia (and then the Soviet Union) had become the major threat, and hence the religio-ethnic bond—though closer than in the Scandinavian countries—was never as strong as it was in Poland, for example, where Catholicism distinguished Poles from the Lutheran Germans to the west and the Orthodox Russians to the east.

The methodological point of this is simple. Taking a range of countries, scoring religious vitality, urbanization, industrialization and diversity, adding a number to represent the degree to which the religious market is inhibited by state support for religion, and loading these data into regression equations is an unhelpful exercise. The positivistic assumption that the details of political history can be ignored produces meaningless results. Or to put it more bluntly, if the supply-siders knew more about the religious history of the countries they sought to describe in their regression equations, they would not be able to sustain the fiction that the structure of the religious economy explains most of the cross-national variation in the degree of religious vitality.

I do not have the scope to address this in detail but a related failing of the supply-side approach is that it neglects differences in confession. Any brief review of religion in the countries of the former Warsaw Pact should show that there is a considerable difference in the extent to which religion becomes embedded in nationalist movements of opposition to communist rule. In the three Baltic states, the Catholic Church in Lithuania (as it did in Poland) long served as a repository for national identity. The Lutheran Churches in Latvia and Estonia were not similarly to the fore in anti-Communist movements. In part this difference is related to diversity. The Catholic Church could claim to speak for the Lithuanian people to an extent that the Lutheran Churches in Latvia and Estonia, where there had been deliberate planting of foreigners, could not. In part it is a question of how competing groups differ in religion (or not!). That the local rulers of the Baltic in the eighteenth and nineteenth centuries were Lutheran Germans blurred the lines of conflict for Latvians and Estonians and weakened the ties between religion and national consciousness. But if we consider the record of the Lutheran Churches in East Germany and Hungary we can see the importance of confession. Whereas the Catholic Church in most Communist states was able, despite enormous political pressure, to retain its autonomy, the Lutheran Churches often collaborated with the regime. A full explanation would explore both the differing attitudes of Lutheranism and Catholicism to the mundane world and their global structures (Bruce 1999). Clearly the international organization of Catholicism gave it the resources to resist being coopted that Lutheranism lacked. My purpose here is the limited one of establishing that understanding the nature and fate of religion in modern Europe (let alone the world) requires attention to the specific histories of the countries in question and to the content and structure of the religions in question. In that vital respect Martin's *A General Theory of Secularization* towers above the shallow positivism of the rational choice theorists who routinely but mistakenly claim him as a critic of secularization.

Socio-logic

The above gives some idea of how Martin's own work and that which he inspires differs from the positivistic sociology promoted by such organs as the *Journal for the Scientific Study of Religion* and the *Review of Religious Research*. I suspect that the rational choice theorists would deny it the status of social science and dismiss it as mere reportage. It is worth stressing, then, that Martin's enterprise is sociological explanation. As he puts it (1997: 1):

> Sociology seeks to give an account of the patterns and sequences of social action. Human activity is not random. It gives rise to observable regularities which are susceptible to systematic statement and so allow modest anticipations concerning what is likely to happen next.

As he makes clear, that sociology's raw material is 'human interaction in all its existential variety' (1997: 2) means that its model will inevitably be messy but nonetheless the project of generalizing from the particular means that, while it may rely greatly on the work of historians, it is not the same thing. Although we can rarely express them in the terms favoured by the positivists, we aim to discover 'socio-logics'. Martin's observation, quoted above, about the effect of the voluntary principle on Protestantism is a good example. Although there is no simple causal connection between the core ideas of the Reformation and either secularization in modern industrial societies or the spread of Pentecostalism in Latin America in the last quarter of the twentieth century, complex causal connections can be identified. Once one concludes that religious merit cannot be transferred from one person to another but that each of us is severally rather than jointly responsible for our salvation, then some options are closed and others are opened. The individualism of responsibility promoted by the Reformers can only become the nineteenth century's individualism of rights under certain social conditions (most importantly the replacement of the organic community with an overarching hierarchy by the differentiated society with a variety of task-specific hierarchies) and that complexity means that attempts to uncover socio-logics must themselves be complex. Which merely makes all the more impressive Martin's elucidation of such logics. Some of his work is difficult but the reader who perseveres with *A General Theory of Secularization* will be rewarded with rich insights into the nature, role and fate of religion in the modern world: perhaps older but certainly wiser. The reader who labours through the mathematical modelling of the rational choice theorists will merely end up older.

Conclusion

It would be impossible in a brief homage to assess fully David Martin's work. I have said nothing about his writings on music, popular culture, and education, nor about his theology, or about his careful attempts to bring theology and sociology into creative conjunction. I have mentioned only in passing his pioneering work on the spread of Pentecostalism in Latin America. Instead I have tried to demonstrate the importance of his general approach to sociological explanation.

With the post-1960s expansion of the universities and the number of professional social scientists and the proliferation of sociology books, it has become ever harder for one person to leave an enduring mark on the discipline. Nonetheless, both in his own work and in the example he has set others, David Martin has had a profound and beneficial impact on the sociology of religion.

BIBLIOGRAPHY

Berger, P.L., and T. Luckmann
    1966   *The Social Construction of Reality* (London: Allen Lane).
Bruce, S.
    1990   *A House Divided: Protestantism, Schism and Secularization* (London: Routledge).
    1996   *Religion in the Modern World: From Cathedrals to Cults* (Oxford: Oxford University Press).
    1999   *Choice and Religion: A Critique of Rational Choice Theory* (Oxford: Oxford University Press).
Iannaccone, L.R.
    1991   'The Consequences of Religious Market Structure', *Rationality and Society* 3: 156-77.
Inglehart, R., M. Basanez and A. Moreno
    1998   *Human Values and Beliefs: A Cross-Cultural Sourcebook* (Ann Arbor: University of Michigan Press).
Martin, D.
    1969   *The Religious and the Secular* (London: Routledge & Kegan Paul).
    1978a   *The Dilemmas of Contemporary Religion* (Oxford: Basil Blackwell).
    1978b   *A General Theory of Secularization* (Oxford: Basil Blackwell).
    1997   *Reflections on Sociology and Theology* (Oxford: Oxford University Press).
Young, L.A. (ed.)
    1997   *Rational Choice Theory and Religion: Summary and Assessment* (London: Routledge).

The Functions and Dysfunctions of the Belgian Bishops' Public Interventions

Karel Dobbelaere

Accepting the central thesis that secularization is a consequence of functional differentiation, Casanova rejects two sub-theses of secularization theory, to wit the decline of religion and the privatization of religion (1994: 19-39). The process of functional differentiation is central in Martin's explanation of secularization, although, he, more than anyone else, stresses that the outcome of this and related processes depends to a large extent upon 'the particular cultural (and generally linguistic) complex within which they operate' (1978: 3). It was Berger (1967) and Luckmann (1967) who most of all stressed the privatization of religion as a consequence of functional differentiation. It is on the basis of five case studies, representing forms of 'public' religion, that Casanova rejects the privatization thesis. One of them concerns Catholicism in the USA, 'From Private to Public Denomination' (1994: 167-207), where the argument is based on episcopal speeches and actions regarded as public events. Casanova refers to the episcopal letters *The Challenge of Peace* (1983), and *Economic Justice for All* (1986); episcopal public statements against abortion; and the Roman Catholic Church's political activities in seeking to reverse the 1973 *Roe* v. *Wade* Supreme Court decision, among others, by a constitutional amendment and by interventions in the presidential campaigns of 1976, 1980 and 1984.

Casanova admits that by using the criteria of rational-strategic action 'one would have to admit that the bishops' public speeches have not been very effective' (1994: 201). A pro-life constitutional amendment did not pass and the bishops did not control the so-called 'Catholic vote'. American economic policies did not change, and the change of American nuclear policies was a response to change in international circumstances and not to the bishops' letter. However, he states that criteria of rational-strategic action are 'inappropriate, indeed fallacious, to attempt to measure the public relevance of the bishops' public speeches' (1994: 202).

According to Casanova, such 'speeches challenge successfully liberal and secularist claims that religion ought to be restricted to an allegedly private religious sphere' (1994: 202). That bishops claim an overarching role for religion is evident, and typical of most religions. However, that in itself does not establish what Casanova claims, namely, 'the right and competence of the church to intervene in public affairs'. This is something which must be researched. Casanova thinks further that the bishops did not claim this right only for themselves. By stating that they did not enter the public debate on nuclear or economic policies as experts, they questioned the attempts of experts to withhold these policies from public debate and threw the debate open to all citizens. What Casanova suggests might be in his opinion a latent function. However, it seems to me that it could be a latent dysfunction. Indeed, it could very well turn out to be a dysfunction for their own position. By extending discussion to the religious field, the consequence could be that laypeople might claim the right to intervene in the public debate about theological and moral questions. This certainly was not a function of their public speeches, since the *magisterium* concedes this right neither to laypeople nor to theologians who may be considered to be experts. Ultimately, according to Casanova, the most relevant aspect of their political intervention was that they occupied the public square, left 'naked' by academic philosophy, the specialized social sciences, the universities, the press, politicians and intellectuals (1994: 204-205).

Are these the functions of the public speeches of the Belgian bishops? Are there no other (dys)functions linked to such speech acts? Casanova suggests two dysfunctions linked to the actions and letters of the American bishops (1994: 205-207). First, it became very clear that the Catholic bishops lacked the power to mobilize Catholic laypeople and politicians: 'At times the bishops sound much like prophets clamoring in the desert'. Secondly, by taking a public stand, the bishops exposed 'Catholic normative traditions and ecclesiastical institutional structures to public scrutiny'.

I shall analyse the public speeches of the Belgian bishops in the light of Casanova's analysis. I will also confront some of these letters with the reactions in the Belgian press, which is appropriate since the bishops always give a press conference when publicizing their points of view. Since 1976, they have published 22 letters, some of which are pastoral letters written for their flock. Here I am interested only in letters addressed to the whole population, that is, to the public at large, which reduces the number of letters to be analysed to nine. The topics were: Europe; disarmament; the child; handicapped persons; the law on abortion; care for the dying; migrants and refugees; and marriage.[1]

How Did the Bishops Legitimize their Declarations?

The bishops took up some United Nations' 'themes of the year' which had an elective affinity with the teachings of the Church: namely, children and handicapped persons. However, they did not take up the theme of 'the year of the woman'. Indeed, prudence must have guided the bishops since Catholics who think that the rights of the women are suppressed by the Church might have taken such a letter to reinforce their claims. Moreover, the elective affinity with this theme of the United Nations is, to put it mildly, not very great. Suffice it to confront the standpoints defended by the women's movements on contraception and abortion with those of the Church and, more specifically, of the Church's representative at the Fourth World Conference on Women (Peking, 4–15 September 1995) (see Dobbelaere 1998: 85).

The letters of the bishops on the selected themes of the United Nations and on Europe were addressed to the Belgian population at large, and were legitimized by stating that 'the radical demands of the gospel are not in conflict with what non-Christians feel when they listen to the deepest motives of their own hearts'. For that reason they submitted their thoughts on these themes to all people of good will. The same argument was used to legitimize their letter on migrants and refugees.

---

1.   All these letters were published by their own publishing house, Licap, in Brussels: *La vocation d'Europe* (1976),with comments *Construire l'Europe*; *Désarmer pour survivre* (1978a); *L'année de l'enfant* (1978b); *L'année internationale des personnes handicapées* (1981); *Désarmer pour construire la paix* (1983); *La loi relative à l'interruption de grossesse* (1990); *L'accompagnement des malades à l'approche de la mort* (1994); *Migrants et réfugiés parmi nous* (1995); and *Choisir le mariage* (1998).

Peace and disarmament were a grave theme in the early 1980s. The second special session of the United Nations on disarmament had not kept its promises, and there were demonstrations in the country against the installation of nuclear weapons, culminating in a massive demonstration in the Belgian capital. In their letter, the bishops stated that they had to speak out, since their silence would have been understood as a 'resigned acquiescence, which is in itself a standpoint' (1983: 3-4).[2] They further argued that they were aware that the installation of nuclear weapons was a complex problem, and that they did respect the competence of those who had to take decisions. In such a complex situation, a wise moral standpoint implied that 'the evangelical and ethical claims are confronted with a serious analysis of the facts', and they stated further that there seemed to be room for different choices within certain boundaries. They continued (1983: 4; my italics):

> In such cases those responsible in the Church will generate their own opinion depending upon their evaluation of the situation in the light of the gospel. *However, they cannot put forward their opinion with the same authority that they have in other circumstances.* It is, however, their duty to call Christians and to recommend to all persons to inform themselves sufficiently, to think thoroughly about the question, and to be willing to enter into a real dialogue.

The text makes clear that they respected the competence of experts and decision-makers, contrary to what Casanova suggested, and that they asked for a real dialogue between well-informed people who had thought seriously about the matter. Conversely, the bishops claimed that they could impose binding commandments with regard to abortion, euthanasia and marriage.

After the adoption by parliament of the law on the termination of pregnancy, the bishops issued a public statement (1990). In an appeal to the population at large, they expounded their doctrinal and pastoral standpoints, and pointed out to Christians that persons who co-operate 'effectively and directly' in abortions 'exclude themselves from the ecclesiastical community' (1990: 8). They legitimized their intervention by pointing out that in fact their standpoint did no more than reaffirm 'the juridical and moral principles which regulate the state',

---

2.   The dates refer to the documents of n. 1, but the pages to the Flemish edition of the document.

to wit that the law 'should at least ensure the respect of the fundamental rights of the person, to start with the right to life'. Otherwise, one introduced 'into the law itself a new discrimination…more awful than all social, racial, and sexual discriminations which everyone agrees to prohibit' (1990: 15-17). The bishops stated furthermore 'that one cannot prevent Christians and those in charge of the Church standing up for their convictions. It would be another matter to impose them with coercive or non-democratic means' (1990: 17). In this way they distanced themselves from certain acts perpetrated by Christian movements in the USA. They clearly wanted to stay within the legal system.

A large part of their letter on care for the dying dealt with abortion, and was addressed to 'our compatriots' and 'those governing our country'. The bishops legitimized their intervention by referring to the historical care of the Church for the sick and the dying (1994: 11), and more specifically, in light of the fact that a range of arguments existed in public opinion in favour of euthanasia 'out of compassion'—which has a great resonance—to 'claiming the individual right to die' (1994: 6-7). Another argument was given at the press conference: the bishops felt obliged to speak out, 'since euthanasia is creeping into Belgian society quietly and without much resistance'. They argued in their letter that euthanasia was consciously to kill a person, an act which they confronted with the ancient norm, 'thou shall not kill'. They furthermore asserted that life was a gift, and that people were here 'for one another' and, consequently, might not totally dispose of themselves. Other pages were concerned with good medical, psychogical, human and pastoral care for the dying, stressing the need for good functioning palliative care.

Their most recent letter was on marriage. They referred to some changes in Belgian society, such as the decreasing number of marriages and the existing alternative patterns of relationships to marriage. Since parliamentary commissions were discussing adaptations of the law, such as had occurred in some neighbouring countries, they anticipated that the law would be changed to accommodate the new situation, and this prospect they regarded as legitimizing their intervention. Consequently, they forcefully defended marriage and the family, and expressed their opposition to any equality of treatment of those alternative patterns of relationships and marriage proper (1998: 23). At the same time they urged the authorities legally to protect marriage and the family, and to make them socially and fiscally more attractive.

It is clear that the legitimization of interventions is more elaborate when more controversial issues are discussed: the bishops relativize their own authority in matters of peace and disarmament, but claim both absolute authority over Catholics in matters of life and death and the right to inform the public at large about their standpoint in these matters. As a last resort, the bishops defended their interventions by stating that their silence would be explained as acquiescence, and that no one could prevent Christians and ecclesiastical authorities standing up for their convictions. There is also a noticeable change in the timing of their public interventions. They did not write a public statement about abortion until after the law had been voted upon. Earlier, they had written a pastoral letter to Catholics, and had vocally expressed their opposition to the intended changes of the law. As far as euthanasia and the recognition of alternative patterns of relationships alternative to marriage were concerned, they anticipated, in a public statement, the possible changes of the law, and addressed explicitly the Belgian authorities.

How Did the Press React to the Episcopal Statements?

The secretariate of the Episcopal Conference was able to inform me about the exact publication date of only the last three letters: consequently, I limited my study to these and added the letter on peace and disarmament.[3] In this way, I have two letters on social morality—disarmament, and migrants and refugees—and two on interpersonal morality—death and marriage. I analysed six Flemish and two francophone newspapers which were available in the university library; five of these newspapers have a rather Christian tendency, three have a non-Christian tenor.[4]

All but one of the newspapers being studied provided an account of all four episcopal standpoints and reported on the press conferences.

---

3.   Looking up the reactions of the press without an exact date would have taken too much time; finding the exact date of the press conference on disarmament and peace in the newspapers had already taken more than an hour.

4.   The Christian newspapers are: *De Standaard*, *De Gazet van Antwerpen*, *Het Belang van Limburg*, *Het Volk* and *La Libre Belgique*; the non-Christian newspapers are *De Morgen*, *Het Laatste Nieuws* and *Le Soir*.

An analysis of the titles of the articles, the pages where they were reported in the newspaper, the number of lines allocated to the articles, and where appropriate the photographs used, allowed me to conclude that newspapers of a Christian tendency devoted much attention to the episcopal standpoints.[5] Some even found certain standpoints so important that they included an editorial comment to the letter in question.

The headlines of the Christian newspapers correctly reported the point of view of the bishops. The articles were always published on one of the first pages and they were quite often illustrated with photographs on the subject to attract the attention of the readers. The non-Christian newspaper, *De Morgen*, also reported the episcopal letters on one of its first pages; *Le Soir*, also a non-Christian daily, informed its readers on page 18. The interpretations of neither of these newspapers was as meticulous as those of the Christian papers, and they were more critical. For example, the headline of the article on marriage in *De Morgen* was 'Bishops plead for a liberal conception of marriage', contrasting with the headlines in all other papers, which emphasized that the bishops had defended marriage, and declared themselves explicitly against unmarried co-habitation. The position of this daily must be attributed to the fact that the bishops expressed understanding for the fact that people co-habitating 'demand a special statute that is socially and juridically recognized'. However, the bishops immediately added to this: 'but, this is a purely legal arrangement, and not a equalization with a marriage' (1998: 20).

The title of *Le Soir*'s article on the bishops' declaration on disarmament read: 'A text of compromises typically "Belgian" '. *De Morgen*'s headline was '*Only* a question mark about missiles' (my italics), and stated that as clear as the bishops were in their disapproval of nuclear force, they remained vague about the installation of nuclear missiles. *De Morgen* also reported the discord within the Christian community that emerged at the press conference: some parts of the Christian Workers Association felt let down. Conversely, the conservative Christian daily, *La Libre Belgique*, felt happy that the bishops distanced themselves from some of the associations mandated by them which sought to impose their so-called evangelical standpoints on the whole Christian community. It was clear that in the Christian community

5.   For a more detailed analysis see Dobbelaere (1999: 227-30).

different viewpoints prevailed on the efficiency and opportunity of the installation of nuclear missiles. The bishops recommended people to inform themselves on the issue, to think about it and to enter into a real dialogue. This the Catholic newspapers emphasized, calling the episcopal declaration a balanced, pragmatic and realistic approach to a complex problem. They certainly did not call it 'a Belgian compromise'. The non-Christian newspapers, *De Morgen* and *Le Soir*, however, were critical of this episcopal declaration, which they also called less radical than the standpoint of the American bishops, but less conservative than that of the German bishops.

Whereas the letter on migrants and refugees was well received by all newspapers, this was not the case with the episcopal letter on caring for the dying. The Christian newspapers reacted positively: they called the approach 'Christian and humane'. Positive editorial comments were published, and the titles of the articles clearly expressed the standpoint of the bishops. To the contrary, *De Morgen*'s headline was 'Danneels[6] anticipates the political discussion. According to the Belgian bishops, only palliative care is ethically acceptable', and *Le Soir* put it this way: 'Church and euthnasia: No, but... In principal, the Belgian bishops confirm their opposition, notwithstanding an overture to appropriate "analgesics" and a eulogy of palliative care.' *Le Soir* interviewed a representative of the 'Association for the Right to Die in Dignity', who reacted negatively to the episcopal standpoint. The newspaper entitled the article: 'A very timid move of relative little importance'. According to the spokesman of this association, the Church permitted only what had since long been accepted. However, he said, the bishops still negated the will of sick people and their agony, since in 2 to 5 per cent of terminal cancers pain cannot be relieved. Clearly, these standpoints were in opposition in principle. The Church's line of reasoning was based on deeds with a double consequence, accepting the risk of an early death if it was the unintended consequence of a particular medicine administered to alleviate pain. The other party argued that the medical actions of a Christian and a non-Christian medical doctor are the same, differences are only 'in the head' and not in the act. At the press conference, the cardinal had exactly pointed out the importance of what is 'in the head', to wit the ethical *attitude*, and he condemned *deliberate* killing. *De Morgen* also

6. The Archbishop of Belgium.

gave the opinion of a freethinking professor of medical ethics. He made the same remarks and went on to trivialize the Church's standpoint 'with an anecdote about a usher who threw the money that he had collected in the church in the air, saying: "what God takes is his, what falls on the floor is mine" '.

Factuality predominated in the reactions of the non-Christian newspapers. That the medical act was the same gave rise to an incomprehension of Christian ethical teaching. Facts were also pointed out to show that the standpoint of the Church on marriage was superseded. *Le Soir* argued that the standpoint of the bishops was resolutely contrary to the factual tendency of cohabitation, which not only took precedence over church marriage but over civil marriage as well. Reading these comments, the impression is conveyed that the bishops were engaged in a rearguard battle. It should be added that all newspapers emphasized the fact that the bishops did not want alternative patterns of relationships to be discriminated against, but this did not imply that new laws should put these patterns of relationships on the same level as marriage. For the bishops, the importance of marriage as an institution came clearly to the fore in their preference for a civil marriage above all other forms for those who might not want to marry in church, since 'it expresses better the definitive and exclusive character of the contract and…the potential openness for children' (1998: 19). The Christian newspapers also discussed some pastoral aspects which the bishops developed in their letter about divorce and re-marriage. This gave rise to letters from readers to *De Standaard*, which indicated that the press coverage of the episcopal letters was being read.

The Functions and Dysfunctions of the Bishops' Public Speeches

Reading the comments in the press, I concluded that newspapers of Christian persuasion reported the standpoints of the bishops positively. The Christian newspaper replaces the pulpit of yore, but the priestly role is now taken over by a journalist, who has not been socialized by the Church. The message is transmitted—be it interpreted by journalists—and, consequently, selectively divulged. Journalists do not simply relay the message, rather they have their own agenda which emerges in reporting it, and their priorities may conflict with the Church's agenda. Furthermore, the message is quite often also stripped of its references to Christian sources, depriving it of its legitimizing tradition (Hervieu-Léger 1993: 142). To the extent that the message is read, the letters of the bishops are certainly an episcopal instrument to catch the attention of politicians, management and staff of Christian institutions on the ethical expectations of the Church. What the effect of such messages is in the Christian community is, however, hard to discover. As Voyé has argued before, we know that the rules of the Church are mostly translated in terms of general values (1988, 1994), and so function as a type of 'civil religion' (Dobbelaere 1986). Since the bishops do not address their letters only to Christians, we have to research the possible effect of those letters on non-Christians. The reporting of the episcopal standpoints in the non-Christian press suggests that these messages are not very 'performative', especially in matters of marriage and death. We should, however, also evaluate the bishops' standpoints from the point of view of the characteristics of our modern society.

On the dimension of individualism versus communitarianism, the bishops situate themselves resolutely on the communitarian side. Values such as ambition, assertiveness, freedom and self-determination are defined as non-values, together with hedonism, inequality, material-ism, permissiveness and the undue pursuit of profit and power. The negative attitude towards individualism was also clearly manifested by the representative of the Vatican at the Fourth World Conference on Women in Peking (Dobbelaere 1998: 85). He expressed his reserva-tions about the excessively individualistic interpretation of human rights in the accepted resolutions by which the *universal discourse* about these rights had been reduced to a *libertine dialect*. To the contrary, charity, fraternity, hospitality, mercifulness and solidarity, together with austerity, fairness, fidelity, goodness, justice and responsibility, were the core values which the bishops emphasized in their letters. They also stressed the importance of societal cohesion on the basis of these communitarian values, and defined the family as 'the revitalizing cell of a sane society' (1998: 10). Consequently, they underlined the great significance of the socialization into the communitarian values in the family. However, I should stress that family relations have become less compelling and more optional in our modern society than in former times. In an interview, a student, expressing the overwhelming views of the interviewed youngsters, formulated it this way: 'She is more than a sister, she is a friend'. One may ask also if such socialization prepares children sufficiently for a *gesellschaftliche* society in which secondary relations prevail. The bishops seem to pass over the fact that modern societies are no longer integrated by value consensus but by functional differentiation.

In such a society, there are no longer any core values that are applicable in all sub-systems: at most they are specific for a particular sub-system. The maximization of profit is typical for the economic sub-system and 'love thy neighbour' for the religious sub-system. This example clearly reveals that different sub-systems have institutionalized contradictary values. In the light of this, it seems that the standpoints of the bishops are quite often pious wishes which do not take into account the characteristics of social sub-systems. For example, since the medium of the economy is money and the value pattern includes the value of success, some of their recommendations for the European economic development are no more than pious wishes. Among others: 'There should be a willingness to invest available capital in enterprises that seek to promote the vitality of underdeveloped regions' (1976: 6); 'While redistributing salaries and pensions, he [who follows the gospel] should take into account needs as well as performance. He should look for creative ways to…use profit first of all for the conservation of jobs and as seed for the creation of employment' (1976: 9). From a theological point of view one may define such messages as 'prophetic', as what sociologists call the challenging function of religion. However, in reference to 'civil religion', one should point to the fact that such speech acts are rhetorical rather than performative, and that they chiefly belong in the field of ritual (Dobbelaere 1993).

Furthermore, values are general in nature and in need of specification: what is 'life', for example, in a conflict of values and duties concerning abortion (1990: 6)? Do we mean by it pure 'biological' life or a 'decent' life? Even these specifications still imply a problem of translation, since, as Luhmann has put it, options may not be deduced logically or by rational reasoning from basic values (1981: 303-305). In fact, modern societies are based on procedural values and not on substantive values, which posit ultimate ends: not value rationality but functional rationality prevails. Absolute goals, such as peace, are reduced in an infinite regress to proximate ends, such as the controlled reduction of atomic weapons. Such functional rationality evaluates the means to achieve this, whereby procedural values are central, and a gradual disarmament is also constantly evaluated on the basis of the interests of the parties involved. In fact, functional rationality examines if the available means are efficient to realize the proximate end, and for whom this end is advantageous (Wilson 1982: 166-67). To the contrary, value rationality presupposes absolute, substantive values based on beliefs, and often legitimized by religion. In their public statements on disarmament, the bishops have an eye for functional rationality typical of our social system (1983: 9). However, in questions of life, suffering and death, marriage and family, they hold on to substantial values. This is expressed in their absolute statements on these matters, for example 'the first human right is the right to live' (1990: 14), and 'the Church endorses the one and indissoluble marriage bond, faithful and fertile' (1998: 17).

Casanova points out another possible dysfunction: Catholic normative traditions and the structures of the Church may be subjected to critical questioning as a consequence of episcopal public statements. My analysis might be an example of this. On the one hand, I have criticized the societal vision of the bishops, and, consequently, the foundations of their normative tradition. On the other hand, criticism of the Church's structure was also implicit in pointing out the selective support for the United Nations' themes of the year. The non-Christian newspapers used facts to suggest that the episcopal standpoints were outdated, and, furthermore, they pointed out that the bishops were not informed about the real problems that medical doctors face when trying to control pain, and in not wanting to respect the will of patients. The idea that life was a gift of God was also criticized. However, this argument was only implicitly present in the episcopal letters: 'Humans receive life as a gift' (1994: 10). Life is seen as a gift from father and mother and *ultimately of God*, and, according to the bishops, people may not totally dispose of it. However, a Flemish maxim emphasizes that a gift is given once and for all, that the donor definitely loses his rights over it, and that the receiver has full control of it. The argument of the bishops would be valid only if it explicitly stated that life and death exclusively belonged to God. Were such an argument explicitly stated by the bishops, that argument would be valid only for those believing in God and not for all members of the Belgian society to whom the bishops were addressing their message. Consequently, the reference to God could not be used to legitimize a societal norm. Perhaps this is why the argument was not explicitly stated, which makes clear the fact that the episcopal argument does not hold. The Church is placing itself more and more in the position of a 'third party', above and beyond the parties involved, claiming to be a moral authority with a discourse that is valid for all, Christians and non-Christians. To achieve this, the Church needs to legitimize its arguments on general and not on its own particular principles (Voyé and Dobbelaere 1994: 99-103). But since the anchoring of the reasoning is lacking, the argument, as I have indicated, is liable to criticism. Moreover, since some of the principles which the *magisterium* used—for example, universal human rights and the notion of subsidiarity—are not applied *ad intra*, its discourse loses credibility. Finally, it should also be noted that, since its moral discourse is formulated as coming from a specific sub-system—that is, the religious sub-system, which, in a secularized society, has lost its overarching claims, such discourse will always be seen as religiously bound and, consequently, not universally valid.

It is clear that the episcopal standpoints have a manifest function for the Church. However, do they also have a societal function? Of course, they point out societal problems; however, they treat only those problems that have an 'elective affinity' with the Christian message: the family; life, suffering and death; handicapped people; marginalized people; and children. Moreover, their social standpoints sometimes concern only changes which *they themselves* define as problematic, for example alternative patterns of relationships. It is very questionable that in this way they occupy what Casanova called the 'naked square'. On the one hand, the social problems that they have discussed have been very selective, and, on the other hand, the discussion has concerned topics that were already in the spotlight, and the bishops were only one voice in the discussion. The 'square' certainly was not 'naked'.

To occupy the so-called 'naked square' also implies risks: the bishops must venture into the political domain, for example, concerning alternative patterns of relationships, which, in a functionally differentiated society, they must do cautiously. Indeed, they are denied to overstep their specific competence, which is restricted to the religious domain. If, nevertheless, they do so, they need to legitimize this transgression. In taking a standpoint in politically sensitive problems, the bishops have always legitimized their interventions (see pp. 24-27 above); however, in so doing, they have implicitly confirmed the functional differentiation of society.

The episcopal discourse may also be used as a legitimization by activists, although they tend to welcome with rancour the nuanced standpoints of the bishops. The episcopal letter on disarmament, which promoted reflection and dialogue, was seen in these circles as curbing their efforts. Furthermore, in their opinions, the Belgian bishops have always stressed that only democratic means may be used to achieve goals, a point of view that activists do not always share. Recently, this came to the fore in actions concerning closed detention centres for refugees who lacked documents: some activists destroyed the fences to liberate them. The Church may also be in a difficult position when activists refer to episcopal letters to legitimize their actions. This was recently the case when refugees without documents occupied churches, explicitly referring to the episcopal declaration of 1995 in which the bishops argued that the government should revise its policy of regularization of refugees without papers. According to a well-known authority in the field of law, Belgian criminal law prohibits the participation of members of the clergy in political actions against the government, and with their occupation of churches refugees transgress the Belgian administrative law that forbids political actions in a sacred places (Robert Senelle in *De Standaard*, 31 October–1 November 1998). On 12 November 1998, the bishops were compelled to take a stand concerning this so-called church asylum. They acknowledged that there might be divergent views about such actions, even among believers. However, they did not see this gesture as a political action but rather as 'a sign and signal' which might appeal to public opinion and to the political authorities, the explicit condition being that such actions were 'backed by the local Christian community'. In fact, they defused what was intended as a political action and regarded as controversial by some of the parishioners.

Finally, when the bishops engage in a political debate, the attention of members of a coalition government is drawn to the fact that the Church condemns potential changes in the law and seeks to use its moral authority to prevent this—which may cast a cloud on the relations between the coalition partners. The Christian parties may also consider such episcopal interventions as hampering a political compromise. That is why the then president of the Christian People's Party (CVP) qualified the position of the bishops on disarmament as an important *moral* document. However, as I have emphasized already, an episcopal document, even qualified as a moral document, will always be seen as a particular, that is, a religiously bound, document, and, consequently, not universally valid.

We must therefore conclude that episcopal public speech acts will be performative at most for Christians who are open to such an ethical and prophetic appeal. Their letters might be more performative if the bishops took into account the functionally differentiated structure of our society and its sub-systems. Episcopal letters also have a diagnostic function, since they draw the attention of the population to societal problems. However, the scope of their speech acts is limited to those social problems that have an elective affinity with the Christian message and is only partially determined by the socially defined relevancy of the problems. Episcopal perspectives may also legitimize activists, but this is not without dangers for the Church itself, as we have seen. All in all, it is very doubtful whether episcopal interventions prove 'the competence of the church to interfere in public affairs', as suggested by Casanova. Nobody denies the right of the bishops to speak: this is a democratic right that all citizens enjoy as long as they respect the laws of the country. It certainly must be a delicate task for the bishops to weigh the functions and dysfunctions of their interferences in public affairs—the most obvious function being that the Church comes under the spotlight and loses for a while the veiled character, which, for most members of our modern societies, it normally possesses.

BIBLIOGRAPHY

Berger, Peter L.
    1967   *The Sacred Canopy: Elements of a Sociological Theory of Religion* (Garden City, NY: Doubleday).
Casanova, José
    1994   *Public Relations in the Modern World* (Chicago: University of Chicago Press).
Dobbelaere, Karel
    1986   'Sociaal-culturele christenheid en publieke religie', *Tijdschrift voor Sociologie* 7.4: 653-79.
    1993   'Civil Religion and Functional Differentiation: A Critical Study', *Schweizerische Zeitschrift für Soziologie/Revue Suisse de Sociologie* 19.3: 509-534.

1998   'Relations ambiguës des religions à la société globale', *Social Compass* 45.1: 81-98.

1999   'Over het publicke spreken van de Rooms Katholicke Kerk in een geseculariseerd België', *Onze Alma Mater* 50.2: 204-32.

Hervieu-Léger, Danièle

1993   *La religion pour mémoire* (Paris: Cerf).

Luckmann, Thomas

1967   *The Invisible Religion: The Problem of Religion in Modern Society* (New York: Macmillan).

Luhmann, Niklas

1981   'Grundwerte als Zivilreligion', in Niklas Luhmann, *Soziologische Aufklärung* 3: *Soziales System, Gesellschaft, Organisation* (Opladen: Westdeutscher Verlag): 293-308.

Martin, David

1978   *A General Theory of Secularization* (Oxford: Basil Blackwell).

Voyé, Liliane

1988   'Vision of the Church, Vision of the World', paper presented at the Annual Meeting of the Association for the Sociology of Religion, Atlanta, USA.

1994   'Les étudiants de l'UCL (Synthèse)', *Revue Louvain* 51: 41-44.

Voyé, Liliane, and Karel Dobbelaere

1994   'Roman Catholicism: Universalism at Stake', in Roberto Cipriani, *'Religions sans Frontières': Present and Future Trends of Migration, Culture, and Communication* (Rome: Presidenza del Consiglio dei Ministri: Diparti-mento per l'Informazione e l'Editora): 83-113.

Wilson, Bryan

1982   *Religion in Sociological Perspective* (Oxford: Oxford University Press).

Reflections on Secularization and Toleration

Bryan Wilson

In an age in which ecumenism is a much-canvassed goal of Christian leaders; when churchmen of divergent traditions together lament the absence of Christian unity; and when conciliatory gestures are directed to other major faiths—the adherents of which were once regarded as appropriate objects of missionary endeavour—it is easily supposed that toleration is an embedded feature of the Christian inheritance. More than this, it is even assumed that Christianity has stood historically for complete religious liberty. Such suppositions and such assumptions are remote from the truth. Christianity may today stand for toleration, but it does so only as the result of a profound change in its stance towards other faiths and by having relinquished its erstwhile theological teachings. The inherited position of the Church—based on the gospel that declared that Christianity has a monopoly of access to salvation, that Christ is the only way to redemption—has been one of an intolerance perhaps unparalleled among world religions. If Christianity has relinquished its extreme claim to be the sole purveyor of salvific truth, and has moderated its earlier soteriology, it has done so only in the face of compelling secular forces. Where these forces, the forces of secularization, have lacked vigour, so the intolerant aspects of Christianity have persisted and remained vibrant. One may see such evidences in the retarded exercise and laggardly endorsement of toleration in countries dominated by the Orthodox Church, such as Greece, Serbia and Russia; and, at least until a decade or two ago, in such Catholic countries as Spain and Portugal.

Secularization, as the process by which religion loses its significance in the operation of the social system, has been a phenomenon most marked in the most advanced countries. Where secular forces have wrought change conducive to the exercise of increased toleration, they have done so, one need hardly say, not by virtue of the efforts of self-styled secularists. Indeed, secularists have sometimes appeared to be as obdurately intolerant and as ideologically committed as the religionists they have set out to oppose. Rather, the process of secularization has been a consequence of changes in social structure and technology, and the endorsement of rational procedures in modern social systems, and not a response to secularist ideology as such. Secularists may have challenged, and have certainly criticized church dogma and the dominance in society of religion, but the factors stimulating the secularization of society owe incalculably more to socio-economic change which has occurred involuntarily as an autonomous and largely endogenous process, and as an unintended and perhaps unanticipated consequence of that more fundamental process of change. In accounting for the major impetus to secularization, we may leave the influence of secularist ideology comfortably to one side.

That Christianity should, today, continue to manifest its atavistic dispositions of intolerance in less developed—less civilized?—societies is by no means surprising: in those contexts, the constellation of primitive value-orientations have undergone less exposure to challenge. What, then, were these core characteristics on which is predicated the contention that Christianity is inherently committed to religious intolerance? There appears, from very early Christian times, to have been commitment to four key dispositions, which operated together in a unique combination. To discussion of these elements I shall shortly turn, but it should first be noted that Christianity stands in sharp contrast with the religions prevailing in some oriental countries. In those parts of the world, the adherents of one system of beliefs—or as may often be more appropriately said, the practitioners of one set of rituals, or the devotees of one particular deity—live alongside, tolerate and often associate easily with those who practise in other ways and who worship other entities. The same people may quite voluntarily and readily participate in a diverse variety of worshipful activities. In India, polytheism, pantheism, henotheism, eclecticism and syncretism are all to be found, while in Japan many people regularly engage in the rituals of both Shinto shrines and in Buddhist temples or maintain in their own homes, on the one hand a Shinto god-shelf and, on the other, commemorative ancestral monuments for a Buddhism already infiltrated by the concerns of ancestor worship.

For these peoples, religious boundaries are fluid and even permeable; pluralism is normal, and, despite occasional outbursts by fundamentalists in this or that religious community, toleration generally prevails. The historical legacy of Christianity has been quite different.

As a consequence of its circumstance of origin, and the diversity of the ethnicity of those whom it recruited in its earliest years, Christianity, from its beginning, was preoccupied with the firm demarcation of the community of the faithful. The early Christians were people of diverse tribal, racial, geographic, social and cultural origins, drawn together by virtue of their acquisition of a shared religious commitment. For these heterogeneous adherents to be welded into a viable community required that all these other bases of identity be relegated as of no more than secondary importance when compared with the transcendent claims to fraternity based on the principle of fictive kingship: believers designated themselves as brethren because they claimed spiritual descent from the same father. In the ultimate scheme of things, these converts made affirmation of their identity specifically and explicitly as Christians. In staking everything on that commitment, they totally discounted all other bases of affiliation and allegiance. For the individual, this choice instanced an early example of the displacement of the primacy of ascribed status by achieved status—and a spiritually achieved status at that. It indicated a status gained by change of normative dispositions, not by dint of the effort of work, intellect or force. For the Christian community as a whole, its self-chosen boundary rested on the supernatural legitimization of Christians as a unique and separate people, a people 'neither Greek nor Jew...bond nor free' (Gal. 3.28).

The inclusiveness of the community of the faithful certainly implied one sort of toleration—we may call it ethnic toleration, that is toleration which extended to all *Christian* peoples of whatever tribal, racial or linguistic stock. But the implications for toleration of people who subscribed to a different religion were of quite the opposite kind. Christian commitment entailed the exclusion of those who were beyond the religious pale. Christians were taught that their god was not to be seen as one god among many: he was no longer the god of one particular ethnic group surviving among many different ethnic groups. He was, rather, the only god. To worship him was to be committed to an exclusivistic faith allowing neither other deities within the faith, nor a dual allegiance to other so-called gods beyond the Christian community. From being the ancient Judaic tribal god, who from among many ethnic groups had chosen his own people, a people ethnically defined, the god of the Christians had come to be seen as the putative universal God, the only eligible god, indeed the only god for all mankind (sic), even if at any given time he was acknowledged only by a people who were self-chosen. Christians were not content to see their deity as one among many tribal gods: their god, so they claimed, was the universal god.

It is a paradox that the self-chosen, voluntaristic character of the Christian community itself became a basis of exclusivity. Proper religious choice became a moral matter: not to choose the Christian faith in itself became a sin against God. Thus, although there was a principle of voluntarism in Christianity it was compromised by the assumption that although there was choice, there was only one right choice: although there was freedom, it was only freedom to serve, as the dictum, that service of the Christian god amounted to perfect freedom, averred. Absorbed into Christian philosophy, this prescript was proffered as a transcendent truth of Christian superiority, a con-cluding argument for Christian triumphalism, which later opened the way for what purported to be freedom of choice to succumb to coercion. Whatever may have been the parameters of freedom for early Christian converts, by the time of the Treaty of Augsburg in 1555, freedom was available only to princes, whose choice of faith was, thereafter, with varying degrees of constraint, imposed upon their subjects.

The possibility of choice of religion as the basis for social identity in the disordered world of the Roman Empire entailed another feature of Christianity—proselytism. The Christian community had firm boun-daries, but new converts could always be incorporated. Christianity, and herein lay its uniqueness, combined four elements: exclusivism, universalism, voluntarism and proselytism. It was this combination which established the significant difference between Christianity and all previously established faiths. Those pre-existing religions were confined to groups of common ethnic origin, or confined to particular constituencies of tribe, territory or nation. Christianity, in contrast, claimed to be not only superior to other faiths, but to be the only true faith, to possess a monopoly of truth, under the one and only true God. And this claim forged for Christianity a mandate for religious intolerance, leading the Church to adopt a rigorous approach in matters of belief and practice. As, in its early history, doctrine became progressively systematized, and as contending parties were suppressed, so deviation from what eventually came to constitute orthodoxy and orthopraxis was to be censured even more severely than commitment to some other non-Christian religion. Professed religious beliefs were the touchstones of Christian identity. The self-affirmed status of Christians as the children of God was, after all, the basis for their claim to citizenship of heaven, to being joint-heirs with Christ (Rom. 8.17).

Determining just who were the true children of God led to the condemnation of those who deviated from orthodoxy. Thomas Aquinas, although hoping for the predicted ultimate conversion of the Jews to Christianity, accorded, and thus legitimized, limited tolerance to Jews to perform their rituals. He did so because the Jews could be said to have pre-echoed and foreshadowed Christianity. Yet he showed no such toleration towards self-styled Christians who departed in any minute particular from the authority of the Church in matters of faith and order, even though they accepted so much more of the Church's prescriptions than did the Jews. Of these wayward Christians, he declared:

> In regard to heretics...there is their sin, by which they have deserved not only to be separated from the Church, but to be eliminated from the world by death. For it is a graver matter to corrupt the faith, which is the life of the soul, than to falsify money which sustains temporal life. So if it be just that forgers and malefactors be put to death without mercy by the secular authorities, with how much greater reason may heretics be not only excommunicated but also be put to death, when once they are convicted of heresy? On the part of the Church there is merciful hope of conversion of those in error [but] if the heretic remains pertinacious, the Church, despairing of his conversion, makes provision for the safety of others, and separating him by the sentence of excommunication from the Church, passes him to secular judgement to be exterminated from the world by death.[1]

Aquinas and the Inquisition must stand as testimonies of the traditional position of the Roman Church on the matter of toleration, and although that Church is not now anywhere in a position to require the secular authorities to exact the death penalty for heretics, where the Roman Church remains privileged, it tends to persist in attitudes of

---

1. Aquinas, *Summa Theologica*, Secunda Secundae Partis Qu. 10. Art. 11 'Tolerance of Non-Christian Cults'.

intolerance—a posture that is evident in the current atavistic attitude towards religious minorities displayed by Catholic France and Belgium, in the recent publication by governmental agencies in those countries of indiscriminate indictments of contemporary new religions. Nor did the Reformation, despite the intimation of religious freedom in the commitment to an 'open Bible', initially affirm principles of toleration, except where it was politically expedient to effect compromise. Both Luther and Zwingli, after early affirmations favouring a measure of toleration, subsequently reneged on those earlier sentiments—Luther in declaring the Mass to be a blasphemy, and Zwingli in his dealings with the Zürich Anabaptists.

If, then, traditional Christianity is not the seedbed for an ethic of toleration, one must look to other agencies to explain the steady groundswell of that sentiment that favours a 'live and let live' approach to religion which is now so much more in evidence than in earlier times. The major trend in Western religion in the past couple of centuries, despite recurrent revivalist movements, has been secularization. That development has stemmed largely from the rationalization of social organization. Rationalization has occurred spontaneously and, in the first instance, without specific reference to religion. It has not, however, simply been an inevitable endogenous outworking of latent potential in Western society: it has also been specifically stimulated by the adventitious and unique historical circumstances prevailing in North American society, without which model the dislodgement of religion from its earlier institutional presidency in nation–State social systems would perhaps not have occurred, or at least would not have occurred so widely or so quickly.

Secularization is the process in which religion ceases to exert control over other social institutional spheres as these become autonomous and clearly distinguished one from another. Over time, these other major departments of the social system acquire their own specialist language, apparatus, personnel and organization. As the modern state develops, so these institutions become recognizable as the major departments of social organization, linked, but now relatively autonomous, under the central political authority. The coordination of institutions brings into being a complex pattern of social integration, which depends on formal and rational systematic planning. This form of social integration—as the way in which society is 'held together'—replaced the former dependence on social cohesion, which was achieved by the diffusion of shared values, procedures and rituals, and the cultivation, through religion of a common *mentalité*. In that earlier situation, there had been a recognized dependence on a common belief system as an established agency that served to legitimize leaders in the various (perhaps as yet undifferentiated) institutional sub-systems. A change was now occurring from dependence on consensus in matters of belief, ideology and practice as the guarantee of social cohesion. The social system was increasingly coming to rely on a more rational and systematic pattern of social integration. It had been the common assumption that, perhaps more effectively than any other disposition, shared religion sustained social cohesion, but as nation states came to form, so this dogma was steadily relinquished. With new devices to create or reinforce social solidarity, so older dispositions—shared religion, patriotism, nationalism, paternalism, deference, mythology, and the like—began to lose their significance. Simultaneously, as the social contribution of dissenters— of Hutterites and Anabaptists, and later of Quakers and Huguenots— was increasingly acknowledged, so limited gestures of toleration could be progressively conceded, first to one group and then successively to others, without too openly challenging the core values of the traditional concern for social cohesion. Those values suffered attrition rather than direct refutation.

Of course, mere toleration is in itself not an avowal of religious liberty: it is in itself no more than a limited licence. It implies only the absence of prohibition and persecution: it is a concession by those who possess power to those who are excluded from it. As a policy it assumes that religious practice occurs in the public domain, and that the governing authorities prescribe and underwrite religious orthodoxy. The persisting intolerance fostered by the churches and reinforced by the political authorities was supported by the assumption that religious dissent was in itself a portent of a more general and potentially more explicitly political form of dissidence. In the sixteenth and seventeenth centuries, the political authorities in Europe sought to coerce their populations to adopt a common religion, a policy which they saw as their best guarantee of ensuring social solidarity. It was only as reliance on shared values, on the commitment of people to their prince and their prince's religion, gave way to the new technology of a more rationally instituted state, that religious conformity ceased to be—and ceased to appear to be—a guarantor of social cohesion.

Secularization made possible the supersession of religion's erstwhile proclaimed role of fulfilling functions that sustained social cohesion. Once the state itself became an effectively secular agency, toleration of diverse kinds of religion, or, initially at least, of the received religious tradition and of dissenters specifically thereto, became a practical possibility. The state itself, no longer perceived by its ruling class as threatened by religious dissenters, could then act as an agency transcending divergent religions. Indeed, to ensure peace and harmony, the state was then not only able to 'hold the ring' for at least a number of acceptable religions, but became virtually obliged to do so, and gradually to act so as to sustain increasingly common rights for all of them.

Belying any historicist tendency, we must recognize that the 'accident' which occurred in the settlement of the United States, as the first new nation, powerfully influenced the general secularization process, not merely on that continent but throughout the Western world. The appropriate conditions for widely applied acts of tolerance, as distinct from the piecemeal, ad hoc and incremental concessions accorded over time, came into being in the United States. Here was the first avowedly secular state, founded as secular not because its founding fathers were in any sense secularists—far from it—but because they saw that the state itself could be, indeed should be, secular; that religion of any and all kinds might flourish without promoting discord for the polity. In the establishment of the new state; the old theory that religious consensus was indispensable for social cohesion, finally received its deathblow. The new nation was forged from a cluster of federated states peopled by immigrants of diverse cultural origins and of heterogeneous religious persuasions, many of them, indeed religious refugees, seeking escape from oppressive regimes in which people had often experienced coercion in the attempt by state authorities to establish religious conformity. There were Puritans in Massachusetts, Baptists in Rhode Island, Quakers in Pennsylvania, Catholics in Maryland, and sooner or later, a variety of German and Dutch Sects—Pietists, Anabaptists, Moravian Brethren Mennonites, among others—scattered in various states, as well as those who were not refugees, Anglicans in large part, in Virginia and the Carolinas. If all these religiously diverse states were to form a stable federation, and hence one new world society, then religious toleration and not religious consensus must become the premise to which all men (sic) gave allegiance.

In America, then, there was discovered a higher principle than that of religious conformity. It was clear that the principle of toleration was the only basis on which a new state and a new nation, forged from so many disparate elements, could possibly hold together. Had religion been accorded primacy over other bases of civic obligation, could there have been anything other than the prospect of constant division and perhaps of social conflict? Given the diminished place publicly accorded to religion, when civil conflict did occur in America, denominational religious differences played no part either in the causes or in the legitimization of the struggle. A significant implication of accepting toleration of the divergent religious traditions as a transcendent principle was that religion per se became relativized, and in effect relegated to a secondary place in people's commitments, certainly in as far as the sources of identity were concerned. Furthermore, this arrangement effectively removed religion from its former role as a paramount phenomenon of public life, and this may be seen as the beginning of its increasing engagement with the private sphere. In contrast to Europe, religion no longer provided the official public expression of orthodox belief and required practice: it was no longer an essentially public and civic concern. Religion now became a matter of private, individual choice. And choice became increasingly emphasized, as the recurrent resurgence of revivalism and revival campaigns makes evident. Those individual states that had initially created official state churches, disestablished them. Henceforth, neither the states, much less the federation, would endorse religion, and, while leaving religious people at liberty to pursue their own devotions in their own way, governments now eschewed all official involvement with religious practice. And, as we have observed, this development was in no sense a consequence of ideological secularism, but the application of the rational principles of social organization which prised religion out of its former connection of reinforcing political authority and national identity.

We may note in passing that where a secular state is instituted not as an accommodation of the diversity of religious bodies functioning among its constituents, but as the result of ideological secularism, the consequences for toleration are different. The secular states of the

Soviet Union and China, far from endorsing toleration, sought to suppress religion of all kinds. It is where the secular state has emerged as a consequence of the rationalization implicit in structural differentiation (which is the epitome of the secularization process), or where the political authorities have recognized an imperative need to treat religions equally, lest their adherents, still in bondage to Christian exclusivism, turn on each other, that religious toleration has been more likely to become institutionalized.

The implication of the first amendment to the American constitution was that there was indeed a principle that stood higher than the truths proclaimed by any religion, and that was the principle of toleration. Religious pluralism was accepted as the norm, and toleration became the fundamental concern of the new type of state being created in America. Nor was the degree of toleration that was acclaimed merely the negative concept of restraint on the use of the state's coercive power against dissenters, which was all that the initial gesture of 'toleration' had amounted to in Europe. What, in America, was additionally entailed was a great deal more, namely, the equal rights of people of every religion to worship, preach and proselytize in their own way. Embraced and proclaimed by international agencies as fundamental human rights, these demands have shifted the basis of toleration from permission for distinct denominational *groups* to worship publicly in their own way to the guarantee of freedom for *individuals* (within the confines of the criminal law) to believe and practise virtually what they will. This has opened the way for the development of privatized religion, in which religion is no longer a group property, protecting and disseminating a group culture in the way in which this occurred among the older dissenting denominations, but has been the starting point for the spread of 'please yourself' movements which tolerate, and indeed, at times enjoin, a more permissive ethic.[2]

In the interests of equality of all religions, the state has necessarily become a secular state—a marked concession to secularization. State-endorsed toleration relegated each particular faith to a subordinate place. Each sect now had the prospect of rising in status, and was to be accorded parity with already established denominations, but equally, each self-acclaimed church had now to accept that there were other

---

2.   For a related discussion on these themes see my essay 'Religious Toleration, Pluralism and Privatization', *Kirchliche Zeitgeschichte* 8.1 (1995), pp. 99-116.

faiths which implicitly challenged its traditional claim to possess a monopoly of truth as God's one true church. The law stood now as an ethically charged arbiter over and above all religions of whatever provenance and antiquity. This was the groundwork for American 'civil religion', a belief in a higher abstract principle of justice transcending the moral claims and ethical particularities of each and every religious denomination, with its source of authority the—perhaps not inappropriately designed—'Supreme Court'.

To relate toleration to the structural conditions which facilitated its inauguration and its progress is by no means to derogate the idealism of the various intellectuals who canvassed tolerance from the sixteenth century onwards. For many of them, however, what was sought was a relatively modest advance in the liberty of worship for particular groups and not total religious freedom. Some such secular 'martyrs' sacrificed their lives, and thereby engendered, in exponents of the 'great man' theory of history, a certain hero worship. It is far from the present point to detract from the commitment to principles of men such as Servetus, Castellio, Gentile and Acontius, yet, it may be contended, that the real credit for the advance of religious toleration lies elsewhere.

David Martin:
Sociologist of Religion and Humorist*

Christie Davies

David Martin is best known for his contributions to the sociology of religion, a field in which he is an acknowledged leader and enjoys a worldwide reputation. However, this essay concentrates rather on David Martin the humorist, the begetter of many erudite, insightful and downright funny radio scripts and talks, essays, journalism and book reviews. It is worth studying this at first apparently ephemeral work for three reasons. First, it is important in itself because of the sheer quality of the humorous writings which demonstrate a remark-able talent to amuse. David Martin's humour, particularly in relation to religion, is as entertaining and insightful as that of the Revd Sydney Smith (1854) and has far more relevance to the contemporary world than, say, the tired paradoxes and orthodoxes of G.K. Chesterton (1987). David Martin's humour demands the same kind of analysis of technique and sociological consideration appropriate to such writers as these. Secondly, large parts of his humorous output are also vehicles for his sociology of religion and his other sociological ideas. Two of Martin's humorous radio talks (1968a, 1968c) have been reprinted in his eminently serious book *The Religious and the Secular* (1969a). Humour is one more way of making a serious point. Finally, the humorous works cast light upon Martin's best-known books on the sociology of religion. We can see in his humour brief mentions of

*   I wish to acknowledge the assistance given to me by the archivists and librarians of the BBC Written Archives in Caversham and of the University of Reading, and in a much broader sense the steady academic support and inspiration I have derived from David and Bernice Martin for over 30 years.

early ideas and experiences that were later expressed more thoroughly in his major works.

David Martin's career as a sociologist and in particular as a sociologist of religion in a sense began when he did his national service in the British army in 1948–50, to be precise in the Non-Combatant Corps where he was attached in turn to the Royal Pioneer Corps and to the Royal Military Police. The latter clearly made a strong impression on Martin for they are given special mention in the preface to his book *Pacifism* (1965: viii). The Non-Combatant Corps, the NCC, was in those pre-politically correct times nicknamed the Nigerian Camel Corps, a phrase which today would be seen as multiply offensive. Martin has written that there were other even 'more opprobrious variations on this, based on the NCC acronym' but does not elaborate (1967 [1998]: 1).

The NCC was largely employed in providing clerical and secretarial back-up to the Pioneer Corps which gave Martin the opportunity to make many shrewd observations about social class and religion, observations later expressed in humorous form in his radio script *The Non-Combatant Corps* (1967 [1998]: 1):

> This symbiosis was surprisingly imaginative for the British Army because the Non-Combatants were everything the Pioneers were not. For example, army educational ratings were ranged on a scale from 11 to 81: the NCC went from 11 to 31 and the Pioneers from 61 to 81. That meant at least a third of the Pioneers were illiterate, including some of their NCOs. They came from the Gorbals, Lime Street, Tiger Bay, Moss Side and East London. I don't remember where the Objectors [to killing] came from but it wasn't those places. Another difference was religious: the Pioneers contained a large contingent of Roman Catholics and the NCC hardly any.

The relationship between class, education, religion and belligerence could not be more clearly stated; the *humour* stems from the indirect way in which this is expressed by excluding the NCC from previous statements about the Pioneer Corps as in: 'I don't know where the Objectors came from but it wasn't those places', and 'the NCC hardly any'. Such devices are, of course, well known in the work of other humorists but they are the very essence of David Martin's style, a style originally developed for radio, that very demanding medium where the broadcaster has to tell a story without seeing or hearing the audience and without being seen by them. It is almost a kind of oral writing; it requires the ability to write a script that can be delivered with perfect timing, a skill of which David Martin was a complete master. Imagine the impact of Martin softly but emphatically *stressing* '… it wasn't those places' or '… hardly any' on the air.

Unfortunately, no one ever did, for *The Non-Combatant Corps* was never broadcast. The 1960s mandarinate of the BBC took exception at the very highest level to a piece of accurate ethnographic observation later on in the script concerning the graffiti on the walls of the Pioneeral lavatories (1967 [1998]: 8-9).

> And on the damp walls they would inscribe and gaily decorate in their own excrement such legends as 'Only another bloody month to go', '90 more bleeding days' and so on.
>
>   These graffiti were so grotesquely abundant that the authorities were concerned. It was decided to forbid the practice in company orders, a sheet which every corporal and sergeant read out to his assembled troop each evening. The Orderly Sergeant dictated the following: 'Any soldier found writing with his own shit on the walls of the company lavatories will be put on a charge.' I typed obediently. Then the Sergeant Major came in and glanced at it. 'Bleeding Hell' he screamed. 'You can't write bleeding shit in company orders; there's a proper military bloody word for that—H'EXCRETA'. I re-typed the offending passage: 'Any soldier found writing with his own EXCRETA on the walls of the company lavatories will be put on a charge.' But the orderly sergeant was not subdued—'Which of these bleeders knows what the hell excreta means,' he rasped. 'Tell all the NCOs to explain it to them,' said the Sergeant Major 'and if anyone still doesn't know put a h'asterisk by it—anyone not knowing what excreta means can inquire from Private Martin in the orderly room.' I don't remember any enquiries.

It is a splendid account, again with the typical Martin technique of ending on an understatement expressed through the use of a 'not': 'I *don't* remember any enquiries'. The mock poetic beginning 'And on the damp walls they would inscribe…' is equally characteristic with its deliberate use of solemn anachronism and inappropriate metre to introduce a modern Miller's Tale of lower-class rudeness and crudeness.

For those gentle readers who know the Reverend Professor Martin's work only through his academic and analytical or religious and inspirational writings, it may seem out of place or even unseemly for me to dig up these long since censored humorous tales of barrack-room language but they are necessary to our understanding of his sociology of religion. Indeed it was at this time that David Martin, then a Methodist, first became fully aware of the value of the 1662 *Book of Common Prayer* (as distinct from its alternative) which he was later to defend with such vigour. He had been given the job of organist at the garrison church (1967 [1998]: 9-10):

> Here were candles and canticles which I began to take to and an intro-
> duction to the consolations of the Prayer Book. The deputy-chaplain
> was from a good northern family and boasted an under-utilised exper-
> tise in the Abyssinian Coptic Church. Every now and then he wrote
> wearily to 'my lord of Norwich' to enquire how much more purgation
> was required of him ... The day before I left the Army for ever he
> pointed out that this was February 2nd and the Feast of the Purification
> of the Virgin. I might, therefore, take the morning off to receive Com-
> munion. I confessed the Feast of the Purification had not hitherto
> played a significant part in my life but was entirely happy to begin.

Clearly purity and purification can only be understood in relation to and in antithesis to pollution. Without the profane the sacred would not exist. It is no accident, as a dialectician would say, that David Martin's exit from the army camp he called 'a nest of theft, violence, collective sodomy and every kind of petty fiddle' (1967 [1998]: 7) coincided with a feast commemorating the end of a fixed period of ritual impurity. It was in the army, too, that David Martin first became aware of the great spiritual energy of the Pentecostals, for that was the profession of the man who occupied the barrack-room bed to his right (1967 [1998]: 4-5):

> Given the slightest encouragement his prayers rose to a high, excited
> monotone and verged on 'tongues'. He never actually spoke in tongues
> although I would lie on my bed waiting expectantly ... He found me
> regrettably gospel hardened and I found him regrettably keen on
> cleaning his equipment. Eventually I agreed to read his tracts if he
> cleaned my equipment. It was quite a bargain for a future sociologist of
> religion.

It was indeed. Is it too fanciful to suggest that here is the original inspiration of David Martin's celebrated study of Pentecostalism in Latin America where the spreading tongues of fire have converted a previously heedless people to the Protestant Ethic (1990: 205-232; Weber 1930)? Can the pacific British soldier fervent in prayer and in equipment cleaning have been the prototype for Latin America's new respectables (Martin 1990: 211-29; Bernice Martin 1998: 128)? The changes in South America were, of course, real but it took an observer

with a certain kind of prior experience to recognize their full significance.[1] Those who laugh at the Protestant Ethic thus acknowledge its
vitality and importance (Davies 1992).

The Non-Combatant Corps is, though, not typical of the radio scripts
and columns that David Martin wrote in his humorous depictions of
Britain in the later 1960s and the 1970s, that strange radical, turbulent
period that now seems almost as far away as Edwardian England. It
was a time when Communist rule in Russia and Eastern Europe
seemed to be permanent, unshakeable and destined to spread to much
of the rest of the world, including what was later to become Protestant
Latin America. In Britain, Lenin's 'useful idiots' were doing their
unwitting and in some cases witting best to hasten the advance of
Communism by advocating unilateral nuclear disarmament (Mercer
1986). Student radicals disrupted the universities (Martin 1968b),
including the LSE where Martin taught and then set off on a short
and victorious march through the Sociology departments (Martin
1978b) which, as Julius Gould (1977) demonstrated with great clarity
and detail at the time, became utterly Marxist dominated. It was not
an easy time to be a sociologist of religion, for religion had come to be
depicted as an unimportant epiphenomenon, a mere legitimation of
bourgeois hegemony, a trivial superstructure controlled by more vital
and all-determining economic agents rather like frivolous postmodern
window-boxes and chalet eaves perched on an oblong office block
designed by an accountant. The Marxists announced that in the past
Methodism had 'artificially' retarded the revolutionary tendencies of
the British working classes, but now in an era of total and universal
secularization the revolution was nigh and the projected Enlightenment project would be completed on time. Today when yesterday's
revolutionaries are portly felines and Blairist bureaucrats it is hard to
believe that they once closed the LSE (Martin 1969b). No doubt they
will do it again in the future but not in the same sense. Meanwhile, far
from fearing secularization, many theologians welcomed its sting and
victory.

David Martin was one of the few scholars willing not merely to

1.   There was, of course, also David Martin's Methodist family background.
His father had experience as an open-air preacher (including Speakers' Corner)
and, though a Methodist, had spiritual sympathies with the Pentecostals; hence
Martin's ability to stress the parallels between early Methodism in Britain and
Pentecostalism in Latin America today.

resist these trends but to make fun of them, sometimes with a gentle humour, sometimes not so gently. He mocked in turn the Bulgarians, the post-1960 Frank Cousins-politicized CND which had led him to reconsider his views on pacifism, secular theologians, student radicals, streakers, Raymond Williams and the British Sociological Association, an odd combination of the authoritarian and the heedlessly unstructured, all of which were nonetheless the antithesis of the morally ordered, religiously informed and empirically based intellectual commitment that David Martin stood for. There was Methodism in his mockery.

David Martin's radio talk *The Bulgarian Ideology* may well be termed postmodernism *avant la lettre française*, for at a time when the French were still propounding the grandest of grand narratives, Martin wrote (1968a):

> 'You will tell the truth—you will speak well of us. We Bulgarians prefer to be praised … '
>
> …'You will tell the truth…' Telling the truth is never easy, certainly not for an outsider relying on three weeks' impressions. In any case truth is always elusive however long you stay: the nearest most of us get to truth is irony. The Bulgarians are masters of irony and so it is not for us to guess at their truth but simply to let them speak for themselves.

David Martin is far too modest here. A visit of a few weeks and an ignorance of the local language never stopped Margaret Mead (Freeman 1983) from writing entire infallible books about any people she happened to visit but she had not irony. Irony is, though, at the centre of postmodernist thought, as is the idea of letting small colonial and post-colonial peoples (the Bulgarians were both, for they had slipped from Turkish yoke to Soviet umbrella) speak for themselves through the anthropologist 'giving them a voice'. But when it comes to humour we cannot be sure that this speaking in voices is not itself ironic as when Martin (1968a) told us of Bulgaria in the 1960s that:

> Religion is dépassé above all else. Did the clergy take an important part in the [Bulgarian nineteenth century] national revival? Then they did so only as patriots. Did some bishops under the Turkish thumb in Constantinople condemn the revival? Then they did so as religious functionaries.
>
> Just how dépassé religion is you can find out by going to the Atheists' Museum in Plovdiv. The largest exhibit of the museum shows two sputniks circling the earth, underneath is the caption: 'Neither the Russians nor the Americans have been able to find God…'

> ...Marxism gives Bulgarians insights denied to empirical science. A
> Marxist has preference shares in reality; he has peeped behind the his-
> torical curtain...empiricists study this trend and that trend but they
> [the Marxists] are able to compare true trends with false. Religion
> remains vigorous in Poland and to some extent in Roumania. This is
> because Poles and Roumanians are retarded by special historical factors.
> Religion is comparatively weak in Bulgaria and it follows that Bulgaria
> is the true case exemplifying the 'real' trend.
>
> For me to argue otherwise was a natural enough result of living so
> long in the miasmal mist veiling bourgeois reality. So they were kind
> and compassionate... They knew well enough the supposed liberties of
> England—legalistic illusions like travelling around the country without
> identity documents or going abroad without permission. They had
> considered our social frame and knew we were as historical dust.

David Martin's talk provides an amusingly accurate picture of the
Bulgarian Marxists of the 1960s; no doubt his critics will dismiss
Martin's humour as a mere satire on crude Marxism, but then what
other kind is there? Just over 20 years later the Bulgarians were to
topple their Communist regime with a general strike. Visiting British,
American and Lithuanian academics were to delight turbulent local
crowds by dancing on Georgi Dimitrov's grave (or at least on the roof
of what had been his mausoleum) and singing 'There's no business
like showbusiness' and 'Oh what a wonderful tractor' from the
Marxist version of *Oklahoma!* All that was solid melted into air
pollution as history repeated itself as farce. The mighty fortress of
Marxism proved to be a cardboard edifice made by stage designers—
much as David Martin had humorously suggested in 1968. Even more
important for our present purposes, his observations on the thriving
of religion in Poland and Roumania relative to Bulgaria provide a
preview of the findings of his later masterpiece *A General Theory of
Secularization* (1978a). What is crucial is Martin's recognition of the
key methodological point that we cannot deduce what is real or true
by recourse to Marxism or any other kind of sociological theory. Such
limited approaches to a knowledge of the truth as we are able to make
can only be achieved through the systematic examination of the
differences between one society and another on a comparative basis.

In a later radio script, *Sociologist Fallen among Secular Theologians*
(1968c) David Martin placed himself in the central role noting that:

> One of the persons secularizing theologians most delight to honour at
> their conferences is the sociologist. They believe that he is one of those
> 'modern men' with whom and about whom they wish to discuss. And

they have a fair expectation he will have something pretty funereal to tell them about why the church is dying and must die. No doubt he can also be prodded into dilating on the character and dilemma of modern man, confirming in his own inimitable sociological jargon the pregnant obscurities of Tillich and Bonhoeffer... However it has not escaped my notice, moving from conference to conference, that I am usually the next-but-one most (theologically) conservative person present...there is nearly always one person present more conservative than myself and he is generally a physical scientist, a biochemist perhaps, or worst of all a physicist... So it would seem that while the theologians joyfully proclaim the death of God and the death of the Church in the name of 'modern man', the only two modern men present watch the whole exercise with sad and wondering eyes.

No one need doubt man's rational control of his environment is vastly increased, and maybe this magnificent creature of the theological imagination does exist or at any rate scattered fragments of his body. Nonetheless he is barely known to empirical sociology. He makes only a marginal impact on the gallup polls which more usually document gullibility, illogicality, insecurity and rank superstition. Hence I am encouraged to carry my vulgar empiricism not only to the point of asking 'Who is modern man?' but in addition 'Where is modern man?' I even asked one theologian just how many examples of modern secular man were extant. 'What', he said, 'in a percentage?'

'Yes', I replied, confirming his worst suspicions.

The incident confirmed mine as well. Theologians never lose their habits, not anyway their habits of *mind*. They know modern mind man exists *de fide*. Why so gross a sceptic as not to believe in modern man? In a style reminiscent of Marxist theology all who do not conform to the thesis or agree with its proponents are suffering from 'false consciousness'; they are just behind.

As was the case with the Marxists, secular theologians are shown by David Martin to be what I would term Grindgradians. Grindgradians are the obverse of Dickens's Gradgrind, men and women who utterly abjure facts in order that their meta-meta theories can flourish unhindered by reality. The resulting theoretical frameworks are then taught to unfortunate and uncomprehending undergraduates as an exercise in vital and necessary obscure uselessness. They are literally a grind for grads. It is fair enough for a traditional theologian to express faith in events and processes that are by their very nature untestable such as the Incarnation or the Resurrection. But for secular theologians or Marxists or sociological theorists who make no claims whatsoever to believe in divine revelation and who seek legitimation through a spurious association with science to seek to evade empirical investigation and testing in this way is bad faith and an expression of bad faiths. It is, though, a truth much better expressed above by David Martin in the indirect and humorous form of his satire on the purveyors of secular theology.

In his account of the theologians' conference Martin later recounts an incident embodying a heavy clash between the vacuousness of secular theology and the vacuity of political correctness, for as Newton pointed out long ago, there is gravity in vacuity. There is also considerable levity in this particular incident (1968c):

> Some of those really determined to finish the Church off attacked a proposal to celebrate Holy Communion. The arguments proceeded and violently until two coloured delegates rose, arguing in favour of a celebration and incidentally dropping the reminder that they happened to be the servers. The progressive mind agonised, caught between the desire to eliminate a ritual and the patent illiberality of depriving coloured people of an honourable role. It was decided to celebrate, but at the same time to declericalise the occasion; the officiating minister wore an open-necked shirt—just to give it that necessary touch of ultimate reality.

The radio scripts *The Non-Combatant Corps*, *The Bulgarian Ideology* and *Sociologist Fallen among Secular Theologians* represent the very peak of David Martin's humorous writings. They are even funnier than his other humorous radio scripts such as *The Politics of Peace* (1968d) or 'The Delicate Streak' (1974d) because they deal with first-hand experience and observation. David Martin really was in the Non-Combatant Corps, really did travel to Bulgaria to meet sociologists and philosophers and really did attend conferences with secular theologians. By contrast, so far as I know, he has never had the chance closely to scrutinize naked ladies running through the streets of London, though he did once attend a lecture by Talcott Parsons at the LSE where three members of the audience were stark naked except for Viet Cong headbands (Ho! Ho!). His radio talks on peace and streaking were funny, extremely learned and made telling points notably in relation to the high-minded pacifism of the Protestant left-free-traders (a flashback to *Pacifism* [Martin 1965] and a preview of *Does Christianity Cause War?* [Martin 1998]) and to the early sectarian streakers such as the Quakers who sought to escape an artificial, hierarchical and behatted social code by shedding clothes. Nonetheless, *The Politics of Peace* and *The Delicate Streak* lack the sheer sense of exuberant fun of the three talks quoted extensively above, a fun comparable with that to be found in H.G. Wells's (1928; see also Davies 1990, 1998) great comedies such as *The History of Mr Polly* or *Bealby*.

David Martin's radio talks on Bulgaria and on the secular theologians were even funnier as broadcast than they read in manuscript. They were both written as 15-minute talks, probably to fit into an interval in a longer broadcast such as a concert (thus also boosting the number of listeners) and David Martin was and is a master of the techniques needed for such a slot—brevity, crispness, the ability to tell a story, particularly a comic parable, an attractive speaking voice and of course perfect timing, notably his use of a very slightly longer pause before the punchline, that key word or phrase that reveals the comic meaning of what might have seemed a purely serious tale (Raskin 1985). Too many compilers of scripts for radio write sentences that they can't actually speak; they lack the imagination to write not for readers but for listeners they can't see. It is clear even from the text of David Martin's scripts that he had fully mastered these arts and it is a tragedy that the tapes of his broadcasts do not seem to have been preserved. They would make an excellent audio-cassette to brighten up a motorway journey with their wit, exuberance and insight.

The same qualities are to be found in Martin's humorous (with seriousness) writings on the uses of language (1974e, 1975b, 1975c) and on conferences (1974i, 1978b), two themes which very much lend themselves to humorous comment.

In 'The Fine Art of Academic Denigration' Martin (1974e) has carefully observed the advantages that the practitioners of a discipline gain by 'agreed criteria for denigratory remarks about other subjects' together with 'a resounding unanimity about high standards in one's own subject'. Thus:

> Economists, for example, are very good at this and no number of practical failures or internecine disputes about which policy will have which effects distract them from their steady chorus of self-praise. They are, they tell us, practitioners of a hard, scholarly discipline in which rigorous standards drive out all but the hardiest intellects. Their conversations abound in words like 'hard', 'rigorous', 'scientific', 'analytical', 'disciplined' and 'logical'; their favourite perjoratives are 'soft' and 'unscholarly' … One has only to read their assessments of each other to realize that a discipline which permits such precise ranking must indeed be ordered by rigorous criteria. People are summed up relative

to each other in terms which suggest no uncertainty at the margin. And the assessors are in turn assessed with the same fearless certitude … Another technique is the use of honorific terms which somehow rub off on the user as well as the person honorifically described. 'Eminent' is a word which springs naturally to the lips of economists …

…The difficulty of sociologists arises from their ambiguous position between science and arts which prevents them building up a consistent defensive rhetoric. More genuinely messy subjects can make a virtue out of sheer messiness in a way that sociology cannot. The historians, for example, positively glory in the loose and indiscriminate employ-ment of categories and manage to convey the feeling that their intellectual mess is derived from the endearing muddle which is the substance of historical reality. They turn confusion into a virtue and claim it is based on their conformity to the nature of their material …

It is an unfair world in which you need a consistent rhetoric to defend yourself: either the vocabulary of rigour and 'hard' data or the vocabulary of glorious mud. One also needs a rhetoric based on impurity and ambiguity which eschew misleading rigour and are not content with celebrating the apparent muddle of human affairs.

This essay has the feel of being written after a long, hard day serving on a promotions committee at the LSE, but if this is the case its importance is enhanced for it is at that point that resources and status are distributed competitively between individuals according to subject. One can just imagine the rigor of economic theory battling it out with that sticky colloid, the Sartrean honey-pot of the historians. Rigor to rigor mortis, mud to mud. Yet surely sociology is not an entirely impure and ambiguous category but rather has its own spheres of rigidity (tick-box surveys of trivia) and of mud (the appropriately named 'thick' data of the observer in the field) and also a feature it shares with uncultural studies—the unchallengeable prestige of its incomprehensible, purely self-referential pseudo-theories. By con-trast, David Martin's brief comic essay is a model of clarity. A good exercise for one's undergraduates would be to ask them to rob the extract above of its meaning by rephrasing Martin's dimension that runs from rigored economists to muddied historians in the jargon of Baudrillard or Bourdieu or even both at once. There are only two rules in sociology. The first is the uncertainty principle that points out that the more precise your data the more trivial the deductions you can make from it. The second is that the more opaque and obscure your writings the more they will be feted, especially if written in French. Martin is a shining lone exception to the two rules.

If bureaucracy and the dividing of knowledge into 'disciplines' (shades of Opus Dei) are the key oppressions of the academic world, conferences are its mouldy cakes and sour ale. Perhaps Martin's best description of the comic side of a conference was made of one that he (wise man) never actually attended, the British Sociological Association's annual conference held in Brighton on All Fools' Day 1978. To mock their nonsense, it was enough for Martin to recite the items on the programme (1978b):

> Sunday morning opened with 'Working class Autobiographies' and you could settle for a pleasant Sunday afternoon with 'Language and Discourse' raising questions relating to the 'critique of economism in Marxist theory'. After tea and scones the Women and Film study group investigated inter alia whether Coronation Street has potential for subversion... Monday morning, up early for spiritual exercises with John Berger on 'Cultural Imperialism' or else for 'Marxism, Feminism and Cultural Practice' ... 'Marxist Theatre in Britain', 'The Materialism of the Material Concept of History', 'Feminist Art Practice (a psychoanalytical approach)'. The next instrument of tumbrils included a piece of rock, considering theories of communication 'more particularly those in the Marxist tradition'.
>
> A quick cuppa and we are back for 'Rock and Sexuality' or 'Ideologies of Motherhood and Radio and TV' or 'The Theory and Practice of Counter-Culture' (a gentle presentation this, on vegetarianism, Divine Light and good co-operatives). For hard-core, 'Culture and Crisis in the 1930s' by contributors about to publish a book of that title under the imprint of Lawrence and Wishart.

In this brief canter round the stalls of the righteous lefteous, David Martin was able to tell the British taxpayer in a *quick* and *comic* way what the once 'Revolting Students' of the 1960s were now doing with their money and indirectly to convey to the general public the full thrust of the justly celebrated Gould report into the Marxist and radical penetration of higher and further education (Gould 1977). Menace riding on mockery equals communication. The editorials for 4 April 1978 printed alongside Martin's op-ed piece in a daily newspaper noted sombrely that there were currently 17,000 Cuban troops in Ethiopia and 30,000 in Angola plus numerous Russian military 'advisers' and massive Russian arms deliveries, and that the people of Cambodia under Pol Pot had been reduced to slavery and starvation. None of these items seems to have impinged on the mindset of the British Sociological Association. The Evil Empire has since collapsed and Pol Pot has been defeated but the militants of the BSA were not exactly involved in the people's struggles to bring about these changes; they were too busy undermining their own society. Anyone in our post-socialist world who doubts the continued relevance of David Martin's message about the ideological obsessions and the intellectual triviality of the BSA's annual *general* conference (the separate sections can be quite good) need only scan one of their more recent programmes. The old whingers have merely been poured into new whine bottles. David Martin was right.

In many of his later columns and reviews Martin comes up against two problems that all would-be serious humorous writers encounter. First, the tension between the humorous and the didactic. Humour is by its very nature ambiguous and elusive and can be construed in many ways by its readers; indeed it has these qualities more than any other kind of text. Exhortatory, instructive or instructing messages by contrast have to be clear and straightforward as in '*Nicht hinauslehnen*', 'Last exit for Brooklyn', '*Défense de cracher*', 'Do not exceed the stated dose', '*Cave canum*'. The presence of humorous ambiguity undermines such messages as with, say, 'In case of fire, alarm the caretaker', 'Stop when flashing' or 'Look out, monsieur'. This is a problem even for a master humorist like Martin for he is likely to be misunderstood.

Many of David Martin's polemical writings have been concerned with the decay and decline of Britain's system of primary and secondary education under the influence of progressive ideologies, which have downgraded learning in favour of a perverse egalitarian individualism, that is, the child may do anything except excel. At a time when Chris Woodhead, later as Chief Inspector of Schools known for picking his way through the ruins and planning postwar reconstruction, was a mere teacher of field courses, David Martin was already one of the educational system's major critics (1974a, 1974f, 1974h, 1975d, 1975e). If only we had listened to him then, we would not be stuck with the numbing bureaucracy of Ofsted today. It is one more proof that progressive revolutions aimed at undermining traditional standards always end up with an oppressive centralized dictatorship.

David Martin's essay 'Schools are Nurseries of Democracy' (1974f) states its central message with great clarity at the very beginning: 'It is very difficult to face the fact that one's children are now likely to receive an inferior education to one's own.' Yet many missed the real meaning of the ironic account of progressive education that followed and believed that he was praising the progressives for having made schools into not merely nurseries of democracy but of all that was enlightened and worthwhile. Martin noted of these schools (1974f):

> Naturally enough there is no insane insistence on the regular production of homework: a modern school is not a forcing house or a factory. Instead homework is 'indicated' and if it happens that a pupil wishes to explore further the fascinating problems encountered in his latest collective project he will inevitably want to take up the indications given him.
>
> Teachers for their part need not sully his work by 'assessment', let alone by grading because such external appraisals spoil the sense of unique personal involvement...
>
> ...Parents who ask to know about homework (or about progress) are told (I quote): 'We don't think it proper to impose it on them if they don't want to do it', 'They are doing a project and it is difficult to say what they ought to be engaged on at any particular time', 'We've given up sending out reports, they're so misleading', 'We don't believe set written work is appropriate at this stage (fourteen year olds). We try to keep them from writing things down as long as possible' ... 'If he wasn't taught cursive script in the primary school, then we're inclined to let him print; we don't like to interfere in these matters' [these were real answers given in response to queries at a parents' evening at one of his children's school].

In intention this is a mocking criticism of a risible system of education. Martin had seen the future and knew it wouldn't work. Indeed he had seen it at first hand for before joining the staff at the LSE in 1962,[2] David Martin had spent seven years (1952–59) working as a teacher in a primary school, including a spell at a school where the headteacher was a typical progressivist bigot who would not allow his teachers to teach the children their multiplication tables. Martin, mindful of his higher duty to the children, had his charges whisper their tables instead of reciting them so that the authoritarian progressive in charge of the school would not find out. It was a dangerous thing to do; what if the strange murmuring hush had led the head-

---

2.   David Martin was appointed to the LSE in 1962 having previously taken a first class honours degree (BSc Sociology) at the University of London as an external student, an achievement based on wide, self-chosen reading and independent thought. This route to obtaining qualifications may well be one reason for his amazing creativity; it was not stifled by the horrid deadliness of most mainstream sociology teaching.

teacher to believe that the children were being encouraged to say their prayers.

Now we *are* the future and we *know* that it didn't work, although 'respected' Professors of Education famed for the monosyllabic contractions of their Christian names still defend the old lie that it is sweet and fitting to be made illiterate in the cause of social engineering. Yet it is also possible, if perverse, to ignore the irony in Martin's essay altogether and to read it as a simple, descriptive and laudatory account of recent advances in education. In fairness, such readers might have been deceived by context. Praise of such compulsive and compulsory progress is just the sort of nonsense that a Professor of Sociology might have written or the *Times Higher Education Supplement* might have printed. Such are the perils of humour.

The second question that faces the serious humorous writer is the role of aggression in humour. According to Thomas Hobbes (1840) all humour consists of a put-down of someone else (or of our own past) in order to elevate our present selves, as a way of experiencing 'sudden glory'. The most recent writer in the Hobbesian tradition, the American scholar Charles Gruner (1997) sees humour as a game and as in all games there are winners and losers. Humour is thus a form of aggression. The problem with this argument is partly that humour is ambiguous and incongruous (Oring 1992) and that the 'victims' of a satire may feel they have been praised and partly that even when the 'victims' do get the point they may enjoy the skill and contrivances of the humorist so much that they do not mind being attacked. Politicians are notorious for wanting to buy the originals of cartoons that have savagely caricatured them. It is easy to conceive of a Bulgarian official philosopher, a secular theologian, a sergeant in the military police, a BSA member or a rigorous economist reading or listening to that piece of David Martin's humorous output that impinged directly on them and enjoying laughing at it. This should not surprise anyone who has ever been amused by Shaw or Brecht or Althusser, despite their bizarre ideological tendencies. Humour exists in a world of its own beyond good and evil and must be judged as such. If I am right that those mocked by David Martin could and did enjoy his work, then this is both a strength and weakness. It is a tribute to his skill as a humorist but also a statement of the limits to which wit can be used as a weapon.

The only exception to the dominance of humour over serious attack that I can find in David Martin's more playful work is his celebrated review 'Words Master Him' (1976a) of Raymond Williams's book *Keywords: A Vocabulary of Culture and Society*. *Keywords* was an unfortunate title for Williams's book; it was a sad reminder that keys are designed to lock doors as well as open them. Here may be seen a rare glimpse of Martin using a truly aggressive humour in which the desire to raise a smile is utterly subordinate to the serious purpose of demolishing a book that might have become a celebrated, inane and dangerous attack on the sociological tradition in and for which Martin stood. Where humour is used by Martin in this review it is merely as an auxiliary weapon in the battle against fashionable nonsense.

In his sole note of praise for Williams's work, Martin commented 'Indeed if you have not time to consult the *Oxford English Dictionary* on which Williams so largely relies then his extensive borrowings from that work can prove very useful. (It is perhaps as well that the OED is in the public domain.)' (1976a). Later Martin wrote that (1976a):

> Williams refers to what he regards as the subtle ideological bias of the OED (though he characteristically omits to say where this lies) but his own compilation shuffles unhappily between factual information and moralistic puffs. He might have been well advised to write a mini-essay on the word 'fact'. But maybe 'fact' is surreptitiously included under 'fiction' since he argues that the supposed contrast between them is 'artificial'...
>
> ... Perhaps the trouble is that basically Williams is a muddler with a talent for moralizing... Here I must distinguish between high-mindedness about society as an object of fastidious and prissy contemplation and genuine sociological seriousness. Raymond Williams is a high-minded man who has exactly caught the right set of attitudes and knows how to strike them for other people's benefit. But as to the profoundly funny business of serious sociological analysis he hasn't an idea and probably never will.

No one had ever dented the charisma of this mumbling while exhorting icon (and a real Cambridge professor, mark you) in such a fashion before. It was a moral revolution. The *Times Higher Education Supplement*, which loves savage book review controversies because they sell copy, added insult to injury by maliciously adorning David Martin's review with a singularly unflattering photograph of Williams in his eminent middle years. Williams's long, lank, proletarian-greasy hair was combed across the top of his ears to fall where his collar would have been had he been wearing one in order to distract attention from a noble brow created by incipient male pattern baldness. Below the high hairline and Williams's invisible eyebrows projected a craggy, creased, pseudo-Welsh-miner's face peering out against the harsh overground light. There was bound to be a battle.

Until then I had thought of 'The Dinosaurs Danced' only as a popular ballad written and sung by the talented composer Adrian Shaw but now they really did. Led by Professor 'Vic' Allen (famously described by E.P. Thompson as the hero of 'Professor Noddy's Trip to Utopia' [Mercer 1986: 383]) the Marxists emerged from the seams of their Jurassic ideology (Mercer 1986: 232, 258) and charged and bellowed at this impudent, large-brained, agile mammal who had challenged the hegemony that was theirs by right. How dare David cast a slingshot at the Goliatherium! Martin (1976b) replied coolly and with wit saying:

> I am not surprised that Professor Allen declares himself impressed by the 'bafflement' induced by Raymond Williams. Many a reputation is enhanced by bafflement and many a reputation would be lost by the descent to clarity. I see he is also baffled by my *Tracts against the Times* since he says it is muddled about Marxism. It contains no discussions of Marxism … I omitted the entry [i.e. Williams's entry] on bureaucracy out of kindness but it comprises one or two quotations, almost *all* from the Oxford English Dictionary, and the pious observation that we have here 'a real and indeed a growing issue'. Indeed we have but what *is* the issue? A gesture in the direction of difficulty is not enough.

Game, set and match to Martin. But why was it funny? It was funny in quite a different way from the gentler humour for which David Martin is renowned. It was a truly Hobbesian flash of sudden glory and the mighty and pompous were unexpectedly laid low by David Martin's dexterity. The audience laughed at their defeat much as we laugh at the downfall of a computer-error-sounding Donald Duck or Tom of Tom and Jerry or RSM Claude Snudge or Mr Samgrass. If Williams had been alone and powerless it would have been different but he was powerful and he had powerful friends who sprang ineptly to his defence. No wonder the crowd leaped to its feet to shout *Olé* for Martin.

This savagely accurate and in places comic demolition of Williams's book by its reviewer was not typical of David Martin's humour and perhaps was a sign that the great humorous phase in Martin's writings was coming to an end. In the complicated world of the 1980s and 1990s David Martin's (1990, 1998) hugely creative contribution to the sociology of religion and to both the study and practice of religion continued unabated but he has only made two significant published contributions to humour in the last 20 years. One was 'Cowgirls for Christ' (1988) a comment on religion in Dallas—Dallas, Texas, not Dallas soap—for *The Independent* and the other his essay 'Making People Good Again' (1992). Clearly his talent for humorous writing is still alive as indeed may also be seen from his 1998 revision of his 1960s still unbroadcast script 'The Non-Combatant Corps' but there seems to be something about our flat contemporary world which prevents the rulers of the media from commissioning further humorous work from him.[3] I hope they change their minds.

BIBLIOGRAPHY

David Martin: Humorous Broadcasts, Manuscript and Archive Material

1967	*The Non-Combatant Corps*, unbroadcast radio talk, revised standard version 1998, Reading University Library Archive, David Martin file.
1968a	*The Bulgarian Ideology*, BBC Third Programme talk, broadcast 4 February 1968, BBC Written Archives microfilm. Printed in Martin 1969a: 131-36.
1968c	*Sociologist Fallen among Secular Theologians*, BBC Third Programme talk, broadcast 21 March 1968, BBC Written Archives microfilm. Printed in *The Listener* 25 April and revised version in Martin 1969a: 61-78.
1968d	*The Politics of Peace*, BBC Third Programme talk, broadcast on 17 June, BBC Written Archives microfilm.
1975a	*Words*, BBC Talk, 8 June.

David Martin: Humorous and other Published Journalism, a Selection

1968b	'Trouble in the University', *The Listener*, 7 March.
1968c	'Sociologist fallen among Secular Theologians', *The Listener*, 25 April 1968. Reprinted in Martin 1969a: 61-78.
1968e	'Bands and Bowls: Review of Brian Jackson, *Working Class Community*', *The Listener*, 30 May 1968.
1969b	'High Dry Love: Review of Harry Kidd, *The Trouble at LSE 1966-67*', *The Listener*, 11 September.
1970a	'Technocracy's Children (Book reviews)', *The Listener*, 26 March.
1970b	' "Literarism" versus "Scientism" (with Bernice Martin)', *Times Literary Supplement*, 16 July.
1973a	'The Grain of Things', *New Statesman*, 1 June.

3.   Also his humour tended to be about controversial matters and David Martin largely withdrew from public polemic after his long and exhausting campaign to try to save the *Book of Common Prayer*.

1973b	'Postgraduate's Lot Is not a Happy One', *Times Higher Education Supplement*, 16 November.
1973c	'Paradoxical Deaths of Humanism and Religion', *Times Higher Education Supplement*, 23 November.
1973d	'The Importance of Being Different', *Times Higher Education Supplement*, 14 December.
1974a	'In Defence of Middle Class Values', *Times Higher Education Supplement*, 11 January.
1974b	'Streaking', *The Listener*, 21 March.
1974c	'The Ugly Face of Participatory Democracy', *Times Higher Education Supplement*, 8 April.
1974d	'The Delicate Streak', *The Listener*, 25 April.
1974e	'The Fine Art of Academic Denigration', *Times Higher Education Supplement*, 14 June.
1974f	'Schools are Nurseries of Democracy', *Times Higher Education Supplement*, 12 June.
1974g	'Bringing Light to the Unbelievers', *Times Higher Education Supplement*, 9 August.
1974h	'In Praise of Authority and Assessment', *Times Higher Education Supplement*, 16 August.
1974i	'Good Place to Acquire a Hole in the Head', *Times Higher Education Supplement*, 4 October.
1974j	'The Self Educated Man: All Alone, He's So all Alone', *Times Higher Education Supplement*, 1 November.
1975b	'Speaking the Speech Skilfully', *Times Higher Education Supplement*, 24 January.
1975c	'Blindfold Pretence of Bureaucracy', *Times Higher Education Supplement*, 13 June.
1975d	'The Issue of Paintboxes: An Analysis in Retrospect', *Times Higher Education Supplement*, 18 July.
1975e	'Will a Welsh Furnacewoman Learn to Love DES 456/789?', *Times Higher Education Supplement*, 17 October.
1976a	'Words Master Him: Review of Raymond Williams, *Keywords*', *Times Higher Education Supplement*, 13 February.
1976b	'Keywords', *Times Higher Education Supplement*, 27 February.
1976c	'Prestige versus Porn: Review of Louis A. Zurcher Sr and R. George Kirkpatrick, *Citizens for Decency*', *Times Literary Supplement*, 24 December.
1978b	'The Revolting Student is Alive and Well and Living on the Higher Education Budget,' *Daily Telegraph*, 4 April.
1979	'After Marcuse: Multi-Dimensional Man', *The Listener*, 9 August.
1988	'Cowgirls for Christ,' *The Independent*, 11 July.

Books and Chapters in Books by David Martin Referred to in the Text

1965	*Pacifism: An Historical and Sociological Study* (London: Routledge & Kegan Paul).
1969a	*The Religious and the Secular, Studies in Secularization* (London: Routledge and Kegan Paul).

1978a	*A General Theory of Secularization* (Oxford: Basil Blackwell).
1990	*Tongues of Fire: The Explosion of Protestantism in Latin America* (Oxford: Basil Blackwell).
1992	'Making People Good Again: The Role of Authority, Fear and Example', in D. Anderson (ed.), *The Loss of Virtue, Moral Confusion and Social Disorder in Britain and America* (London: SAU, 1992), pp. 231-41.
1998	*Does Christianity Cause War?* (Oxford: Basil Blackwell).

Further Bibliography

Chesterton, G.K.
    1987   *Collected Works* (San Francisco: Ignatius).

Davies, Christie
    1989   'Making Fun of Work: Humor as Sociology in the Comedies of H.G. Wells', in P. Parrinder and C. Rolfe (eds.), *H.G. Wells under Revision* (Selinsgrove: Susquehenna University Press): 82-96.
    1992   'The Protestant Ethic and the Comic Spirit of Capitalism', *British Journal of Sociology* 43.3: 421-42.
    1998   *Jokes and their Relation to Society* (Berlin: W. de Gruyter).

Freeman, Derek
    1983   *Margaret Mead and Samoa: The Making and Unmaking of an Anthropological Myth* (Cambridge, MA: Harvard University Press).

Gould, Julius
    1977   *The Attack on Higher Education: Marxist and Radical Penetration* (London: Institute for the Study of Conflict).

Gruner, Charles R.
    1997   *The Game of Humor: A Comprehensive Theory of Why We Laugh* (New Brunswick: Transaction).

Hobbes, Thomas
    1840   'Human Nature or the Fundamental Elements of Policie' (1650), in *The English Works of Thomas Hobbes* (London: Bohn).

Martin, Bernice
    1998   'From Pre to Post-modernity in Latin America: The Case of Pentecostalism', in Paul Heelas, David Martin and Paul Morris (eds.), *Religion, Modernity and Post-Modernity* (Oxford: Basil Blackwell): 102-46.

Mercer, Paul
    1986   *Peace of the Dead* (London: Policy Research Publications).

Oring, Elliott
    1992   *Jokes and their Relations* (Lexington: University Press of Kentucky).

Raskin, Victor
    1985   *Semantic Mechanisms of Humor* (Dordrecht: D. Reidel).

Smith, Sydney
    1854   *The Works of the Rev Sydney Smith* (London: Longmans, Green).

Weber, Max
    1930   *The Protestant Ethic and the Spirit of Capitalism* (London: Unwin).

Wells, H.G.
    1928   *A Quartette of Comedies* (London: Ernest Benn).

French Protestants and the General Theory

Grace Davie

The 'Introductory Comments' in Martin's magisterial *A General Theory of Secularization* indicate that the initial sketch—the five-finger exercise on which the subsequent pages are based—commenced life in a graduate seminar in the London School of Economics in 1968. I was not able to be part of that seminar in any developed sense, but I was undoubtedly influenced by the thinking that emerged from it in my attempts to understand the particular 'minority within a minority' that was the subject of my own doctorate. Like so many graduate students at the LSE, I benefited enormously from Martin's wisdom, direction and knowledge of the field.

What, then, was this minority and how was my thinking coloured by the 'general theory' that was emerging at that time? The first two sections of this essay will be concerned with these questions. The third will look at the evolving nature of the French situation in the later postwar decades, using as a point of reference Martin's more recent writing on secularization. All three sections will underline the greatest debt that I, like so many others, owe to Professor Martin—the encouragement to discern patterns in religious life; patterns which have profound sociological resonance but in no way compromise the faith of those involved.

Right-Wing Politics among French Protestants 1900–45: A 'Minority within a Minority'

My doctoral thesis (Davie 1975) was concerned with a small group of French Protestants, who—in the interwar period in particular—embraced markedly right-wing political views. The most extreme among them were members of a royalist organization known as the *Association Sully*. The easiest way to grasp the nature of the *Association Sully* is to consider it a Protestant version of the *Action Française*—the *Action Française* being the most prominent of a series of nationalist *ligues* in twentieth-century France, all of which endorsed an extreme right-wing political agenda. This agenda included, and at times prioritized, attacks on a series of minorities felt to be hostile to the nature of Frenchness. Charles Maurras (brilliant journalist and leader of the *Action Française*) named four such groups: the Jews; the Protestants; the Masons; and the *métèques* (i.e. foreigners).

A proper understanding of this situation—namely, one in which a small section of an already limited minority embraced political views that at least in part were directed against itself—requires considerable historical background. The following is but a thumbnail sketch.[1] Twentieth-century French Protestantism emerged from a history of persecution. French Calvinists were victims of the re-alignments of European history in the early modern period in which the emergence and definition of the nation state became inextricably linked with the religious factor. Hence the two centuries of European history known as the wars of religion, at the end of which France had established herself as a Catholic nation barely tolerant of its Huguenot minority. The connections between this stage of French history and the situating of French Protestants (and indeed French Jews) on the French political left are more complex than is sometimes imagined. The process continued throughout the nineteenth century and had as much to do with the contemporary *re*-assertions of the alliance between throne and altar as it did with the wars of religion as such. Whatever the case, by the late nineteenth century (i.e. as the Third Republic became established) the vast majority of French Protestants were ready to endorse Republican values—attitudes which were to last at least until 1945, and in some cases well beyond.

Why, then, did a small minority of Protestants turn in a different direction and in the 1920s and 1930s embrace the ideas of the political right, a section of French society closely aligned with Catholicism often in its most intransigent forms? There are various reasons for this, one being the markedly ambiguous legacy of Calvinism from a

---

1.   A considerable sociological literature on the French Protestant community has emerged since the completion of my thesis. Notable within this is the extensive work of Jean Baubérot and Jean-Paul Willaime.

political point of view (see below). The nature of the French left was, moreover, changing as the twentieth century developed—it began among other things to take on a socialist rather than radical hue. No longer were the more prosperous elements of the French Protestant community able to align their economic and ideological interests and while, for the great majority, the latter dominated in the interwar period, the former could not be entirely ignored. Nor could the political instabilities of the Third Republic as France lurched from one crisis to another. For some, including some Protestants, the attractions of strong government became increasingly compelling, despite the resonance of past authoritarianism of which the Protestants had all too often been the victims.

How a small section of the French Protestant community came to terms with these pressures and established a series of organizations, including the *Association Sully*, was the subject of my doctorate (Davie 1975). The final chapter, in particular, attempted to place the material within the larger frame of the as yet unpublished 'general theory'.

The Calvinist Pattern

There are two starting points in this discussion: the French (Latin) pattern and the Calvinist pattern (Martin 1978: 6), each of which pulls in a different direction. The Latin pattern—of which France is a prime example—involves the elimination of religious dissent in so far as this is possible, endorsing a strongly centralized religio-political power. Dissent, in this case the Huguenots, was subject to ruthless and prolonged persecution, a policy which eventually achieved its goal despite protracted and bitter resistance. In the long run, however, the eradication of religious alternatives leads to a different sort of conflict as forces of discontent not only build up but take on a secular— frequently anti-clerical—character. Political life, moreover, is increasingly dominated by such divisions, a situation well exemplified in France at least until the second war. This is a situation in which the great majority of Protestants will locate themselves in the radical, anti-clerical camp—unsurprisingly given that their very existence as a public or legal body depended on the post-Revolution settlements.

The Calvinist pattern works rather differently. In some way the Calvinist inheritance encourages both secular and liberal tendencies. The Church is declericalized from the inside, radically so, in a movement which encourages the autonomy of the individual, felt by some (notably Bruce 1996) to be a necessarily secularizing process. This is even more the case if the movement to greater individualism is linked to rationality. There are, however, strands within Calvinism which push in the opposite direction: they resist rather than encourage the secular. Or to put the same point more directly, Calvinism is both radical *and* restrained: radical in the sense of new understandings in theology based on the doctrines of predestination and redemption, but restrained in terms of its stringent moral and at times political codes. (The effect of this particular combination on the subsequent economic development of Europe has provided inexhaustible material for an ongoing debate among historians and sociologists alike.)

Part of the ambiguity lies, in fact, in the understanding of the term 'Reformation'. Does this imply innovation and the breaking of new ground? Or does it involve a return to and rediscovery of primitive excellence? Were those who endorsed the theological changes taking place in the sixteenth century looking primarily for radical change or for the restoration of order but on a different basis? Motives were bound to be mixed. The more conservative interpretation, however, was bound to appeal to those political rulers anxious to establish independence from external authority, but with a careful eye on stability within. In the early modern period, both were possible within the concept of the 'godly prince' as certain parts of Europe (mostly the Lutheran countries) rejected papal interference but were markedly more cautious about economic and social change inside their designated territories.

Some of these ideas can be applied to the Protestants of the *Association Sully*—a necessarily mixed bunch, many of whom (it must be said) were motivated primarily by political opportunism. Others were seduced by the journalism of Charles Maurras. A rather more thoughtful group, however, took seriously their theological heritage and drew from Calvin theological reflections which legitimated conservative rather than radical political views (Davie 1975: 108-113). In a larger frame, these perceptions form part of the neo-Calvinist revival in the French and Swiss Protestant communities in the interwar period, eventually paving the way for Barthism. The essential point to grasp is the following: there is no necessary connection between Calvinism and rightist (or for that matter leftist) political tendencies, but there *are* currents within Calvinism that can turn towards the right (even an extreme right) given appropriate circumstances or motivations.

Hence the 'minority within a minority'. *Association Sully* Protestants opposed the political views of most of their co-religionists, a group already aware (acutely so) of its minority status. The double minority factor was further compounded by the anti-Protestant views of the French political right. This, in fact, is one reason for the separate existence of the *Association Sully*, an organization (albeit tiny) which permitted Protestants to embrace royalism without becoming part of the *Action française* itself, a movement which by its very nature was hostile to Protestantism. Given such a situation, it is hardly suprising that the *Association Sully* spent considerable time and effort justifying its necessarily vulnerable position—not only in terms of the Calvinist inheritance but also with respect to French history. Regarding the latter, the most encouraging features lay in the Orleanist period (the second quarter of the nineteenth century)—that is, in two decades or so of constitutional monarchy under which French Protestantism flourished.

All this is very small scale. It invites nonetheless a comparative perspective. Hence in the final chapter of the thesis the introduction of a series of Calvinist cases—South Africa, Northern Ireland, Scotland, the Netherlands, Switzerland and France[2]—in terms of the following variables: majority/minority existence; the economic and social status of the Calvinist community; the existence or otherwise of a rival church (asking whether this was traditionally hostile to the Calvinism); the existence or not of an element of persecution; and finally the nature of territorial patterns (the existence of geographical enclaves or, alternatively, of a scattered population). Cases and variables were plotted against each other (Davie 1975: 262), paying close attention to the patterns which emerged—the combinations of which provide the sociological frame within which to place the case study. By and large it is not unusual to find Calvinists on the political right. In this respect it is the French Protestant community as a whole which is 'unusual' (albeit for obvious historical reasons), not the minority within it which, initially, had seemed so odd.

At the same time, I had my first experience of establishing sociological patterns and the multiplicity of variables that have to be taken into account in a proper understanding of sociological process. I

---

2. Some reference was also made to the Russian Baptist community.

also learnt the difference between sensitive and well-informed modes of analysis and crude forms of reductionism in which the theology in question becomes simply a justification for economic or political advantage. In Martin's analysis the theological deposit is always taken seriously, but it takes root in a particular economic and social context which colours, inevitably, the forms of religious life which emerge. The result is a profoundly incarnational form of sociology.

In a collection of essays published very much later (Martin 1996a), Martin makes the same point in socio-theological language. Between the specificities of each situation and the exigencies of the gospel lies 'an angle of eschatological tension'. Documenting and explaining the sharpness of the angle are, essentially, sociological tasks. So are suggestions of possible resolution if the tension becomes unbearable. The tension did indeed become so for many *Association Sully* members once the realities of war had taken hold. Like many others on the French political right, they found themselves sucked into the conflict on the 'wrong side'—a paradoxical state of affairs for those who had embraced the nationalist cause so vehemently. And for some the tragedy was inevitable: the gospel gave way to, or (worse still) was used to legitimate, extreme and anti-Semitic political views. But for others—not least the 'theological' group—precisely the reverse happened: increasingly dubious political views collapsed under the pressure of the gospel despite, at times, considerable cost to the individual concerned (Davie 1972, 1975).

A Re-appraisal: France in the Year 2000

What can be said 25 years later? There have, first of all, been marked changes not only in the French Protestant community itself, but in the religious situation of modern France taken as a whole. Such changes amount to significant modifications in both Latin and Calvinist 'patterns'. This section will start by outlining the principal changes that have taken place; it will conclude with reference to Martin's later work on the 'general theory', specifying its relevance to the French case.

The important point to grasp in relation to the religious life of France (as indeed of other European societies in the late twentieth century) is the presence of several different factors, all working at once but not necessarily in the same direction.[3] On the one hand France has become a markedly more secular society—the statistical decline is one of the sharpest in postwar Europe. In the late 1950s, for example, 90 per cent of French people declared themselves Catholic, a percentage which has dropped to less than 70 per cent in the final decade of the century. A CSA poll in 1994[4] produced a figure of 67 per cent, a drop which mirrors the fall in regular practice (now about 10 per cent on a weekly basis) and in the proportion of infants baptized within the Catholic Church (slipping under 50 per cent for the first time). A whole range of other indicators tell the same story, the most striking of which is the fall in the number of vocations to the priesthood. A country which ordained close to 1000 priests a year in the immediate postwar period, now ordains just over 100 (Willaime 1996: 168). A dramatic change has undoubtedly taken place, which, in many respects, can be described as the collapse of clericalism—a central feature of the Latin pattern.

There are, however, countertendencies. Certain forms of religion flourish in France, as they do elsewhere at the turn of millennium, notably the one-off gatherings for a special occasion (a papal visit or a particular anniversary). One such took place in the summer of 1997, when more than a million, mostly young people, took part in the papal Mass at Longchamp racecourse which marked the climax of the twelfth celebration of the biennial World Youth Days. That such numbers were possible in August (essentially a holiday month) and in an increasingly secular France astonished the pundits. It seems that young people, those most disenchanted with regular churchgoing or with Catholic dogma, are still attracted by the emotionality of the large gathering and respond to the charisma of those whose lives embody other than worldly values (Hervieu-Léger 1994). Theirs is a spirituality easily missed by the conventional statistics of religious attendance or credal statements. It requires a rather different sociological awareness.

An analogous shift can be found in the growing individualism of

---

3.　Again there is a considerable sociological literature on the changing religious situation in modern France. A useful point of entry can be found in the three summary articles published in *Social Compass* 45.1 (1998) (Baubérot, Hervieu-Léger and Willaime). Davie (1999) covers the essential points in English.

4.　This was published in *Le Monde*, 12 May 1994; it is set in a sociological context by Willaime (1996).

French religion, a movement with equal—but paradoxical—significance for the Protestant community. The size and significance of this community remains difficult to estimate: in 1995, 1.7 million French people (3 per cent of the population) declared themselves 'close to Protestantism', though 27 per cent of these were members of the Catholic Church. A figure of 2 per cent is probably closer to the mark. More to the point, the Protestants, like the Catholics, have lost considerable numbers of those prepared to support their churches financially and regular practice continues to fall (Willaime 1996: 168-69). Conversely the Protestant constituency still produces disproportionate numbers of individuals who become prominent in French public life—notably, though not exclusively, in the *Parti Socialiste* (old habits die hard) and in the business world (the countertendency already noted). Indeed there is a school of thought that suggests that the real problem for Protestant identity is the 'protestantization' of French culture as a whole. In such circumstances, it becomes more and more difficult to delineate a Protestant specificity, a necessary element in the formation of identity (Baubérot 1988; Willaime 1992). In some ways French Protestantism has achieved its ultimate goal, but at the price, almost, of its own existence. The distinctiveness of the Calvinist pattern is eroding fast.

How should this material be interpreted? Again the data should be looked at from different angles. It is evident, first of all, that the traditional churches (both Catholic and Protestant) are losing ground not only in terms of their institutional presence but also in terms of their capacity to control both the beliefs and practices of most French citizens. There is a growing emphasis on the notion of choice, as French people—like most Europeans—work out their own religious destinies, selecting their material from the growing range of alternatives on offer. Individual conscience is, it seems, a better guide for most people than the teachings of the historic Church, notably in the area of personal morality.[5]

Such a situation should not be exaggerated: the vast majority of French people will return to the fold at death, if not before. Choices, moreover, are framed by history and French history is indisputably Catholic. The parameters of French society cannot be altered that

5.   More precisely, 83 per cent of the population indicate that individual conscience is their most important guide in the important decisions of life (ISA poll, 1994).

easily: time (public holidays) and space (the presence of a church spire) remain resolutely Catholic. Also enduring are deep-seated regional differences in religious practice or denominational (including Protestant) distribution. Despite the mobilities of modern French society, some aspects of the Latin pattern endure—the cultural legacy is particularly marked. Significant shifts have, however, taken place. In terms of confessional attitudes, for example, ecumenism has begun to replace mutual animosity. Even more significant are the mutations in the political agenda—as clericalism dimishes, so too does its alter ego.

An illuminating example of the latter can be found in the celebrations, in September 1996, of the fifteenth centenary of the baptism into the Catholic Church of Clovis, King of France. The anniversary itself was a strange and recondite affair with little relevance to modern French people. The decision, however, to combine its celebration with a visit of the Pope to France provided a further trigger to the unresolved debate about the place of religion in public life (a legacy of the clerical/anti-clerical controversy). Much of the argument turned on the costs of the papal visit; how much of these were or should be borne by the secular authorities? Rather more significant for the argument of this essay, however, was the increasing realization that the capacity of the free-thinkers or anti-clericals to rally their troops is even more impaired than that of the Church. Quite simply, the issues no longer resonate.

This much is relatively straightforward, but a further question lurks beneath the surface. It can be summarized quite simply. Is it possible to achieve a greater sense of moderation in the religious life of modern Europe (including modern France) without losing sight of the religious factor altogether? Or, to put the same question in a different way, is it necessarily the case that once Europeans cease to dispute the place of religion in modern societies, it ceases for the great majority to matter at all? Holding the balance between these two extremes is not only essential to the maintenance of a healthy democracy, it forms the basis of courteous relations between different religions. Mutual respect between faith communities is as difficult to achieve in a climate of indifference as it is in an atmosphere of hostility.

An example of ongoing controversy in this respect can be found in the *affaire du foulard*, an episode which also reflects the increasing religious pluralism of modern France (one of the most significant features of the postwar period). The central issue in the dispute lies, once again, in the place of religion in public life—this time in the school system. Was it, or was it not, permissible for young Muslim women to attend a state school wearing a *foulard* (the traditional Muslim head-covering for women)? The debate has been intense, prolonged and at times very bitter as significant numbers within the Muslim minority felt that their daughters or sisters would be (or indeed were already) excluded from the education system unless they removed an essential item of Muslim dress. The point at issue concerns the nature of the French education sysytem: this is free, *laïque* and universal—and for the more uncompromising educationalists (frequently of an anti-clerical persuasion), the *foulard*, though not, it seems, a discreetly worn cross or skullcap, violates the principal of *laïcité*.[6]

The notion of *laïcité* is, however, ambiguous and contains within itself more than one interpretation: on the one hand there is a universalist claim based on reason and the exclusion of all religions in the public space; on the other a more pragmatic emphasis which attempts to come to terms with the specificities of the situation in each generation. Not only did both exist from the outset (Bauberot 1990, 1997, 1998), but both continue to resonate in the 1990s with reference to the *affaire du foulard*, within which each understanding of *laïcité* points in a different direction. The first, fearful of the destructive forces of Islam in Europe, adopts a primarily defensive attitude and rejects the possibility of the *foulard* in a state school. The second is more pragmatic and continues to look for new definitions of *laïcité* and new accommodations as France becomes an increasingly plural society. Questions, however, are easier to come by than answers. The unresolved status of the *affaire du foulard* is indicative of the difficulties involved in the second position. Realistic in its intentions, it has yet to produce an enduring solution to this problem.

But what of the future? Will the exigencies of the old patterns endure (albeit with certain modifications) or is something more radical likely to happen? One clue can be found in Martin's renewed attention to the issue of secularization and the ambiguities embedded therein (Martin 1991, 1996). Crucial in this respect is a growing

---

6.   The term *laïcité* is almost impossible to translate into English. It denotes the absence of religion from public space (from the state, from the school system etc.), but is not in itself anti-religious. All religions meet as equals in the public arena; none receives favours, financial or otherwise.

awareness in the work of Martin and others (notably Berger 1992, 1999) that European patterns of religious life are distinct. They derive from the deposits of European history and should be considered in such terms; they are not a blueprint for religion in the modern world. Or to put the same point in terms of the 'general theory', the significance of contigency in understanding the place of religion in developed societies is both sharpened and specified—with the effect that Europe becomes increasingly a special case.

Following Martin (1991) two conclusions emerge from this perspective. First, that the existence of vibrant and growing forms of religion is entirely 'normal' in the modern world. Such forms are neither leftovers from an earlier civilization, nor are they 'really' something else (e.g. justifications for nationalism). They offer, in contrast, a rich and challenging agenda for the sociologist of religion, indeed for all sociologists since they epitomize what it means to be human in a rapidly changing society. The West European case, on the other hand, was brought about by particular circumstances; first by the collusions of religion and power over many centuries and, second, by the ongoing battles between the Church and the forces associated with the Enlightenment. But even in Europe (Martin's second point [1991: 473]), considerable change has taken place:

> [W]ith regard to Europe itself, where the secular dynamic was originally generated, the two supports of that dynamic are in terminal dissolution. On the one side the establishments of religion which gave it a negative association with power and particular elite styles are either things of the past or ineffective facades of the kind remaining in England or Scandinavia. On the other side, the rationalistic passions unleashed by the French Republic have now diminished to the status of a puppet show; and Marxism is rapidly caving in everywhere.

The French case illustrates both dimensions of the argument. That the decline in both clerical and anti-clerical forces has been uneven—with the old reactions continuing to jerk from time to time—does not challenge Martin's conclusion.

A further question follows on. Will the shifts in European religion result simply in collapse and fragmentation, or will the spaces cleared prove receptive to new forms of religion—either generated from within or imported from outside? Either is possible at the turn of the millennium. Martin's close observation of the field for several decades leads him, however, to suggest that the latter might indeed be the way forward. Interestingly it is a point of view that derives from Martin's later work on Latin America (1990)—Europe is examined from the outside rather than from within (Martin 1996b: 41):

> Initially, about a quarter of a century ago, I asked myself why the voluntary denominations of Anglo-American culture had not taken off in Latin America as they had in the U.S.A., and concluded that Latin America must be too similar to Latin Europe for that to happen. But now I am inclined to reverse the question and ask why the burgeoning denominations of Latin America have not taken off in Latin Europe ... There are new spaces being cleared in which a competitive denominational culture can flourish (citations taken from the English original).

Given the erosion of earlier patterns, there is no reason why the voluntary denominationalism of the New World should not find a place in the old, alongside if not always replacing, the historic churches.

Not all sociologists of religion are persuaded by the notion of European exceptionalism. Bruce (1996) and Wilson (1999), for example, continue to embrace an understanding of secularization that includes considerable sections of the modern world, notably—in their view—the United States. Others, including José Casanova and indeed myself, are inclined to follow Martin, whether working on the specificities of the European case (Davie 2000) or within a broader global perspective (Casanova 1994). Either way Martin's work both instructs and provokes—the debt to him among sociologists of religion is and will continue to be enormous.

BIBLIOGRAPHY

Baubérot, J.

    1988   *Le Protestantisme doit-il mourir?* (Paris: Seuil).

    1990   *Vers un pacte laïque* (Paris: Seuil).

    1997   *La morale laïque contre l'order moral* (Paris: Seuil).

    1998   'La laïcité française et ses mutations', *Social Compass* 45.1: 175-87.

Berger, P.

    1992   *A Far Glory: The Quest for Faith in an Age of Credulity* (New York: Free Press).

Berger, P. (ed.)

    1999   *The Impact of Religious Conviction on the Politics of the Twenty-First Century* (Grand Rapids: Eerdmans).

Bruce, S.
1996   *From Cathedrals to Cults: Religion in the Modern World* (Oxford: Oxford University Press).
Casanova, J.
1994   *Public Religions in the Modern World* (Chicago: University of Chicago Press).
Davie, G.
1972   'The French Protestant Church under the German Occupation', *Proceedings of the Huguenot Society of London* 32.2: 127-41.
1975   'Right Wing Politics among French Protestants (1900–1945), with Special Reference to the Association Sully' (thesis, University of London).
1999   'Religion and Laïcité', in M. Cook and G. Davie (eds.), *Modern France* (London: Routledge): 194-215.
2000   *Religion in Modern Europe: A Memory Mutates* (Oxford: Oxford University Press).
Hervieu-Léger, D.
1994   'Religion, Experience and the Pope: Memory and the Experience of French Youth', in J. Fulton and P. Gee (eds.), *Religion in Contemporary Europe* (Lewiston, NY: Edwin Mellen Press): 125-38.
1998   'La recomposition religieuse et les tendances actuelles de la sociologie des religions en France', *Social Compass* 45.1: 143-54.
Martin, D.
1978   *A General Theory of Secularization* (Oxford: Basil Blackwell).
1990   *Tongues of Fire: The Explosion of Protestantism in Latin America* (Oxford: Basil Blackwell).
1991   'The Secularization Issue: Prospect and Retrospect', *British Journal of Sociology* 42.3: 466-74.
1996a   *Reflections on Sociology and Theology* (Oxford: Clarendon Press).
1996b   'Remise en question de la théorie de la sécularisation', in G. Davie and D. Hervieu-Léger (eds.), *Identités religieuses en Europe* (Paris: La Découverte): 25-41.
Willaime, J.-P.
1992   *La précarité protestante: Sociologie du protestantisme contemporain* (Geneva: Labor et Fides).
1996   'Laïcité et religion en France', in G. Davie et D. Hervieu-Léger (eds.), *Identités religieuses en Europe* (Paris: La Découverte): 153-71.
1998   'La France religieuse entre l'Europe du nord et l'Europe du Sud', *Social Compass* 45.1: 155-74.
Wilson, B.
1999   'The Secularization Thesis: Criticisms and Rebuttals', in R. Laermans, B. Wilson and J. Billiet (eds.), *Secularization and Social Integration: Papers in Honor of Karel Dobbelaere* (Leuven: Leuven University Press): 45-65.

Reservoir Gods: Religious Metaphors and Social Change

David Docherty

Introduction

David Martin's engagement with religious symbol systems and social change has been a defining aspect of his work, never more powerfully and intensely expressed than in his book, *The Breaking of the Image*.[1]

Written in the mid-to-late 1970s, it was a companion piece to the more sober, conventionally sociological studies contained in his *A General Theory of Secularization*;[2] but *The Breaking of the Image* cut free from its predecessor's structural mooring and sped off in pursuit of the profound double-meanings contained in transcendent symbolism of Christianity. *The Breaking of the Image* demonstrated Martin's intoxication with religious imagery and his ability to 'see' connections between these symbol systems and the social orders that dammed them in reservoirs of contained meaning. In examples drawn from music, architecture, liturgy and rite he shows the ways in which the walls of the dam time and again were swept away in great transcendental surges triggered by time and circumstance.

Although written at a time of great pre-occupation about the role and importance of semiotics and linguistics, *The Breaking of the Image* (hereafter *The Image*) contains mainly glancing references to such theories. Martin suggests that he is working with a codified transformational grammar of religious symbolism, but there is no labouring over Saussure's signifier and signified, no agonizing over Peirce's

---

1. Oxford: Basil Blackwell, 1980.
2. Oxford: Basil Blackwell, 1978.

triptych of icon, index and symbol, no impish—but dangerous— appearance by Foucault or Lacan, no technical discussion of Eco's semiotics or Barthes's radical subversion of the role of the reader. No postmodern hall of mirrors.

The study of symbolism in the *The Image* stands alone, certainly in the sociology of religion. It creates a world in itself. This, as I shall show, is its strength but may also be its weakness. Although it stops Martin being dragged into arid semiotic wastelands or postmodern fairgrounds, it may leave his theoretical work without a methodological anchor. You somehow suspect at the end of *The Image* that you have to be David Martin to practise the kind of analysis he is advocating.

However, if you accept, as I do, that Martin is saying something of deep sociological importance about religious metaphor and social change, it is reasonable to look for ways to make his approach both generalizable and replicable. At the very least, it should inform the methodical practice of the kind of sociologically based hermeneutics of religion that those in the Weberian tradition have been striving for most of the twentieth century.

There are two gaps in *The Image* that must be addressed. First, it seems to lack a formal or technical engagement with the kind of language with which it is dealing—namely, analogy and paradox. (Although, again, I suspect that as far as *The Image* is concerned, a sober, technical discussion would have slowed down the power of Martin's tumultuous engagement with the double meanings.) In Paul Ricoeur's major study of creative language—*The Rule of Metaphor*[3]—he develops precisely the kind of language analysis which can be applied to the symbolic order required by *The Image*. By lowering Ricoeur's analysis into the social world of struggle and change, we can see how Martin's double-meaning can be grounded. More than that, in a classic hermeneutic fashion, it is the merging of the horizons of both pieces of work that will allow us to unpick the lock of the ways in which religious metaphor have been—and may yet be—engines of profound social change (including, crucially, changing the way we think).

The second gap is an explicit recognition of the social mechanisms that detonate major shifts in meaning. Most of these mechanisms

3.   London: Routledge & Kegan Paul, 1986.

were analysed in detail in *A General Theory of Secularization*, but both books miss one crucially important group who play a pivotal role in the reinterpretation of metaphor, the priests and the religious intellectuals, who play a kind of armourer's role in the use of symbolic power.

So, I want to do three things: outline Martin's basic argument; then show how Ricoeur's theory of metaphor, appropriated in a sociological frame, answers a methodological need in *The Image*; and finally sketch out the role of casuistry in detonating tradition and leading the re-formulation of social order.

Breaking Up Is Hard to Do

In *Does Christianity Cause War?* Martin argues that there is 'an irreducible religious realm of transcendental possibilities that cannot be straightforwardly realised on the plane of politics'. Religion, he argues, 'erects symbolic platforms in consciousness'.[4] This theme is first advanced in *The Image*, in which Martin seeks to capture what he calls the grammar of monotheism and to explore its paradoxes. He isolates the key symbolic tensions in Christianity and demonstrates their uneasy and uncomfortable relation with natural religion.

For Martin, natural religion codes the language of social necessity. It generates a sacred weight around the channels of power, the pattern of obligation and the understood ways.[5] The crucial sociological ties of degree, blood and generation are symbolized and made sacred. If this is symbolic form of natural religion, what about that of the transcendental world faiths that grow out of the Judaic root—Islam and Christianity? (Although it is the ur-text of the monotheistic traditions, Judaism does not conform to the idea of a transcendental faith in the sense that Martin is interested in—i.e. it remains tied to blood and has no appeal to universal brotherhood.)

Christianity, according to Martin, is about radical contingency and

---

4.   David Martin, *Does Christianity Cause War?* (Oxford: Clarendon Press, 1997), p. 135.

5.   Martin, *The Image*, p. 20. See also Martin, *A General Theory of Secularization*; David Martin, *Tongues of Fire: The Explosion of Protestantism in Latin America* (Oxford: Basil Blackwell, 1990) for examples of how Martin uses conventional social analysis to explore the ways in which Christian symbolism interacts with society.

risk—and therefore fundamentally at odds with natural religion. The risky nature of the transcendental faith is expressed in its characteristic linguistic style. He notes that 'Christian language is analogy, paradox, oxymoron, inversion, conversion. And it is set in the active-passive voice. And this new language mounts an attack on the frontier of social possibility.'[6]

The universal brotherhood proclaimed by Christianity and expressed in its symbolism inevitably pushes against social boundaries. Therefore, a transcendental faith breaks up the natural images of blood and brotherhood to open up a unified social space. And it attacks the previously constructed meanings that it borrows from the everyday world. For example, scarring, marring and bruising are sources of power rather than of weakness. The power of wholeness is brokenness. Nietzche articulated a similar thought when he noted that God was the will to nothing sanctified. Nothingness equals godhead, and slavery equals freedom. Martin's work brings clear focus to this 'disputed zone where grace confronts nature'. It is precisely in the process of disputation that disruption occurs in the social order and social change can occur.

To sum up in Martin's own words from *The Image*: 'A world religion must code the underlying structure of social necessity: inertia, contiguity, hierarchy. But it will also code the transcendence of the underlying structure…which embody intimation of change, universality and equality.'[7]

The fascination of *The Image* lies not in the opposition between the symbols of natural and transcendental faiths, but in the analysis of the way that the former appropriates the latter only to discover that it has swallowed something alien, something that at some stage will burst out and consume the social order that initially consumed it. Each age may be pregnant with the next, as Marx would have it, but in Martin, each age is pregnant with alien possibilities; the foetus of each age has many fathers, and is the product of many seeds. He points to the ways in which radicalism, striving to invent the new world order, has to save itself and in the process appropriates the world of blood and hierarchy from which it seeks to escape. Breaking the image is hard to do because those who seek to break also seek to build.

6. Martin, *The Image*, p. 129.
7. Martin, *The Image*, p. 170.

Rounding Up the Radicals

The central moment in *The Image* is the argument that Christian 'images lie poised in the realm of symbols awaiting the moment of release. And when they are released they fragment and disperse in the collective psyche, achieving their end by another route and under another name.'[8]

Christian symbols are reservoir Gods. They are stored and dammed up before they can be released slowly into the body politic and body religious. The radical explosion must protect itself and the faithful gather into cells that become churches that become state religions that turn again to sects and cults. Throughout this journey the symbols continue simultaneously to proclaim control and release. Martin isolates the universal nature of this complex double meaning.

> The necessary instruments of openness can lead to closure. The partition which says there is more to come may cut off potentiality. The transfiguration may be used to diminish and not to alter, because the figures of grace have been translated into a completely foreign other world, expropriated and removed from their proper contact with human potentiality.[9]

A protective rail is thrown up around the symbols and rituals of grace and the pursuit of universal brotherhood is carried in small, social units. The radicals round themselves up in the holy space of the monastery, the commune or the holy city. However, the so-called holy city is inevitably a paradigm case of destruction, failure and disillusion. Inevitably hierarchy and discipline are required to deliver equality and brotherhood and the symbols systems must express both potentialities (the chains of freedom).

As the spiral of double meanings is played out into the twentieth century, Martin notes that the sacred has been saved at the expense of its dynamic with social reality. The image has been locked away to preserve its purity and in the process has lost the dialectic with the theodical needs of everyday life. This insight links *The Image* with Martin's work on the structures and processes of secularization at work in Christianity. Unless Christianity is embedded in the needs which natural religion expresses, it can never detonate its transcenden-

---

8.   Martin, *The Image*, p. 15.
9.   Martin, *The Image*, p. 125.

tal bomb, and therefore is pushed to the margins of the store of meanings.

So, Martin has expressed a dynamic theory of Christian symbolism marked by ambiguity, reverse transcription, double-meanings and metaphor. And yet at a conscious level, his theory of symbolism, his semiotic for want of a more appropriate word, curiously pulls on static models of meaning generation. His avowed method is in many ways at odds with the insights he wrestles from the metaphors.

A Note on Code Sociology

Martin appeals to the idea of collective logic and codifications in his model of how symbols operate. He argues that 'Religious thinking, more especially as realised in the major world faiths, is a form of collective logic, with its own rules and modalities. These take up and express a unique attitude to the world.'[10] His task, as he sees it, is to state the fundamental code in which the Christian message is carried.

This hard-line approach was modified some time later in *Does Christianity Cause War?*, in which he argues that faiths have a 'flexible but distinct logic'.[11] He states that he is interested in the 'horizon within which moral rules and prescriptions are set'.[12] In the later book, the language of codes, although still lurking, has become a more suggestive idea that he is interested in the sign language of Christianity.[13] Sign languages share one crucial characteristic of natural languages: they operate at the level of discourse between two or more people, and are shaped and modified in the course of references created in the interaction. By the time of *Does Christianity Cause War?* Martin had also modified the notion that each faith has 'a huge and consistent repertoire of images', to the notion that there is a 'symbolic whispering gallery working through Christian civilisation'.[14]

The methods by which we gain access to the whispering gallery or the code are basically hermeneutic. Martin believes that the history of transcendental double-meaning is 'a secret history which cannot easily be verified by the ordinary processes of historical inspection. The evi-

10. Martin, *The Image*, p. 153.
11. Martin, *Does Christianity Cause War?*, p. 120.
12. Martin, *Does Christianity Cause War?*, p. 133.
13. Martin, *Does Christianity Cause War?*, p. 111.
14. Martin, *Does Christianity Cause War?*, p. 151.

dence is documentary and iconographic. And even this is not evidence but illustration.'[15] Elsewhere, he notes that 'the effect of liturgy, gospel and word is indeed part of a secret history ignored in the chronicles or battles and economic transformations'. We have almost lost the capacity to read such signs, he argues. (The key task of hermeneutics as articulated by Gadamer and Ricoeur is the reclamation of the ability to read the past in terms of being in the world today.)[16]

Martin is obviously patient enough, systematic enough and insightful enough to gain access to the secret history, but he does not leave a clear guide-rope for the rest of us to follow. Martin uses what one might call methodological metaphors to explain his own approach. He argues that he is trying to provide 'a map of sacred and secular which contains a transformational grammar'. But surely transformational grammar is too precise an idea to carry the load of meaning that Martin lands on it? First developed in Noam Chomsky's seminal *Syntactic Structures*,[17] the term transformational grammar refers to the box of rules by which grammar, in an ideal situation, relates deep and surface sentence structures. (Or more precisely that each sentence has two structures—deep and surface—and grammar provides a set of rules that relate them.) It is a precise, technical map. There is no room for interpretation, no shimmering horizons of meaning.

The best way to illustrate why this does not remotely apply to the kind of analysis actually performed in *The Image* is to offer one of Chomsky's transformational grammar rules—the so-called 'number transformation':

Present --- {s/NPsing___
          Ø/elsewhere

'This is a context-sensitive rule which says that Present is to be rewritten as "s" if and only if it is immediately preceded in the under-

15. Martin, *The Image*, p. 44.

16. Martin, *The Image*, p. 179. See Paul Ricoeur, *Time and Narrative*, I (Chicago: University of Chicago Press, 1990); Hans-Georg Gadamer, *Truth and Method* (trans. Garret Burden and John Cumming; New York: Seabury Press, 1975).

17. See John Lyons, *Chomsky* (London: Fontana, 1970), still the clearest introduction to Chomsky. See in particular chapter 7 on transformational grammar, from which I have drawn the example. See also Chomsky's 'Conditions on Rules of Grammar', in Roger W. Cole (ed.), *Current Issues in Linguistic Theory* (Bloomington: Indiana University Press, 1977).

lying string by a sequence of one or more elements dominated by the *NPsing* in the associated phrase marker, but is to be rewritten in all other contexts as zero (i.e. as the absence of suffix).'[18] There is no semantic tree that can remotely deal with God is Love in a transformational way. There is no universal grammar of symbolism in which surface and deep structures can be translated by mathematically precise transformational rules.

I labour the point only because the idea that the interplay between transcendental metaphors and natural religion (by which I mean all theodical solutions to the problems of everyday living) can be reduced to a hard and fast set of codes undermines the very breakthroughs presupposed in the double-meaning. Compare, for example, *The Image* to Louis Marin's *The Semiotics of the Passion Narrative*, with its detailed and precise delineation of toponymic networks.[19] Martin's work is definitively sociological and rich in its 'feel' for the world he describes; Marin offers a conventional semiological reading of the Passion narrative which is insightful but difficult to apply to the real world in which the Passion narrative is a discursive multi-media experience filled with paradoxical illusion and allusion.

That Martin knows himself that he is not dealing with a recognizable semiotic is shown by the way he reaches for other descriptions of his method—calling his analysis 'a geography of signs',[20] (still too static, arguably, given that geography is about discovering a pre-existing world rather than that which is constantly being created). And finally he argues that 'Music is closer to religious thinking than either ordinary logic or poetic tradition. Ordinary logic is too unified and impersonal; poetic tradition too fragmented and personal.'[21]

Given that he is dealing with multiple reversals of meaning and with symbolic plenitude waiting for release, he is handling a great deal more than just a grammar and vocabulary of signs. He is trying to understand the well-springs of creative imagination as it relates to major sociological transformations. And he is searching for it in the real stuff of life. He is looking for it in the practice of religion in terms of celebration, remembrance and proclamation, and every invocation

18. Lyons, *Chomsky*, pp. 72-73.
19. Louis Marin, *The Semiotics of the Passion Narrative* (trans. Alfred M. Johnstone, Jr; Pittsburgh: Pickwick Press, 1980).
20. Martin, *The Image*, p. 59.
21. Martin, *The Image*, p. 159.

of the transcendent in act, image, word and musical sound. As he says, this is a multi-media environment that organizes life completely.

And yet the organized life is broken, transformed, transcended and re-made. The media collapse in on themselves or are tumbled over in iconoclastic surges. This is possible precisely because Christian speech (and the multi-media environment) is rooted in analogy just as it is rooted in paradox.[22] When the invisible is made flesh it makes its appearance in the world of analogy: it proclaims that 'the transcendent is like this or that' (God is like a father, or a shamrock) or, more powerfully, 'the transcendent is this or that' (God is the father, or God is the word).

What we need, therefore, is a theory of language and of symbolic development that is active and imaginative; that does not rely on code, although does not reject it; that operates at the level of people engaged in the stuff of their everyday lives; that can gain insight into the moment when individuals and collectives are switched on by the transcendental implications of the metaphoric world in which they live and have their being. Paul Ricoeur's study of metaphor can usefully be examined for insights into how Martin's approach may be grounded. As Martin himself says of his approach, watch carefully to see how it connects.[23]

Enigma Expressions: Ricoeur on Metaphor

Paul Ricoeur shares much in common with David Martin. Like Martin, he is a Protestant preacher as well as being a social theorist. Both men are religiously musical and have an open engagement with Christianity and religious experience, and both are fascinated by the power of religious symbolism. But there are clear differences. Martin is obviously more engaged by sociology and the careful gathering, ordering and assessment of evidence, whereas Ricoeur is on an intellectual journey that has ranged from the phenomenology of *The Symbolism of Evil*, through complex engagements with Freud, linguistic philosophy, Habermas, semiotics and semiology. But always he returns to hermeneutics and to the questions of what it is to be in the world. From this large canvas, I want to focus on the small square that is his theory of metaphor (although I harbour the suspicion that if you

22. Martin, *The Image*, p. 120.
23. Martin, *Does Christianity Cause War?*, p. 138.

blow up the small square you will see the large canvas writ small.)

One of Ricoeur's phrases for ideas such as the kingdom of God or the Son of Man is that they are enigma expressions.[24] These cannot be decoded like the Bletchley Park enigma code; enigma expressions cannot be cracked by reading numbers off in a precise manner. They cannot be reduced to the words from which they are composed.

Similarly, Ricoeur argues that parable is a metaphor in narrative form. Its structure has the capacity to shock us into new ways of thinking and being. This idea of being-shock goes to the heart of Ricoeur's theory of metaphor and how it can be appropriated within a sociology of cultural change. In his book, *The Rule of Metaphor*, Ricoeur tackled the problems of the emergence of new meanings in language and of the referential claims raised by such non-descriptive languages as poetic discourse.[25]

The conventional definition of metaphor is that of a figure of speech in which two unlike objects are compared by identification or substitution of one for the other. For the past 50 years or so, following Roman Jakobson's ground-breaking work on aphasia, linguists and semiologists have contrasted the combination and substitution implicit in metaphor with that of similarity and contiguity implicit in metonymy and synecdoche (in which the change of name of some object or idea is substituted for another to which it has some relation). These latter parts of speech operate by contiguity to the object—the sceptre represents the monarchy, No 10 means the Prime Minister. Metaphor, by contrast, operates by intruding an unusual object of reference into the sentence (The King is like a wolf. The King is a wolf).[26]

For Ricoeur, 'metaphor is what separates a meaningful self-contradictory statement from a self-destructive self-contradictory statement'.[27] It is a figure of speech that presents in an open fashion, by means of a conflict between identity and difference, the process that,

24. Paul Ricoeur, *Essays on Biblical Interpretation* (London: SPCK, 1981), p. 45. See also Paul Ricoeur, *Figuring the Sacred: Religion, Narrative, and Imagination* (Minneapolis: Augsburg–Fortress, 1995).

25. See *Essays on Biblical Interpretation*, p. 41, for Ricoeur's own description of his study of metaphor. Also see Paul Ricoeur, *The Rule of Metaphor* (London: Routledge & Kegan Paul, 1978), pp. 92-94.

26. Ricoeur, *Rule of Metaphor*, p. 198.

27. Ricoeur, *Rule of Metaphor*, p. 194.

in a covert manner, generates semantic grids by fusions of differences into identity. He argues that metaphors are models for redescribing reality, and that metaphor organizes our view of humankind.

According to Aristotle, metaphor has two distinct goals: persuasion in oral discourse and the mimesis of human action in tragic poetry. These two social functions have profound effects when translated into Martin's world of symbols carrying *at one and the same time* reactionary and revolutionary implications (with both meanings capable of being reversed at any moment, the revolutionary becoming reactionary and vice versa). In imitating Christ, we know that he is come to set brother against brother and father against son, but we know also that he had an intimate loving relationship with his father ('I and the father are one'). It is the power of metaphor that being set together words take on qualities they do not possess in themselves, which even contradict those they possess otherwise.

Metaphor is the rhetorical process by which discourse unleashes the power that certain fictions have to describe reality. It operates at the level of the sentence, and therefore it is about semantics and not semiotics. Following the linguist Benveniste, Ricoeur distinguishes between semantics, in which the sentence is the carrier of the minimum complete meaning, and semiotics in which the word is treated as a sign in the lexical code. As he says, 'to say with de Saussure that language is a system of signs is to characterise language in just one of its aspects and not in its total reality. Semantics are not reducible to semiotics.'[28]

Semiotics is aware only of the intralinguistic relationships, whereas semantics takes up the relation between the sign and the thing signified. And it takes account of the situation in which the discourse occurs and the speaker's attitude to the world and the context. Metaphors are therefore powerhouses of meaning and work hard with and on the imagination.

How Do Metaphors Do their Work?

It is a consequence of their being set together that words take on qualities they do not possess in themselves, which even contradict those they possess otherwise.[29] For Ricoeur, committed as he is to

---

28. Ricoeur, *Rule of Metaphor*, p. 69.
29. Ricoeur, *Rule of Metaphor*, p. 76.

operating at the level of discourse, it is not enough to suggest that the metaphor can be reduced to its linguistic components. It is also motivated by resemblance and reference. Resemblance must be about predicates rather than just the substitution of names, and resemblance can be seen as the site of the clash between sameness and difference; it is therefore resemblance where the double-meaning is at its most dangerous. When the sword becomes a cross and the cross a sword, those who 'see' the metaphor set in motion the cross-sword as the defender of the faith, but also, of course, as the way in which the cross nullifies the sword and crosses it off as a means of imitating Christ.

According to Ricoeur, metaphors have the power to break categories in order to establish new logical frontiers on the ruins of their forerunner. They are agents of revelation. The essence of metaphor is to present an idea under the sign of another idea that is more striking or better known. Therefore metaphor liberates thinking, whereas metonymy, because it is anchored in current social reality (it is only a part representing an existing whole), is inherently conservative. In its poetic form, metaphor extends the power of double-meaning from the realm of the cognitive to that of the affective. Metaphors move people, both emotionally and sociologically; they move the symbolism on. Metonym may do for natural religion what metaphor does for transcendental symbolism.

Ricoeur argues that as you go from analysing sentences to exploring poetry, plays, prayers and liturgy you go to a hermeneutic plane. And when he himself does so, he connects back to the same concerns as Martin. For example, he argues:

> Just as the world of poetic texts opens its way across the ruins of the intraworldly objects of everyday existence and of science, so too the new being projected by the biblical text opens its way across the world of ordinary experience and in spite of the closed nature of that experience. The power to project this new world is the power of breaking though and of an opening.[30]

Therefore when Martin says that the problem of Christian logic turns compulsively on the relationship between father and son,[31] or that the primary oxymoron is the warfare of the cross and whole armour of salvation,[32] or that universal illumination must focus down

30. Ricoeur, *Essays on Biblical Interpretation*, p. 104.
31. Martin, *The Image*, p. 157.
32. Martin, *Does Christianity Cause War?*, p. 113.

on a particular spot and be contained in a particular body, we know that we should look for the conditions under which such metaphors are created, appropriated and reinterpreted.

To recapitulate: Ricoeur points to the fact that metaphors are agents of revelation; they are more powerful than metonymy in re-defining the world; they operate at the level of discourse and not words; they require a fluid hermeneutic rather than a static semiotic analysis; and they are ways in which creative intelligence operates to appropriate meaning in the world. The double-meaning of the metaphor is a powerful mechanism for social change, and we can return to the themes of *The Image*, armed with a sense of how the broken images can, as Martin puts it, 'slide under the net of sociological prohibition and reappear in disguise, carrying explosive charges which have to wait on time and circumstances'.[33]

Acid Drips: Transcendetal Metaphors and Social Change

Why is it that transcendental symbolism becomes tamed and only occasionally bursts through to become entangled in social change? Martin's explanation is that there has to be a long period of imprinting in which the visionary acid cuts deeper and deeper into the psyche, that the structures of communication and image cannot bear the load, and that the vision is inevitably captured by the need to reproduce it in human communities.

But as the vision drips away—occasionally erupting to produce 'heterodox' social responses, such as the Albigensians, Cathars or German flagellants, or the intense socially 'orthodox' forms such as the Franciscans or the Italian flagellants—it is storing up trouble for the prevailing natural version of the transcendental faith. This is because the vision is at war with its natural imprinting and because, as Martin notes later in *Does Christianity Cause War?*, there is a common dynamic shared between the realm of politics and religion, namely the 'persistent human struggle to secure peace, to acquire access, to institute equality and ensure that communication takes place as far as possible between persons of equal worth and dignity'. Transcendental religions are deeply implicated in the impulse to seek freedom, despite their appropriation by the enemies of that freedom.[34]

33. Martin, *The Image*, p. 159.
34. Martin, *Does Christianity Cause War?*, p. 136.

The question remains: why do the metaphors only ignite under certain circumstances? The answer, in part, I would argue, lies with Weber's insight that casuistry drives change as well as stasis. The priests break the image.

Moving and Shaking:
The Religious Role of the Chattering Classes

Religion is articulated by metaphor and metonymy. You cannot do religion without engaging the creative imagination in trying to explain the invisible from the visible means at your disposal. And in transcendental faiths the teachers, the priests, the community leaders, are dedicated to the word and the explication of the mysteries.

The great revivals and breakthroughs are by those members of the chattering class who are displaced by their engagement with the word. They see the double-meaning and commit themselves to the transcendental vision with an intensity that turns it into a mission. In Jesus, Paul, Augustine, Luther, Wesley, Martin Luther King and the myriad of modern schismatics the words are fleshed out and made flesh. As Martin notes, in transcendental revolutions the failure of the priesthood to represent Christ means that it will represent the anti-Christ.

There is a double-meaning to the notion of chattering classes. It refers to those who do the chattering and those in the classroom absorbing, challenging, internalizing and uniting around the message. Through these little workshops of meaning the collective work that produces revolutions and breakthroughs takes place. In the chattering classes metaphors become loaded with new meaning as their transcendental implications are absorbed. The double-meaning becomes part of the discourse about what it means to be in the world and how to make the world perfect. As the members of the chattering class talk they create new meaning. As they discuss the tongues of fire, they acquire a fire in their belly. The laity learn to talk in the act of talking and in the act of talking they learn to act. To paraphrase Walter Ong, chattering is consciousness-raising.[35]

Groups engage in selective readings of metaphor according to time and place, social position and the implications of religion in social structure. As structural circumstances lead to (or are produced by) a

35. Walter J. Ong, *Orality and Literature* (London: Methuen, 1982).

new reading of metaphor, the fusion of sense and senses in the Christian multi-media framework becomes stuff to look at and not through. And in that moment of looking at, rather than through, the chattering classes can see the symbol system as oppressive rather than liberating; as closure rather than an opening. To return to Ricoeur: metaphor is not limited to suspending natural reality, but that in opening meaning up on the imaginative side it also opens it towards a dimension of reality that does not coincide with what ordinary language envisages under the name of natural reality.[36] Transcendental Christian analogies as explored in the chattering classes strive to appropriate new realities and to disinter the symbolic body of Christ for re-inspection.

Martin hints at the role of clerics in driving liturgical change but does not approach the issue of revolutionary casuistry as an engine of social change. However, he does point convincingly to the idea that the pre-condition of freedom is probably a deep, internalized experience of the chains in which the believer is being held.[37] Unless you live with the symbols and have a deep, rhythmic relationship with them, Martin argues that it is impossible to use them to transcend their current meaning. Without the understood rules and sequences no breakthrough of the spirit is possible, argues Martin. Repetition and pattern are the sources of self-hood, and therefore translation, transport, transcendence depends on the received, the recorded, the recognized (or at least the symbolic half-life of the received; revivals among the un-churched, including that of the original Methodist movement, rely on echoes, which have been increasingly attenuated as secularization's own acid drips into the symbolic heart of society).

Conclusion

David Martin's work, taken as a whole, has struggled with a Jacob's ladder of structure and meaning, trying to read the messages and social patterns as they impinge upon and re-define one another. *The Image* is unique in his work, in that he allows himself the liberty of focusing more steadfastly on the symbolic realm and the double-meanings at the heart of Christianity. I have argued that the project would benefit from a more systematic engagement with theories of

36. Ricoeur, *Rule of Metaphor*, p. 211.
37. Martin, *The Image*, p. 85-101.

metaphor and the role of the casuistic classes in explicating and making real the transcendental crisis at the heart of the metaphor. However, this does not detract from the power of the work or the persuasiveness of the argument. Aristotle offers an observation on language: 'the greatest thing by far is to be a master of metaphor'. David Martin is.

The Sociologist as Stylist: David Martin and Pentecostalism

Graham Howes

The social sciences in general, and sociology in particular, have long suffered from what might be termed SED—Stylistic Expression Deficiency. The roots of this lie partly in sociology's positivist provenance and especially in the presumption, among many of its founding fathers, that the academic legitimacy of a so-called 'science of society' rested heavily upon its capacity to demonstrate scientific method, scientifically expressed. The price of empirical orthodoxy was often stylistic paucity. A second source was, of course, 'classical' sociology itself, and especially Max Weber, whose breadth, penetration and intellectual power were accompanied by elaborate syntax and dense, allusive prose. Its over-literal translation, not least by Talcott Parsons (whose own prose suffered as a result) led, especially in North America, to a neo-Teutonic house-style, overloaded with subordinate clauses, and to theory invariably couched in highly dysfunctional language. British sociologists, situated institutionally and symbolically between Arts and Sciences, tended to opt, unless they were Marxists, for a stylistic fusion of Spencer and Weber. That legacy remains, albeit with potent Gallic addenda drawn from Foucault and Bourdieu. It might be described as 'Germano-Gallic', and its high priest remains Anthony Giddens. Giddens, now Director of David Martin's own LSE, New Labour *savant*, and with an unequivocally international academic reputation, lectures with enviable fluency and clarity. However, on paper his prose is peppered with terms such as 'structuration', 'disembedding' and so on—organizing concepts whose stylistic brutalism almost negates their theoretical originality.

Such observations, although necessarily over-generalized, can be applied to many contemporary British sociologists of religion. However, they simply do not apply to one of the leading practitioners of the postwar generation—David Martin. Whether this is due to his relatively traditional educational and denominational background, or to the more complex and subtle language that his chosen specialism (with its interplay of sociological, historical and theological modes of thought and expression) demands, remains problematic. Yet the stylistic outcome is not merely an effective riposte to routine criticism of sociology's intellectual pretension and banality, but a source of aesthetic pleasure in itself. 'I've been reading David Martin on secularization', the late Lawrence Stone once remarked to me. 'I had no idea that a British sociologist could write like that. It's very unusual, surely?'

Indeed it is, and on re-reading much of the Martin *oeuvre*, one is repeatedly struck by several stylistic features of his writing. One is the constant, often brilliant, fusion of the literal and the metaphorical in his exposition. Another is his capacity for expressing elaborate theoretical pre-suppositions in lucid and lapidary prose. Thirdly, his skill in presenting highly complex models of socio-cultural change both synchronically and diachronically, in vivid and persuasive language. All three characteristics are omnipresent in his writings—most notably in his extended discourse on secularization, his reflections on the relationship between religion and cultural identity, worldwide, and his exploration of the interfaces between sociology and theology. However, there is a fourth subject area to which Martin has increasingly turned his attention in the last decade, and where his exceptional gifts—conceptual, analytical and methodological, as well as stylistic— are clearly discernable. This is his account of the rise of Pentecostalism as a global phenomenon.

This, noted *en passant* in some earlier work, received fuller treatment in Martin's 1988 essay 'Evangelism South of the American Border' (itself not published until 1993, in the Festschrift for Bryan Wilson entitled *Secularization, Rationalism and Sectarianism*), and extended treatment in his book *Tongues of Fire*, published in 1990. A second, more ethnographically explicit, volume is to follow. In addition, a brilliant *summum*, *Forbidden Revolutions*, subtitled 'Pentecostalism in Latin America, Catholicism in Eastern Europe' appeared in 1996, and a recent collection of essays, *Reflections on Sociology and Theology*, published in 1997, contains both material on Pentecostalism and com-

parative sociological and theological worldviews. In each account
Martin's counterpoint between his conceptual schema, the supporting
data, the narrative thrust, and their collective expression on the page is
beautifully judged, and perfectly executed. The explanations for this
are not difficult to find. Indeed they are easily located within Martin's
own writings. To begin with he has a very clear idea of what
sociology, and especially the sociology of religion, should—and
should not—be. He is deeply suspicious of what he calls 'the standard
rhetoric of sociology, which is closely intertwined with the standard
rhetoric of the contemporary Western intelligentsia. For that matter it
is all too closely linked to the jargon of business organization and
political discourse' (1996: 2). Instead he sees sociology as 'a human
science which seeks regularities within the specific densities and local
character of culture as that unfolds over time in an understandable
narrative. It is a mode of telling "the story"… It also subjects the
inwardness of human culture to a certain amount of external re-
description' (1997: p. 2).

Unsurprisingly, therefore, Martin does not see religion merely as an
epiphenomenon of social, economic or political forces—a dependent
rather than an independent variable—but rather as possessing, especially in the Pentecostal context, a cultural autonomy of its own. For
him, 'culture is not merely a derivative sphere that picks up impulses
from the supposed "motors" of change, but one that autonomously
generates its own transformations' (1996: 2). Hence Martin repeatedly
affirms the primacy of culture over structure, and sees Pentecostalism
in the late twentieth century, like Methodism in the eighteenth, as a
historical validation of 'the latent capacity of cultural changes held in
religious storage to emerge over time when circumstances are propitious to activate them' (1990: 44). When this happens, 'the cultural
margin (or rather the margin we call culture) can effect the so-called
centre' (1996: 16).

Finally, Martin's sociological persuasiveness is underpinned (and
more convincingly than Weber's) by his breathtakingly synoptic, yet
detailed, view of the historical process. The perspective is avowedly
contra-dialectical, for 'the direction, or rather the directions, of change
depend not on prescribed and automatic consequences of this factor
or that, but on the circumscriptions flowing from a gestalt of
influences' (1996: 25). Hence Pentecostalism's 'story' is grounded less
in the meta-narrative of secularization, and Christian responses to it,

but rather in 'three major mobilizations roughly a century apart, each with numerous, overlapping derivatives. They are Puritanism, Methodism, and Pentecostalism' where 'each successive mobilization was further away from the Church–State connection, and reached less far into the upper strata and probed further into the lower strata' (1993a: 110). In addition Martin points to the family resemblances between Methodism, as the second wave of Protestantism, and Pentecostalism as the third, acted out against 'the world-historical clash between the Anglo-American and Hispanic worlds over the past several centuries' (1993a: 102).

This is *macro*-Martin at his persuasive best. Yet the *micro*-Martin is also present simultaneously, drawing (especially in *Tongues of Fire*), upon dozens of detailed research monographs, published and unpublished, as well as his own field work, and effortlessly synthesizing both. The net outcome, unlike some other similar enterprises, is sometimes dense, but never dull. One reason for this—and already visible in his earlier work, and especially in *A General Theory of Secularization* (1978)—is that the large-scale mapping exercises that Martin conducts are rarely restricted to the credal and the geopolitical. Instead he constructs detailed relief maps, where sociologists can place themselves 'initially on some very high ground' (1990: 10) and from there identify and monitor every 'free space, in which the old hierarchies are inoperable' (1993a: 122), and within which Pentecostalism is likely to develop. Indeed this lateral, spatial dynamic, whereby for example 'the Pentecostals in Latin America represent the creation of autonomous spiritual space *over against* comprehensive systems' (1996: 10) is, for Martin, at least as significant as their linear, historically engendered, pedigree.

But readers are not only provided with a relief map. They are also given a geologically sectioned one as well, with many geophysical features identified and described. Unlike so many of his Victorian forebears, especially the Christian ones, who were unnerved by geology, Martin repeatedly uses it as a source for some of his most powerful controlling metaphors. Sometimes these brilliantly condense routine empirical observation, as when 'a glance at Pentecostalism in Zimbabwe tells you something of its power to adapt and to run along the lines of fissure in local society' (1996: 38). Elsewhere they homogenize apparently disparate movements. For example 'in Romania, for that matter in Nigeria, Korea and Brazil ... the volcanic action of evangelical churches throws up underground strata and upends them for the first time to public view' (1996: 32). Very occasionally, not unlike his Victorian namesake, the apocalyptic painter John Martin, he is prone to stylistic overkill, as when 'the social world is heaving and cracking with seismic fissures the lava of faith travels in many directions, helping redistribute a new landscape and adapting to a multiplicity of niches' (1996: 59). However, Martin's frequent recourse to geophysical metaphor remains—heuristically at least—very effective, in that for unbeliever and believer alike it both hints at the hidden hand of God and gives high visibility to the often complex dynamics of religious change itself.

Yet for Martin such transformations 'are also achieved at the level of microprocesses and in the texture of intimate personal biographies' (1990: 6). Indeed on the very first page of *Tongues of Fire* he commits himself 'to present a world of actors, as well as of processes', and in a deeply felt aside in the public lectures that became *Forbidden Revolutions*, he reminds us, rather in the manner of E.P. Thompson or Raphael Samuel, that the vast majority of Latin Americans 'are merely spoken *about*. They are described and categorized ... but we never hear their own voices, and would not dream of taking them seriously if we did' (1996: 13). Martin takes them very seriously indeed. Although we still await the detailed ethnographic studies promised in the successor volume to *Tongues of Fire* ('How long, Oh Lord, how long'!), his existing, published material on Pentecostalism, especially in Latin America, contains some vivid and convincing cameos. We meet 'a canny 6-foot preacher in rural Chile, with the features of the Aymara people and a face as lined as a river bed at low tide. He has been a flyweight boxer and left-wing political organizer' and 'the pastor who dug the ditches for the [church] lavatories with his own hands', knowing 'that this is the Lord's doing—and his own' and his flock, who 'literally feel (and are) "good" as they stand respectable and decently suited outside their chapel at the end of the service' (1996: 50-52).

Behind such descriptive empathy lies Martin's clearly perceived understanding of the social psychology of Pentecostalism. Part of this is historically grounded, in the Puritan *classis*, with its voluntarism and religious democracy, and more conspicuously, in early Methodism, which provided Pentecostalism with prototypical 'models of equality, fraternity and peacability in the religious enclaves of culture' and 'set up communities, the political implications of which are fraternal, participatory and egalitarian' (1996: 22). But Martin also provides us, characteristically, with two accompanying metaphorical devices to reinforce sober, empirical analysis of the Pentecostal phenomenon. One, which he applies to evangelical religion in general, is that of 'a protective box in which novel seeds may grow. It contains mutations at the level of culture, and nurtures them by creating a strong boundary between itself and the outside world' (1993a: 108). The horticultural image, with its biblical resonances, is both precise and apposite. A second, and even more striking, image recurs throughout Martin's writings on Pentecostalism, and perhaps derives more from Géricault than Genesis. 'Pentecostals have', he tells us, 'dramatically walked out of society in order to construct their own *raft* away from the pull of the mainstream and of their own past' (1996: 42; my emphasis). They also 'bind themselves together on *rafts* of discipline and hope' (1996: 12). The same image also serves him as a highly suggestive metaphor for sectarian development (1990: 6). For

> In the beginning the religious impulse assembles a network to which men and women lash themselves for safety. Initially most of their energy is spent on constructing the raft, devising fraternities and sororities of mutual aid, of communication, and useful connection. Those who guide the raft may well be politically very cautious and conservative, anxious to avoid the destructive turbulence of political contention and polarization.

In Martin's hands 'raft' is always more than merely a literary conceit. It serves brilliantly to meld the banal sociological orthodoxies of 'structure' and 'process' into a vivid and recognizable whole. One cannot ask for more.

Yet there *is* more to be admired in Martin's account of Pentecostalism than just conceptual clarity and methodological rigour allied to striking metaphors and stylistic grace. There is also his enviable capacity to reach what Max Weber called *verstehen*—that is sociological understanding at the level of meaning—in describing the sociocultural and theological 'life-worlds' of his subject matter. In general he recognizes, and acknowledges, the personal transformations that religion can bring about, and the implicit models of behaviour and organization that it can generate. More specifically, the groups with which he is primarily concerned (1993a: 122-23),

have pitifully few resources; nevertheless they do what they can, which
is to reorient themselves in terms of habits, disciplines and priorities
and in terms of seeking to reunite the family. They create networks for
personal and pragmatic support. A new personal assurance goes with a
communal insurance. People save, and avoid waste. They gain a sense
of self-hood and a capacity to participate which is expressed in learning
how to take responsibilities and to lead and to speak in 'tongues' or
sing. A fresh rhythm supersedes repetitious fatality.

Here, in a few sentences, Martin both describes and evokes the
entire mindset and lifestyle of a discrete Christian subculture whose
transformative potential is, in his judgment, not to be underestimated.
But his 'ideal type' is never a vulgar stereotype, but a scrupulous
distillation—most notably in *Tongues of Fire*—of his own, and others'
observation and reflection. Beneath the compressed cadences of the
passage cited above, there lies professional craftmanship of the very
highest order.

There is also marked *theological* understanding. For while Weber
famously declared himself 'religiously unmusical', Martin is exceptionally attuned to Pentecostal theology, both public and private. He
acknowledges that 'Pentecostalism and the various faith missions do
succeed in becoming indigenous expressions of faith, couched in the
vernacular and spread by ordinary men—and women' (1990: 180).
Most Pentecostalists, too, 'have come in from the margins and now
know themselves to stand on the right side of a line approved by
God—not by society…they have made the great transition. Unless',
says Martin, 'one understands the way that divine validation literally
and psychically turns people around, you cannot understand what is
going on at all' (1996: 51). He does understand, as he also understands
both the Pentecostal 'language of Zion', and how 'believers hold con-
versations with God and the biblical characters' 'as a man speaks to his
familiar friend'. One consequence is not political radicalism, but
quietism and *spiritual* democracy, when, in Martin's brilliantly evocative image, 'the saints vacate their plinths in Baroque space and walk
the street as fellow artisans' (1996: 47). Above all, he perceives how
Pentecostal theology 'recovers a radical dualism, present in early
Christianity, which suspects "the world" as an evil entanglement and
simply regards "the powers that be" as an interim ordinance of God
before the final restoration of all things' (1993a: 108).

It is not difficult to find explanations for Martin's strong sense of
the interplay between theology, theodicy, social action and personal

identity. For many years now he has sought not only to demonstrate that 'movements of the spirit and of social dynamics are intelligibly connected' (1997: 45) but also that—*pace* John Milbank—the theological and sociological understandings of the world are not dialectically opposed to each other, but coexist rather 'in parallel facing columns' (1997: 12)—another memorable image! In his account of Pentecostalism in particular he not only points repeatedly to what he calls 'multiple resonances between message and situation' but produces, especially in *Tongues of Fire*, plentiful evidence to negate any presumption (whether by sociologist or theologian) that there is 'sufficient disjunction between the "external" elements in a sociological account to throw some kind of ontological doubt on the internal account' (1997: 12, 6).

It is also, of course, the case that as a Christian himself, he is, for a sociologist, exceptionally sensitized to the language, liturgies, history, thought processes and worldviews of his fellow Christians. Unlike most social anthropologists too, he already know, and understands, the tribal vernacular. For Martin, one tribal sub-group is especially relevant to the unfolding of Penecostalism—not least in Latin America—and that is Methodism. This he sees as 'one central element in the Protestant pattern of social change as it has worked itself out in Anglo-Saxon cultures' and with a 'close genetic connection' between Methodism 'as the second wave of Protestantism, and Pentecostalism as the third' (1990: 27). He also shows clearly how the problematic of Methodism, especially as established by Halévy (i.e. that 'non-violent and a-political quietism feeds the status quo' and diverts energies 'away from the progressive or revolutionary task' [1990: 44]), is equally applicable to Pentecostalism in Latin America. Such an argument, historically detailed by Martin, is relatively convincing, especially when accompanied by a *sociological* case for their 'elective affinity'. For what Methodism and Pentecostalism 'clearly share', he observes, 'is an emphasis on the availability of grace to all, a millennial hope, and an intense search after "scriptural holiness" ' (1990: 28). Indeed one could go further and suggest that Martin's own Methodist provenance also shapes—but never distorts—his perceptions of that affinity. In an essay on 'The Limits and Politics of Ecumenism' (1993b: 133-47) he makes a rare but revealing autobiographical aside: 'I certainly recollect as a child being simultaneously inculcated with a fundamentalist evangelical Methodism and being taken to any church where my parents could recognise what they regarded as "the gospel" … We fellowshipped with warmed hearts anywhere' (1993b: 143). Such exposure, at a formative age, must surely have played its part in fashioning Martin's exceptional capacity to combine subjective empathy with objective scrutiny, to remain unfazed by Pentecostal outpourings of the Spirit, their theological reductionism and their crude visual and musical aesthetic? In this sense Martin *knows* what it is like to be at the margins of a religious culture. He has been there himself.

At the same time he also identifies at least three other dimensions of Latin American Pentecostalism which are, as it were, at one remove from his own religious socialization, but whose cultural significance should not be overlooked. One is the elision, well documented anthropologically, between the Holy Spirit and the indigenous worlds of the spirits. This, as Martin reminds us, is not confined to Latin America, for 'in Africa, in the Americas, even in Europe, there is a shared substrate' (again, note the carefully chosen geological metaphor) 'of the animated and the animistic, both of which are literally synonyms for "the Spirit" in all its guises' (1990: 164). This also provides a pre-Protestant, indeed pre-Christian context for such apparently quintessential Pentecostal phenomena as spiritual healing, speaking in tongues, and pastoral charism. Indeed for Martin the relationship between conservative Protestantism and shamanism is 'perfectly natural, even though it perhaps comes as a surprise'. After all, he reminds us, 'the world of New Testament Christianity contains "demons" and it announces victory over "the powers" ' (1990: 140).

Secondly, Martin also attempts to set Pentecostalism and its higher profiled Latin American cousin, Liberation Theology, in a comparative cultural context. Both are rivals, but both also share the same social ethos—voluntaristic, pluralistic and participatory—the same structures for mutual assistance, and—he might have added—the same commitment to Bible study. Yet although he notes that some of the 'base communities' 'also tackle social problems by collective action and political advocacy' (1993a: 106), he also makes it clear that paradoxically (and Martin has a strong penchant for paradox!) it is Pentecostalism that carries the greater potential for social transformation. It does not, like Liberation Theology, 'operate within the Roman Catholic Church and thus…connected to inside resources of intellectual and cultural power' (1996: 39), nor does it carry what Martin calls the 'danger of cumulative politicization, and of becoming more Marxisant than Christian' (1990: 25). Above all, it does not (yet?) speak in what he caustically describes as 'a decided middle class and radical intellectual accent alien to the localized needs of "the poor"' (1990: 290). Characteristically Martin rounds off his comparative assessment with a trenchant and telling aphorism. 'Pentecostalists are an option *of* the poor rather that the liberationist "option *for* the poor"' (1996: 38).

Finally, Martin also singles out the visible impact of Pentecostal membership, beliefs and identity on the role, self-image and status of Latin American women. While he recognizes that, as in the Catholic 'base communities' also, Pentecostal women are empowered beyond the limits traditionally set by their culture, the latter find it much easier to operate beyond the parameters of normative patriarchalism and a male priesthood. They develop new roles—albeit rarely as an autonomous pastor—and in so doing make significant inroads into male machismo. 'For women', Martin contends, 'these groups offer a sisterhood of shared experience, and an opportunity for social learning and expression' (1996: 38). More poignantly, they may offer a sense of personal redemption, as when we hear how 'a woman looking round at the assembled faces of her sisters, many of whom were once abandoned or abused, feels that this redemption not only from hell, but from a social abyss' (1996: 50). The reader remains unsure whether this is a piece of sociological reportage or a fictive device, or a mixture of the two. What is clear, however, is not just Martin's evocative skills, but his ability to enter and experience the social world of others, and to describe this without sentimentality or condescension.

It will, hopefully, be clear from this necessarily brief and oversimplified account of David Martin's writings that his approach to Pentecostalism is essentially double-headed. Historically he sees it— primarily, but not exclusively—as moving from the margins of religious culture towards its centre. Sociologically he has, almost single-handedly, redirected the attention of his fellow sociologists of religion in a similar direction, arguing firmly, but without fanaticism, that 'the potential impact of this religious phenomenon is likely to be very powerful indeed' (1990: vi). Indeed one might add that its long-term significance for religion and society, and the study of their interaction, will be far greater that that of such culturally marginal and intellectually trivial objects of study as the so-called New Religious Movements.

Put differently, for all its scope and sweep, for all its skill in large-scale mapping exercises, Martin's work on Pentecostalism is, like his work on secularization, never an empty exercise in Grand Theory. It is always buttressed by a mass of empirical evidence, diligently collected and brilliantly synthesized. In this sense it is not unlike a technically flawless version of Max Weber or the French historian Fernand Braudel, but more stylistically dazzling than either. It is not, of course, that Martin's style—sometimes precise and lapidary, sometimes complex and highly allusive, sometimes redolent of the seminar room, sometimes of the pulpit—is consciously designed to structure and determine his arguments as well as articulating them. It just seems that way. Nor, conversely, is that style—so original, so highly charged with simile and metaphor, so daring—little more than Baroque ornamentation adorning a plain neo-Classical facade. It is in fact, always integral to the entire edifice of Martin's sociological enterprise. The result is a work of art—a rarity in the sociology of religion—and something for its practitioners, present and future, to confront and admire, even if they are incapable of emulating it.

BIBLIOGRAPHY

Martin, David A.
1978	*A General Theory of Secularization* (Oxford: Basil Blackwell).
1990	*Tongues of Fire: The Explosion of Protestantism in Latin America* (Oxford: Basil Blackwell).
1993a	'Evangelism South of the American Border', in E. Barker, J.A. Beckford and K. Dobbelaere (eds.), *Secularization, Rationalism and Sectarianism* (Oxford: Clarendon Press): 101-124.
1993b	'The Limits and Politics of Ecumenism', in Barker, Beckford and Dobbelaere (eds.), *Secularization*: 133-47.
1996	*Forbidden Revolutions: Pentecostals in Latin America, Catholicism in Eastern Europe* (London: SPCK).
1997	*Reflections on Sociology and Theology* (Oxford: Clarendon Press).

PART TWO: THEOLOGY AND SOCIOLOGY

David Martin and the Growth of
Protestantism in the Third World

Paul Freston

Specialist By-Pass or Route to the Future?

From the late 1980s, David Martin's academic interest turned
increasingly to Latin America, a region he had mentioned only in
passing in his book *A General Theory of Secularization*.[1] The object of
this interest was not, however, the then academically fashionable topic
of ecclesial base communities within Catholicism. Instead, he examined
the implications of the rapid growth of evangelical Protestantism.

This interest resulted in two publications which I shall examine
here. The main one was his book *Tongues of Fire: The Explosion of
Protestantism in Latin America*;[2] the second was *Forbidden Revolutions:
Pentecostalism in Latin America, Catholicism in Eastern Europe*.[3] The
interest also led to a research project into the economic effects of
Pentecostalism in Brazil and Chile, in association with the Institute
for the Study of Economic Culture directed by Peter Berger. The
results of this project are as yet unpublished. Having met David in
1989 on a trip to England, when we talked about my doctoral research
at the University of Campinas into Protestantism and politics in
Brazil, I was privileged to be invited to help with the Brazil section of
his project, which resulted in two trips by David and Bernice to
Campinas and visits to São Paulo and Rio de Janeiro.

But Latin America was not an end in itself; it was a stepping-stone

1. Oxford: Basil Blackwell, 1978.
2. Oxford: Basil Blackwell, 1990.
3. London: SPCK, 1996.

to ever broader concerns. Already, *Tongues of Fire* signalled the intent to widen the focus. Instead of merely comparing Latin America with the traditional homelands of Protestantism (although it does plenty of that), the book includes two chapters which place Latin phenomena in the context of what is happening in the Caribbean, South Africa and South Korea. Later, in *Forbidden Revolutions*, Eastern Europe is placed in parallel with Latin America (though in the former context all Christian churches are examined). An even broader geographical focus, restricted to evangelicalism, in found in embryo in two later essays. The first is 'The Evangelical Protestant Upsurge and its Political Implications',[4] and the second is 'Evangelical Expansion in Global Society', presented at the 1999 Oxford conference of the Currents in World Christianity project.[5]

I shall look at these four pieces, which mark an ever-widening investigation into the implications of the growth of evangelical Christianity outside the developed West. While for some Western scholars Martin's trajectory may seem a by-way, for me it exemplifies certain perspectives which the sociology of religion needs at the beginning of the new century. Among these is the question of secularization/desecularization in a global frame, especially in the light of globalized evangelicalism and its increasingly Third World base. As a naturalized Brazilian of British origin, based at a Brazilian university and involved in the sociological study of evangelicalism, first in Brazil but increasingly in the Third World as a whole, I find it easy to identify with Martin's research agenda and with many of his conclusions.

Before looking at his specific contribution, it is worth emphasizing the importance of what he has been studying. This can be expressed in terms of the intrinsic relevance of the phenomenon vis-à-vis the paucity of academic study. The international comparative study of evangelical Protestantism is still in its infancy. After Catholicism, evangelicalism is the largest segment of world Christianity, and truly global in its reach. Its numerical heartland is already in the Third World, and its numerical dynamism even more so. One of the most salient aspects of this has been a trend to political involvement in many countries.

The dimensions of the phenomenon make it one of the most

---

4. In Peter Berger (ed.), *The Desecularization of the World: Resurgent Religion and World Politics* (Grand Rapids: Eerdmans, 1999), pp. 37-49.

5. To be published in a volume edited by Donald M. Lewis.

important religious developments of our time. This importance is as yet scarcely reflected in scholarship on religion and globalization, or on evangelicalism as such. Much literature on globalization disregards religion altogether or discusses it in the abstract, in apparent ignorance of what is happening on the ground, that is, basically in the Third World. Discussions about religion under globalization must take into account what has actually happened to Christianity in recent decades: recession in Europe and stagnation (masked by high visibility political and media activity) in the US have been countered by the expansion of evangelicalism (at the expense largely of nominal Catholicism) in Latin America and impressive growth of all forms of Christianity in Africa and the Far East. But the only significant non-Western religious phenomenon that has impinged on Western academic consciousness is Islamic fundamentalism. The constitution of a global evangelical Christianity is often ignored because it has occurred mostly independently of Western initiatives.

Large-scale conversion to evangelicalism in the Third World suggests that, pace many scholars, a globalized world need not lead either to a relativistic religious homogeneity or to clashing fundamentalisms. Conversion is another alternative, with quite different cultural and political implications. The dynamic of conversion places evangelicalism in a very different relationship to global cultural processes from either pan-religious ecumenism (tending to global homogeneity) or fundamentalism (tending to irreducible pockets of anti-pluralism). The spread of evangelicalism through conversion fits with a picture of globalizing cultural processes in terms of hyper-differentiation, pluralism and de-territorialization.

Even the study of evangelicalism by Western academics too often imagines parochially that what happens in the Anglo-Saxon world is still determinant globally. As recent work by Martin and other scholars has shown, evangelical Christianity has definitively slipped the 'leash' of Anglo-Saxon culture and of Western power and wealth.

David Martin and the Sociology of Protestantism in Latin America

Martin's influential 1990 book *Tongues of Fire* caught a rising tide of academic interest in Latin American Protestantism, by which Pentecostalism came to replace progressive Catholicism as the main focus of study in Latin American religion. *Tongues of Fire* was largely responsible for putting the phenomenon on the map for European and North American academia (and beyond academia). But it was far from being a pioneer study. Latin American Protestantism, especially Brazilian and Chilean, had first attracted scholarly attention in the 1960s. By the late 1980s, attention had switched to Central America, where in some countries Protestantism had grown enormously and was overtaking Brazil and Chile in proportional terms. Even other large previously resistant countries (Mexico, Colombia and Argentina) began to show growth and interest researchers. It became possible to talk of a regional phenomenon, and academic studies on 'Protestantism in Latin America' multiplied.

Many works have come from American scholars, but a high percentage of the most influential authors are European: Émile Léonard, Emílio Willems, Christian Lalive D'Epinay of a generation ago; Jean-Pierre Bastian and David Martin more recently. Within Latin America, the reigning sociological paradigms of modernization and dependency marginalized the theme of religion for a long time. Brazil, with its large churches and sizeable social-scientific community, stands out for the depth of scholarship on its own Protestantism. The almost total lack of Argentine academic interest until the early 1990s is now being rectified. The other country with a strong tradition in the social sciences, Mexico, with its secularist tradition and more restricted Protestantism, has made a smaller contribution.

Far from being a pioneer study, *Tongues of Fire* is in fact a bibliographical survey. But it was a pioneer synthesis. It came out in the same year as two other important books on Protestantism in Latin America, one by the American anthropologist David Stoll and the other by the Swiss sociologist based in Mexico, Jean-Pierre Bastian.[6] Both are Latin Americanists and have a 'feel' for the region which is lacking in Martin's study. Yet the latter brings other virtues to bear. While Stoll is limited virtually to Central America and Bastian to Mexico and Central America, Martin casts the broadest geographical net. His book does far more justice to South America, and especially

6.   David Stoll, *Is Latin America Turning Protestant? The Politics of Evangelical Growth* (Berkeley: University of California Press, 1990); Jean-Pierre Bastian, *Historia del Protestantismo en América Latina* (Mexico City: Casa Unida de Publicaciones, 1990).

to Brazil (which probably has half of all Latin American Protestants).

Bastian's work has been influential in Francophone and Hispanophone regions but less so in the Anglophone world. Stoll was translated into Spanish, but it is noteworthy that Martin's book has not seen the light of day in either Spanish or Portuguese. This has limited its impact in the region and it has often been assessed impressionistically. There has also been, perhaps, a 'closing of the ranks' against this bold incursion by a scholar who is neither a Latin American nor a Latin-Americanist. But there are other reasons why the book's many virtues have not had the impact they might have had within the region.

Since *Tongues of Fire* came out at the same time as Stoll's *Is Latin America Turning Protestant?*, it is often talked about in conjunction. Their simultaneous publication brought one of the major cultural shifts of our time to the belated attention of Anglophone academia: the fact that 10 per cent of the region was now Protestant and that Protestants might soon be a majority of practising Christians.

By the late 1980s, political involvement was following numerical growth in some countries. This political activity, together with some methods used by new Pentecostal groups (with an emphasis on healings, exorcisms and money-raising), was generating a controversy in the secular media and in Catholic and ecumenical circles regarding the 'sects'. Amid accusations of charlatanism and CIA funding, cool analyses were needed of how Protestant growth might look at ground level, what its real political role was, and what its potential for change might be. The social context was that of the 'lost decade' of the 1980s, foreign debt, the disintegration of society in many Central American and Andean countries, and a slide into despair in the whole continent. Protestant growth was often interpreted, very plausibly, as part of the problem rather than part of the solution. This was the context in which Stoll and Martin were first read in Latin America.

Stoll based himself on interviews with Protestant leaders in Central America and the Andean region, a partial selection of the literature (nothing in Portuguese), and the American religious press. Martin produced an impressive synthesis of very nearly the full extent of scholarly production on Latin American Protestantism.

Stoll's focus was on his subtitle, 'The Politics of Evangelical Growth', rather than on the question in the title, 'Is Latin America Turning Protestant?' His central theme was the efforts of the New

Christian Right in Latin America in the 1980s, especially in Central America and Ecuador. He took the bull of the conspiracy theory (i.e. 'fundamentalist sects' grow in Latin America because of politically motivated American money) by the horns. His work, therefore, had considerable immediate appeal.

Martin, on the other hand, did not meet the conspiracy theory head-on, preferring to duck under it and look at the subterranean currents of long-term significance. His study was set on a grand scale: covering the entire region with a wealth of historical material, the whole was projected upon a vast screen framed by classical themes of the sociology of religion and inter-continental comparisons extending over centuries. As against Stoll's greater knowledge of the US evangelical world and missionary efforts, and deeper familiarity with the local situation in parts of the region, Martin brought to bear his stature as a leading theoretician of the sociology of religion, his breadth of reading of the literature and his knowledge of church history, especially of the European experience. While missing or confusing a few trees, he gave a wider view of the wood.

Both authors repudiated the polemical reductionist treatment of Protestant expansion characteristic of many Marxist and Catholic authors. They stressed that the locus of growth was largely independent of American missions, and certainly of the religious right; that there were important ambiguities within the undoubted predominance of political conservatism; and that the future was an open book.

It should be stressed that the question of why Protestantism grows, far from being just a calm academic discussion, is a weapon in political, religious and even commercial polemic. If this is still true today, it was even more so in the 1980s. Catholic analyses had been influenced by ecumenical initiatives since Vatican II, but since the early 1980s it had again become acceptable for Catholic leaders to show concern over Protestant growth by talking of the 'sects'. The latter were perceived as a threat to religious hegemony because they were autonomous groups demanding exclusive affiliation. The analyses revealed a static view of culture in which religions have people and not vice versa. The old conspiracy theory was resurrected: the 'sects' grew thanks to politically motivated American money. Even some progressives adopted a conspiracy theory, seemingly attracted to this elitist position because Pentecostal growth threatened the numerical base of liberationism in the base communities.

'Invasion of the sects' theory obviously built on facts, especially in the geopolitically charged 1980s. Latin American Protestantism has many foreign connections (whose presence is facilitated by Protestant institutional segmentation); the question is how important they are in accounting for Protestant growth. The fact that Stoll focused on the 'invasion of the sects' question more than Martin may explain his better initial reception in Latin America. In addition, Stoll had good 'progressive' credentials in Latin America, whereas Martin's book came prefaced by Peter Berger, a highly respected sociologist but (especially in the Reagan years) a politically suspect figure in Latin American academia due to his connections with the Institute for Religion and Democracy. But Martin's book gave a geographically broader and sociologically more sophisticated overview of the dimensions, causes and consequences of what his subtitle terms the 'Protestant explosion' in the region.

Martin tackles big concerns: the centuries-old clash of 'Hispanic' and 'Anglo' civilizations; regional variations, such as the huge Protestantism in Brazil and its virtual absence in neighbouring Uruguay; the emergence of a voluntary form of faith as part of the process of social differentiation; the implications of Latin America's 'tongues of fire' for the secularization debate. He goes back a long way to identify in seventeenth-century England the birth of voluntary, fissile and participatory religion, which has since spread out over the world in three waves. The first two, Puritanism and Methodism, made minimal impression in Latin America. The last, Pentecostalism, finally broke the barrier, being equipped with 'local adaptors'.

The analogy with early English Methodism baulks large. In the Methodist revival, religion abandoned the core structures of society and lodged in the cultural sphere. 'Methodism and Pentecostalism alike construct models of equality, fraternity and peaceability in the religious enclaves of culture, but do not generalize from these in terms of coherent political world-views... Thus whether or not you take seriously their impact on a society as a whole depends on your estimate of the power of culture'.[7] The apoliticism which generally results causes problems when transferred from a highly differentiated society such as the US to Latin America, where 'politics, violence and religion remain closely intertwined...Latin American societies...do

---

7.   Martin, *Tongues of Fire*, p. 22.

not permit any mass movement to work solely at the level of culture'.[8] This forces Pentecostalism into political positions foreign to its genesis in Anglo-Saxon culture. Its suspicion of politics and corruption is viewed as a conservative withdrawal from commitment to 'liberation'.[9]

This is a sophisticated argument of considerable mileage at the level of generality. I suspect, however, that it underestimates the degree of calculation and intentionality in the responses of the Pentecostal leadership in Brazil and Chile to their respective military governments, and in the Brazilians' post-redemocratization entry into parliament.

The 'Latin Pattern' of confrontation between religion and politics left the Catholic Church seriously weakened in places such as Uruguay, Venezuela, Guatemala and, to some extent, Brazil. Significantly, in the first two nations Protestantism is also very weak; in the latter two, very strong. This points to the optimum conditions for Protestant expansion: where the Catholic Church has been weakened, but the culture has not been secularized.

After painting various 'profiles of evangelical advance' in Latin America, and comparing them with cases from the Caribbean, South Africa and South Korea, Martin examines the implications of Pentecostalism at four levels:

1. As a system of communication, involving healings, tongues, songs and stories, operating at a pre- (or post-) literate level, tapping underground channels of traditional Catholic and animist spirituality, and redefining the male personality and consumption patterns in such a way as to constitute a female ideology for domesticating the Latin American male.

2. As a system of individual betterment, for which people need to have a certain degree of personal independence, either through being petty-bourgeois or through being destitute. Martin proposes a model in which mobility leads to Protestantism which leads to more mobility. 'People look about them, reach after certain "goods", then embrace Protestantism and are equipped with an inclusive vision, the better to pursue those "goods" '.[10]

3. With respect to the classic 'Protestant ethic' debate, Berger's preface, indulging in some wishful thinking, affirms that Latin Ameri-

8. Martin, *Tongues of Fire*, p. 23.
9. Martin, *Tongues of Fire*, p. 24.
10. Martin, *Tongues of Fire*, p. 190.

can Protestantism will lead to 'the emergence of a solid bourgeoisie, with virtues conducive to the development of a democratic capitalism'.[11] Martin himself does not go so far. He stresses that Pentecostalism offers opportunities for developing the skills of expression, organization, propagation and leadership. These skills are relevant to survival and to modest economic advance, especially for the pastorate. But what is the latent economic potential? How far will the sense of individual humanity, generated by the company of the faithful, be transmuted into economic initiative and new aspirations? Economic advancement depends on facilitating economic conditions. People advance by the margins available, pressing on their constraints rather than breaking out of them. What one can affirm is that economic advancement and evangelical religion often go together and appear to reinforce each other. Pentecostalism may console those who lose from social change, or it may select those who can make the most of the chances change offers. But capacities may take two or three generations to bear fruit, says Martin, recognizing that hard evidence is scarce. Without going as far as Berger, he considers Pentecostalism may be building a constituency well disposed to a capitalist form of development.

4.   The same applies to Pentecostalism's relationship to politics; the cultural logic of voluntarist religion lies dormant for a time, assembling a raft to which people lash themselves for safety. 'Initially most of their energy is expended on constructing the raft... Those who guide the raft may well be politically very cautious and conservative, anxious to avoid the destructive turbulence of political contention and polarization'.[12] But in this 'free space', new potentialities are stored up, which may one day overflow. There is no political route which Pentecostalism absolutely precludes, except adherence to a doctrinally atheist movement. At the minority level, virtually every option has been embraced by some Pentecostals.

Martin's arguments regarding latency are very appropriate, introducing a salutary long-term historical perspective, especially important now that the 'spiral of antagonism' between religion and secular political (liberal anti-clerical or Marxist) forces which has characterized Latin countries has unwound. However, one must ask whether a new logic may not come into operation. Since Latin America is not

11.   Martin, *Tongues of Fire*, p. ix.
12.   Martin, *Tongues of Fire*, p. 6.

simply a different autonomous system, into which 'Anglo' patterns are now flowing, but has structural specificities as part of an international system, within which it is peripheral and being steadily pauperized, voluntaristic religion, now running freely into the breeches of the old organic unities, may not produce the same results. If a new 'Latin American' hybrid is being formed from the original 'Anglo' and 'Hispanic' models, we cannot bank too much on 'Anglo' historical analogies. For example, while the United States has a strong tradition of Church–State separation, indeed it is part of the founding myth, and this restrains all religious political actors today, in Brazil the situation is quite different. Martin recognizes the new possibilities of the mating of Anglo and Hispanic patterns with regard to secularization trends, but we need to extend the scope of these new possibilities to the role of evangelical Protestantism itself.

Tongues of Fire's limited penetration in Latin America has been a combination of unfortunate factors. First, Martin's caution on the economic implications of Pentecostalism has been read through Berger's more ideological preface. In fact, Latin American Pentecostalism does not have the classic Protestant work ethic, and it operates in a significantly different economic context. Evidence for upward mobility is scarce, and signs of a macro effect on Latin American economies even scarcer. Secondly, Martin has fallen victim to his own terminology. He speaks of an 'Anglo' pattern, cultural forms originated by the English-speaking peoples, which were loose, plural and available for export: among them, a voluntary, fissile and participatory form of evangelical religion. He structures his work around two large frames: the emergence of voluntarism, contingent on the breakdown of the organic unity of religion and national identity; and the 400-year-old clash between the 'Hispanic and Anglo-Saxon imperiums'.

Martin historically objectifies the religious market model as 'Anglo' and the 'church' model of religious-political alliance as 'Hispanic'. This labelling of models in ethnic terms is sociologically and historically questionable. Martin is actually talking about models of social organization of religion, not about current religious geopolitics, but the terminology suggests something intrinsically Anglo-Saxon about voluntaristic religion and intrinsically Hispanic about unitary religion. Although the 'Anglo' model made its historical appearance in England, albeit with dress rehearsals elsewhere, especially Holland, it is now widespread. To label it 'Anglo' plays into the hands of the 'invasion of the sects' polemicists inside and outside academia, precisely the opposite of what Martin intended.

In 1991, Martin delivered the F.D. Maurice Lectures at King's College, London, published in reworked form in 1996 as *Forbidden Revolutions*. The revolutions referred to are examples of how religion, when located in (or banned to) the sphere of culture, can nevertheless affect the centre: in Latin America, through Pentecostalism's probable effect in future civil society; and in Eastern Europe, through the churches' direct public role in 1989. (The subtitle 'Pentecostalism in Latin America, Catholicism in Eastern Europe' is misleading, since the Eastern European section deals with Orthodoxy and Protestantism as well as Catholicism.) These revolutions were 'forbidden' by false sociological polarities: left–right, liberal–fundamentalist, political–apolitical, structure–culture.

Much wisdom is to be had here. First, the emphasis that the sociology of religion is not primarily about marginal phenomena. Even where religion is separated from the state, its natural partner is political sociology.[13] Secondly, the critique of 'fundamentalism' when applied to Latin American Pentecostalism. Besides having different political implications from Islamic fundamentalism (autonomous space versus comprehensive systems), Pentecostalism is more about the democratic availability of spiritual gifts than a conservative understanding of the Bible.[14] And thirdly, the eloquent summary of evangelical religion among the Third World poor.[15]

The two halves of the book describe very different revolutions by different types of Christianity. The Eastern Europe section talks of recent events; the Latin America section, of potential changes. The temporary marginality of the established churches of Eastern Europe allowed them a role in the collapse of Communism. The closest comparison in Latin America would be Catholic opposition to military regimes. Instead, Martin talks of Pentecostals. Why? Catholicism has sustained losses to Pentecostalism in Latin America but outlasted Communism in Eastern Europe because in both cases the margins of society have been solvents of monopoly power. Disestablishment and withdrawal from power can be good for society

---

13. Martin, *Forbidden Revolutions*, p. 1.
14. Martin, *Forbidden Revolutions*, pp. 9-11.
15. Martin, *Forbidden Revolutions*, pp. 44-52.

and religion, breaking up ideological hegemony, creating social capital, symbolically challenging the 'powers of this world', building potential for change within culture and allowing 'the Kingdom' to hit back—peaceably.

Yet Pentecostalism in Brazil and Catholicism in Communist Poland are very different 'margins'. Martin is right that there are enough detractors of Pentecostalism, and his positive emphasis is a corrective. But adjusting the balance must still allow for Pentecostalism's ambiguous dynamism.

While rightly questioning an ethnocentric view of what is political, Martin skirts over the actual experiences of overt political participation, not all of which point in the direction of the covert potentialities he describes. A 'politics of culture' is no longer the whole picture. While mentioning 'large temptations for leadership' which can lead to large improprieties, he does not link this with the actual politics practised for over a decade by such leaders. 'Whatever the temptations of success', says Martin, 'the local captains of evangelical industry are impressive',[16] and mentions a pastor studying law in his sixties to cope with administrative demands. Alas, this same pastor ended his career in disgrace. His son-in-law, a federal deputy elected by the church vote, acquired 8 million dollars through corruption. Before the scandal broke, the pastor's daughter divorced him, keeping the 2-million-dollar mansion. She then ran for Congress with her father's help; he made illegal deals to pay campaign debts, costing the church some 2 million dollars. A larger impropriety than most, but not unrepresentative of Pentecostalism's relationship to the 'centre' of Brazilian life.

Evangelicalism can mean different things at different times, occupying different positions in society and in each country's religious field. 'Evangelical religion in Latin America is a replication [is it?] (rather than a diffusion [true]) of differentiations long ago achieved in Anglo-American society. [Thus, they] will not seek, as would 'fundamentalist' Muslims, to replace one hegemony with another'.[17] But are replication and diffusion the only possibilities? And while the many statements of Pentecostal intent precisely to replace one hegemony with another are not important if they go against the sociological grain, the question is whether, in a Latin America still marked by the

16. Martin, *Forbidden Revolutions*, p. 54.
17. Martin, *Forbidden Revolutions*, pp. 60-61.

old monolithic relations between religion and society, the supposed logic of voluntarist religion may not be modified.

David Martin and Global Evangelicalism

A similar comment can be made about Martin's 1999 article 'The Evangelical Upsurge and its Political Implications'. As in *Forbidden Revolutions*, Martin emphasizes the cultural potentiality argument: the 'logic' of voluntaristic evangelicalism will supposedly produce everywhere results similar to those in northern Europe and North America. This theory tends to talk almost exclusively of the long-term potential of evangelicalism, rather than looking at actually existing evangelical politics in the new centres of evangelical political militancy in the Third World. Discussion of potentialities, based on macro-historical comparisons with older Protestantisms, is certainly legitimate, but must be tempered with empirical analysis of what is happening, and with the awareness that we do not yet have sufficient evidence that similarities will produce similar sociopolitical effects. Martin implicitly recognizes this: 'Other things being equal (which of course they rarely are), the cultural characteristics of evangelicals— participation, pragmatism, competition, personal discipline—ought in the long run to foster democracy'.[18] Even in Third World countries where evangelicalism may be highly successful, it will come to see itself, on the lines of Italian Catholicism, 'as a potent commentator within a pluralistic framework, possessed at the same time of concrete institutional interests'.[19] While Martin still rightly contrasts evangelicals sharply with Islamic fundamentalists, it is significant that the analogy he chooses here is no longer evangelicalism in the developed West but Catholicism. However, his affirmation that 'the emergence of more and more significant social actors [evangelical churches] whose interests have to be taken into account can only help the prospects for democracy'[20] is dubious. While I myself am far from pessimistic about the implications of the evangelical upsurge for Third World polities, there are many examples to show that a strong civil society does not necessarily mean better chances for democracy. There were historically many different postures in Western Protestant-

18. Martin, 'The Evangelical Protestant Upsurge', p. 49.
19. Martin, 'The Evangelical Protestant Upsurge', p. 48.
20. Martin, 'The Evangelical Protestant Upsurge', p. 41.

ism towards the state, and all are reproduced in Third World Protestantism. Since there are few of the contextual advantages that the historical Anglophone context offered, it is far from certain that it will be generally friendly to democracy. While Martin's optimism is an antidote to the unmixed pessimism of some authors, the empirical data in diverse situations are too complex to allow us to foreclose the discussion.

Finally, David's conference paper 'Evangelical Expansion in Global Society', to which I had the privilege of responding, brings evangelical expansion into close relation to the emergence of a global society. Already in a 1995 article on secularization, he had stressed that the future of religion lies not only in association with localist opposition to globalizing trends, but also as personal choice within the thrust of globalization itself.[21] He sees the salvageable essence of secularization theory as the process of social differentiation which breaks up monopolies, leading to a pluralism which vitalizes the religious field by competition. In this context, which characterizes ever larger parts of the globe, of individualism centred on expression of the self and putting together of fragments of traditions, evangelicalism seems well equipped to flourish, since it takes elements of expressive individualism but controls them with moral obligation and community loyalty.

David's 1999 paper on 'Evangelical Expansion in Global Society' is mainly a demand-side macro-level analysis of the lines along which evangelical Christianity expands globally. It talks basically of two lines of expansion: the attraction of voluntaristic popular Christianity which emphasizes the Spirit, 'spreading in partial alignment with the English language and Anglo-American influence'; and ethnic-minority evangelicalism, 'to do with the emergence of minority self-consciousness which leaps over the pressure exercised by the local majority and links itself to evangelicalism as an expression of transnational modernity'. His paper points to the great diversity of what can be subsumed under 'evangelicalism' today, although it is perhaps still too limited a purview, since he emphasizes Free Church evangelicalism and especially Pentecostalism, but makes little mention of evangelicalism in mainline churches or in the African Independent Churches.

Latin America especially, and the non-developed and/or non-

---

21. David Martin, 'Sociology, Religion and Secularization: An Orientation', *Religion* 25 (1995), pp. 295-303.

Western world in general, have thus become increasingly central to David Martin's preoccupations, and he has pioneered interpretations relating to processes of religious change, above all conversion to evangelicalism, in those contexts. In focusing on such a theme and in such geographical breadth, and in bringing to their discussion a wealth of theoretical and historical knowledge, he has remained at the cutting edge of the sociology of religion and has shown the discipline's continued (or perhaps greater than ever) relevance to broad political and cultural issues.

David Martin's Sociology of Hope

Richard K. Fenn

David Martin has given us both a sociology and a theology of hope. In reading him over the years I have slowly begun to believe that time is on the side of those who are seeking free social and emotional space. Hemmed in though people may be by various enclosures, they will find their way into new fields of relationship and endeavor. The spirit that animates heretics in Eastern Europe will survive various burnings and move Westward, where it will free the poor, the illiterate and those who suffer from their various thralls. Martin is an antidote to those who feel that humans fundamentally want to escape from their freedom.

To be sure, there are times when the spirit is enthralled by secular powers. Take David Martin's recent answer to those who feel that Christianity has served itself too long by serving the powerful. In *Does Christianity Cause War?*[1] Martin has shown that, even though the cross may be incorporated into the insignia of royalty and be indistinguishable from the sword, even though the state may employ the services of the Church in bringing marginal peoples to their knees, nonetheless the cross remains as a sign that cuts two ways and will wound those who bear it in the name of oppression.

Martin sees a dynamic at work in human history. On the one hand are the forces of 'subsumption' and of 'incorporation'. These may be the 'organic community' in which a person's horizons and identity are determined by his or her nativity. These forces may be found in the state's authority to define and suppress various communities that long for compassion and justice. New cities may claim to bring forward

1. Oxford: Clarendon Press, 1997.

what endures of Rome or Athens or Jerusalem into a future shaped by the architecture of the past. New wine may be turned sour by being poured into old bottles.

On the other hand, Martin never takes his eye off 'sequence and transition'. Out of the organic community come individuals who are freed by the Spirit from their obedience to the old masters, to the landlords and padrones, to alcohol and illiteracy, to public opinion and to the neighborhood. They are freed from old burdens that require them to pay crushing tribute to those who oppress them. Religious language provides double-meanings and escape-hatches that free people from the confines of old understandings and limited horizons. As new horizons open up for them, they are initiated into life through a symbolic form of death. Thus their entrance into the city can be liberating. Certainly there is more to be found in the city than the replication of old forms of domination. There, in the center of the city, laying its claim to public space, is the chapel that frees the spirit from its old shackles and the church that blocks the view of the dictator.

Thus there are two voices in Martin's writing: one about cities and incorporation or subsumption; the other about open space and sequence and transition. The latter voice is as strong as the first, but far less harmonious and with fewer overtones. Here it is, as he writes of evangelicals in Latin America:

> The logic of setting up some enclave of protected free space on the margins is that evangelicals should sever the immemorial bonds tying them into local hierarchies and cut the lateral bonds linking them up with the neighborhood and its norms of behaviour. These norms may include corruption, clientship, violence, the abuse and abandonment of women, the neglect of nurture and discipline, and the dissipation of resources—especially on alcohol … What evangelical religion achieves by its very existence is a fundamental tear in the fabric of mediation. They have laid the axe to a major sector of mediated power in the sphere of religion and that has implications for the other spheres.[2]

Thus cities have open spaces. Indeed, Martin is fascinated by the way that the central parks and open places in the city bring face to face the conflicting communities of the country and their respective dreams and memories of what that country is all about. His descrip-

---

2.   David Martin, *Forbidden Revolutions: Pentecostalism in Latin America, Catholicism in Eastern Europe* (London: SPCK, 1996).

tion, for instance, of the revolts in Romania that brought down the Ceaucescu regime all focus on the gathering of tens, even hundreds of thousands of Christians, first on Opera Square in Timisoara and finally in Bucharest itself. Martin notes the sounds of joy in the middle of terror: the saying of the Lord's prayer by thousands on their knees, followed by the turning back of tanks; the firings on the masses of protesters, followed by candles, flowers and crosses where the victims had fallen; finally the Christmas trees and bells celebrating the death of Ceaucescu on Christmas Day. Martin should know; he remembers the sky over London being lit by the tongues of unholy fire during the wartime blitz.

All these close observations are caught up in an arc of meaning that unites each point: village with capitol; Protestant with Catholic; laity with clergy; underground piety with officially orchestrated observance. All these events speak of sequence and transition: a break with past oppression; long silences being broken by the sound of a prayer that many no longer remember. However, these claims on new and free space were also being made even while local communities, tied together or separated as they may have been by faith and blood, were finding their loyalties subsumed and incorporated in a larger, more universal faith.

The hope that Martin sees, then, is in part a result of the tension and play between these two voices: the one singing the harmonies of incorporation, of organic communities or cities that bring the past into the future; the other voice more like a descant going through its own sequences, singing the pilgrimage of the individual from old tyrannies into new freedoms, and heralding a new relation of religious and ethnic groups to each other, to the past, to their shared territory, and to the state. To orchestrate these two voices is a difficult task, I suspect, although Martin can make it look easy through descriptions, such as this one, dense with unspoken theory:

> Religion, including Christianity, institutes a pattern of space and time composed of shifting relations between the sacred and the secular, the transcendental and the mundane, the stabilizing and the transformative, the world mirrored in its proper order, the world turned upside down. It *is* the developing grammar of these polarities. To work that grammar out in prose in a book on religion in Europe is very difficult.[3]

---

3.   'Religion and Politics in the Space and Time of the City', Manuscript, p. 1.

Let us consider for a moment what may be entailed in the 'shifting relations between the sacred and the secular' in a moment; that is the core of the problem that he has set for all of us. The sacred, Martin is telling us, is not where one might expect. Rather than seek the sacred in the precincts of the temple we are to look for it in the streets and the small huts just outside the city gates. Rather than seek the sacred in the usual formulations of the liturgy or the orders of the church, we are to find it where a few are gathered together under some extraordinary leadership that has yet to be ordained. The sacred is a social space filled with longings that have yet to be satisfied, and some of those longings may be for release from various forms of captivity to convention and social authority. Thus there may be something disruptive and anarchic in the sacred: out of these stones, so to speak, Martin can find the new children of Abraham.

If you are given to cybernetic imagery, you might think of the sacred as crucial information that has been lost about what others in the social system might want or might be thinking or might even do. The sacred is a place full of surprise and potential, threat and opportunity. To know the sacred is indeed to probe the environment of every social system. In that environment are all sorts of possibilities that have been excluded from what passes for common sense and are not mentioned in polite or public discourse. The sacred is—in social-system terms—the environment that surrounds and permeates every part of a social system whether the system knows it or not. If there is hope for a system, it is in the potential for change, the need for satisfaction, the passion for justice, the imagination of a more robust or loving social order—that remains in the environment, just outside the scope of what is normally allowed to enter the discussions of policy-makers or the prayers of the people.

There is nothing wishful or unrealistic about David Martin's sociology of hope. He subscribes to what he once called 'the strong programme' that holds sociological feet to the empirical fire. Even in the middle of new freedoms, Martin would acknowledge, the individual may yet be subsumed and incorporated into new forms of constraint or servitude. For instance, using the image of lava for the flow of the Spirit in Latin America, Martin notes that even lava can only enter where it finds an opening, a crevice, a gap in social structure; otherwise it will congeal, cool and harden. Even the hot flames of the Spirit need air. Note the mature and chastened hope in these lines:

> Conservative evangelicalism has very restricted ambitions with regard to the state, and it has no theory of forcible change designed to overthrow state structures. It desires in every sense to live and let live, so it can only advance by the peaceable slow strain of cultural implication, and even then not by direct intention but through the outworkings of the incidental consequences of disciplined faith.[4]

In many ways, then, Martin hopes for transcendence and finds it in the ways that people have of creating lebensraum for themselves. Some may seek an entirely new, free, social space, while others are willing to live in an enclave that allows them a few more degrees of freedom than they have enjoyed in the past, where people pray together and render one another mutual aid. Thus, the open space provided by the Spirit to the beleaguered may simply be a shelter where they are shielded from the blows of machismo males, from demands for tithing and taxes, or from official insistence on recognition and devotion.

> The free space of evangelical activity may pick up and express many different kinds of previous social alignment that it then remoulds in its own image. For example, free space may appeal to many of those most exposed to capitalistic social relations and accelerate that exposure or, alternatively, it may take many most threatened by the advent of such relations and throw around them a protective cordon...[5]

Contrast the Catholic Church, which remains caught up in neighborhood, fiesta, godparenting, and is 'intimately bound up in such ties'.[6] The Catholic Church subsumes and incorporates, whereas the evangelicals are engaged in sequence and transition.

Of course, the contrasts are not perfect, because even the evangelicals find that the open space is not very free and open, hence the 'protective cordon' against those most threatened by market relations, the 'multiplicity of niches',[7] in which evangelicals find themselves stopped in their tracks by resistance to 'more widely based relationships'.[8] Nor with the evangelicals are we in a free and open space

---

4. Martin, *Forbidden Revolutions*, p. 58.
5. Martin, *Forbidden Revolutions*, pp. 58-59.
6. Martin, *Forbidden Revolutions*, p. 60.
7. Martin, *Forbidden Revolutions*, p. 59.
8. Martin, *Forbidden Revolutions*, p. 59.

without precedent. A Pentecostal pastor in Latin America 'illustrated nearly every proposition in Max Weber's "Protestant Ethic" in two hours of unstoppable exposition'.[9]

So superimposed on the polarities is an overarching dynamic in which the past reproduces itself in new contexts. Thus the dialectic between North and South Europe is recreated in the tension between Protestant and Catholic elements in Central and Latin America. The Protestant ethic is found in suburbs of Santiago, Chile and throughout Latin America in the 'buried intelligentsia'.

Rather than rely largely on the dimension of time to articulate a sociology of hope, Martin uses the trajectory of physical and social space to make his point. For Martin, each city is an emblem of the past and refers back to some historic *polis*. However, within each city the outlines of a new society take shape as groups and communities contest for control of the center or take up flimsy habitation on the urban periphery. Similarly, Pentecostal groups combine very ancient postures of devotion with very modern social skills to declare themselves free to inhabit a new social space free of traditional obligations.

However, there is certainly more to Martin's work than a discussion of these chronic polarities. To be sure, Martin is interested in the way societies work out the dynamic tension between transitions into a new social space and reincorporation into an enlarged and vitalized community. Nonetheless, there is far more than a harmony-of-the-opposites working itself out as centers engage peripheries and as peripheries take on the virtues but reverse the vices of the center. There is a powerful tide in these affairs, but it not just that of a civilizing process.

Quite the opposite. There is a powerful undercurrent in these social processes that takes individuals out of themselves and out of their social contexts, introduces them into a new social world, if only at first in their imagination, and makes every social order seem at best to be merely provisional, fictitious or deadening. To hear this theme in Martin's work one does not have to be musical, but that would help. Consider this passage:

> Music, nature, sexuality: this perhaps taps the underground stream running through all the passages of the argument. It is the problem of a potentially free flow that can wreck three systems. One is the sacramental system that preserves the power of God by acts of

9.   Martin, *Forbidden Revolutions*, p. 55.

containment and designation. Sacrament concentrates power by designation. Another is the theological system which does not wish to compromise the divine perfection by allowing God's existence in all experience. Another is the system of morality and social control, which *must* designate certain areas of appropriate delight and other areas of illicit delight and therefor includes even harmless delights in its normative categories. After all it might be dangerous to leave some areas of experience uncovered.[10]

There is something powerfully seditious about this view of an undercurrent that would disturb all the limits placed on experience. The forces to be released are those of Eros, and in its path all the flimsy constructions of societies and ideologues, theologians and the clergy tend to crumble. Marcuse would be pleased; Martin exercises a critical reason to imagine a society other than the one that continues to place its restrictions on gratification and levy its demands for performance on individuals who have forgotten how to imagine another world.

In this passage Martin also foreshadows all his work on the charismatic and Pentecostal upheavals that are indeed the way found by the poor out of their afflictions. Animating the trinity of music, nature and sexuality, and emerging from it, is a charismatic spirit. Like music,

> Charismatic language seeks to reverse babel and to leap over the boundaries of role and the limits to communication. It hints at the universal speech which makes for unity and brings together all nations and tribes and tongues. Indeed, charismatic language overlaps music by breaking into spontaneous harmony ... Music and charisma are the free flow of the spirit. Both work by rules, sequences, references back, but they take the person into a new ordering of social space and time.[11]

There again are the old polarities between order and change, incorporation and transition, but they are caught up in an 'undertow', a free and inexorable flow, that creates a new order: a genuinely new thing under the sun. To be sure, the ecstatic experience of the spirit depends on order but it also breaks through into a new creation. Granted that it takes discipline and practice. It also requires a willingness to break with the past.

10. David Martin, *The Breaking of the Image: A Sociology of Christian Theory and Practice* (Oxford: Basil Blackwell, 1980), p. 144.
11. Martin, *The Breaking of the Image*, p. 147.

Without this dynamic flow that resists all temporal and spatial boundaries on the spirit of new solidarity, it would be impossible to understand why Martin is so hopeful. It is not just that David Martin understands both the positive and the negative aspects of the presence of the past. Of course he recognizes that the cross may be embedded for generations, even centuries, among a society's cultural icons, where it shares with the sword or other regalia of authority the power to compel assent or even sacrifice. Nonetheless, the cross is part of this assault on possibilities. It is a prototypical symbol of human spiritual freedom and, as such, is able to resist tendencies toward idolatry. The cross is therefore always available for peripheral groups to use as a symbol of spiritual and social possibilities that are otherwise excluded from collective imagination. Thus Christianity has been a secularizing religion, and its presence has helped to transform even its own tradition from an object of veneration to the subject of a free discourse.

I prefer Martin's undertow to Marx's notion of capitalism that devours everything in its path and to Marcuse's notion of Eros as the enemy and source of civilization. What they have in common, however, is the possibility of a society that is secular because it does not enshrine any limits on human experience and thought or seek to call for the sort of sacrifices that will transcend the passage of time. By a secular society I do not mean to evoke an image of a nation that has had a cultural lobotomy and is no longer willing or able to remember the past. I *do* mean to evoke a society in which memories, however honored, are no longer consigned to an inaccessible and official zone marked as 'sacred'. That is, these memories no longer have the capacity to dignify some at the expense of others; they can no longer be used as a vehicle for suggesting that some groups or communities, some peoples or even countries, transcend time while others do not. These memories, however honored, will have lost their capacity to shame or exclude. Because no memories are turned into idols, there is no division between devotees and those without the proper faith. Recollection is enough: not devotion.

There is a strain of pure spiritual anarchism in Martin. Like Prince Kropotkin he has confidence in the power of the Spirit to get people to work together with or without the help of clergy. The option chosen by the poor, he notes, is often not the option chosen for them by religious intellectuals and bureaucrats who need base communities in order to have any constituency at all. Martin is not against theologians; he simply finds them outside the guild. The revolution of the Spirit has produced a generation of leaders that Martin calls the 'buried intelligentsia'.[12] These extraordinary and gifted leaders exercise their considerable talents in organization and finances, in construction and communication, as well as in preaching and the liturgy. They are a crucial part of the environment, and any social order that ignores them is unnecessarily impoverished and may be in trouble.

Church officials who think that the Holy Spirit is moving in concert with their own agendas may not be amused to discover that the Spirit may not be what the Church thinks it is. Martin rejects the reduction of operations of the Spirit to the working of ecumenical commissions or to particular revisions of liturgy. Theologians are warned that 'there is no contradiction between believing firmly in the providential ordering of salvation, and saying also that one cannot know its operation by defining the company of the elect'.[13] Familiar as he is with the 'language of transcendence', Martin never forgets how to speak 'the language of limits'.[14]

Martin always keeps his eye on the sparrows of sociological inquiry. He can engage in very detailed examination of a particular context, and find in it the signs of both new freedom and of renewed incorporation into something organic and solidarity. However, watching these sparrows never prevents Martin from remembering the past or seeing the larger social context. The songs newly sung in the rural areas of Latin America repeat the sounding joys of Western England and Wales. In his detailed examination of the context he often looks up to see what ' "the sum of things, for ever speaking", say now to me, that I recognize'. [15] Although he has an eye for the 'dense forest of symbols', he also observes closely the particular symbol in its particular context and how it may be acquiring and losing meaning over time.[16] He is always aware of 'the providential ordering of the human story, and the free choice of humans in making up that story'.[17]

Martin's work should perhaps be sung rather than read. Certainly

---

12. Martin, *Forbidden Revolutions*, p. 52.

13. David Martin, *Reflections on Sociology and Theology* (Oxford: Clarendon Press, 1997), p. 97.

14. Martin, *Reflections on Sociology and Theology*, p. 87.

15. Martin, *Reflections on Sociology and Theology*, p. 92.

16. Martin, *Reflections on Sociology and Theology*, p. 87.

17. Martin, *Reflections on Sociology and Theology*, pp. 94-95.

there are passages that are lyrical. Take this one, for example; it is resonant with one of his voices. Just before this passage Martin may not have been watching sparrows on the ground, but he was 'staring naively at a tiny sentence' about the peculiar relationship of Christians to time, in which Christians are described as being new creatures; for them the old has 'passed away'. After a minute examination of these words in their larger context, Martin goes on to say:

> I could have begun from any of these tiny micro-statements and traversed the whole arc of meaning. Every point on the arc is integral to the complete cycle of related centres. These centres also subsume each other and thereby provide an analogy of their own meaning. By their own inherent nature they mutually subsume and incorporate, and also point to subsumption and incorporation as fundamental to spiritual relationships.[18]

Now imagine that Martin has been looking not at a text but at cities; there is the same constellation of mutual references, so that one place on the arc of cities around the Atlantic and the Mediterranean, say, evokes all the others:

> You do not know Europe unless you set it against its less constricted realisations in North America and South America. Washington, after all, with its Senate and Capitol, is as direct a translation of the Senatus Populusque Romanus as you could imagine and it embodies the strict logic of the central distinction between God and Caesar as no European city has. It takes the ideas of the Exodus and of the millennial hope explicit in the revolutionary war and translates them in the classical language of the Novus Ordo Seclorum, the New Order of the World. What Columbus conceived as for Europeans a 'New World' was a specific millennial project. The redistributions are constant. England and the United States are simultaneously New Israels and new Romes. Santiago de Chile and Buenos Aires are recreations of Paris and Dallas, Texas rebuilds London's Crystal Palace on a new frontier. Edinburgh is new Athens and Los Angeles new Venice.[19]

Indeed the Atlantic is the new Mediterranean and refracts the memories and dreams laid out in the cities of Britain and Europe.

If Martin's sociology outlines the parameters of what can be hoped for, it is because he probes the environment even further than I have so far suggested. Not only are there two voices in his work, one singing of cities and incorporation, the other of departures and

18. Martin, *Reflections on Sociology and Theology*, p. 76.
19. 'Religion and Politics in the Space and Time of the City', Manuscript, p. 4.

sequences and transitions; there is a third voice, very much his own but somewhat more elusive and fundamental. It is the voice in which Martin speaks of subterranean influences that may lie dormant for decades, even centuries, but that eventually surface to create free spaces or mark transitions in a different context. In that voice Martin will also speak of long journeys into the wilderness that end up back in the city: a new Jerusalem.[20]

It is in this third voice that Martin speaks about religion turning the world upside down: about the inversion of symbols, meanings and relationships under the aegis of religious, and particularly Christian, language.

> All these images have been invoked: war and peace, King and Lord, brotherhood and fatherhood, citizenship and inheritance, language and singing, to show how they alter, how they subvert or invert all the usual meanings. They invert and convert; turn upside down and change. Christian language is analogy, paradox, oxymoron, inversion, conversion. And it is set in the active-passive voice…
>
> The new language must mount an attack on the frontier of social possibility. To make the particular universal means releasing the Fathers from their relation to a particular society and placing them in relation a to all nations, tribes and tongues. That requires a rejection of the biological continuity of the chosen people and the new creation of a brotherhood based on choice not necessity, regeneration not generation…
>
> A man who is going to choose to move must face alienation and also carry the covenant and the citizenship inside him. He will need a new language, transcending previous local languages. He must speak in tongues, the speech of those who are renewed in the spirit. To create unity faith must reverse babel.
>
> All these requirements build up the symbolic structures of hope.[21]

Hope is that fragile sense of possibility without which no one sets out from Galilee for Jerusalem in search of a holy city or from Jerusalem to the wilderness in search of a garden. Hope is the sense of possibility that allows brotherhoods to create a new unity in the name of a fatherhood that chooses no favorite son and whose line of inheritance is open to all who choose it. Hope enables peons to cancel their debts to the padrone and create a legacy of their own, one that frees the next generation to realize possibilities that previously could only

---

20. Martin, *The Breaking of the Image*, pp. 45-46.
21. Martin, *The Breaking of the Image*, pp. 129-30.

have been dreamed or imagined. Hope upsets the boundary drawn by clergy and politicians and activists and officials between the real and the unreal, between the possible and the fantastic. With a hope like that, peons can sing a new song, and Protestants, gathering to protect their pastor from the Romanian KGB, can start a revolution.

This is a hope that permits direct access to the sacred: the sacred being that world of possibility, of the dreamed but unimaginable restoration to a lost world, of the latent impulse toward freedom and unity that destroys all barriers and limitations. In *The Breaking of the Image*, perhaps more clearly than in any other of his works, Martin makes it clear that the custodians of the sacred who preserve it also prohibit access. These custodians may take away a prayerbook that was known by heart and that united the working class with the more elegant and inaccessible and brought the classes together around a common table filled with grace. These protectors of the sacred may even build walls around their brotherhoods; even then, as Martin points out, 'the seeds of hope' may escape by being blown over the monastery wall. Outside, these seeds may take root and create revolutionary aspirations for liberty, equality and fraternity. The inscriptions on the columns of monasteries in Southern France become part of a subterranean current of aspiration which surfaces centuries later during the Revolution on the streets of Paris. Hope takes—and gives—time.

For sociologists who are searching for the sacred, Martin thus reminds us to look for it in unlikely places. Speaking of the Christian activist, too, Martin notes the necessity for seeking the sacred where it may be found rather than where it is so often officially located:

> The partition in the Church is precisely what hides the latent godhead from manifestation. The images and pictures and icons which should mediate possibilities have become barriers, the narrow opening onto vision has become closure ... the necessary instruments of openness can lead to closure. The partition which says there is more to come may cut off potentiality. The transfiguration may be used to diminish and not to alter, because the figures of grace have been translated into a completely foreign 'other' world expropriated and removed from their proper contact with human potentiality.[22]

There it is again: the sacred is pure, raw potential, the substance of things hoped for. This is not the custodians' 'sacred' which cuts

22. Martin, *The Breaking of the Image*, p. 125.

people off from their own 'potentiality'. It is the sacred that one enters through the portal of religious language that mounts 'an attack on the frontier of social possibility'.

Had David Martin been a literary critic, he might well have been heralded as a leading exponent of post-colonial theory. Listen to the way he describes his family as being 'out of date by half a century'.[23] This gave them, he acknowledges, a view of the world that was not easily impressed by the symbols and rhetoric of a cultural 'center'. In saying that they were 'out of date', of course, Martin is engaging in the sort of quiet irony that has permeated much of his work (and has occasionally been lost by some of his readers). Although cultural elites might look on evangelicals from the periphery as being behind the times, those very evangelical communities were in fact the harbingers of the future. That future, in which evangelicals have sprung up throughout Eastern Europe, Latin America and Africa, is now upon us, and David Martin's recent work has provided a telling account of their recent encounters with entrenched status and power.

It would thus be a mistake for anyone to look at Pentecostal enthusiasts or evangelical preachers in remote parts of Latin America or Africa as primitive, traditional or merely antique. They are clearly his contemporaries for whom he has a great deal of respect. Certainly they do not resemble the natives who, to paraphrase the nineteenth-century anthropologist Edward Tylor, are like our ancestors and our peasants now. Similarly, he remembers his family as having 'an eschatology, however implicit and shorn of mythic support'.[24] They themselves anticipated the cultural affinities of developing communities with American popular and religious culture. Linking them was the evangelical sense of the world as being full of possibility. Looking back at the past, he finds that to understand his prior life he has to grasp how the future looked to his parents and thus to himself 50, even 60 years ago. A historically oriented sociologist, then, will treat those who seem outmoded or marginal as in every sense his or her contemporaries in time. David Martin, more than any other living sociologist, has been unafraid to honor his parents in his own writing.

---

23. David Martin, 'Personal Reflections in the Mirror of Halévy and Weber', in R.K. Fenn (ed.), *The Blackwell Companion to the Sociology of Religion* (Oxford: Basil Blackwell, 2001), pp. 23-38.
24. Martin, 'Personal Reflections'.

'Reason Delivered in Sweet Language': Image and Argument in the Theology of David Martin

Jessica Martin

Izaak Walton says that Richard Hooker planned the *Lawes of Ecclesiastical Polity* to 'show such Arguments as would force an assent from all men, if Reason, delivered in sweet Language, and void of any provocation, were able to do it'.[1] The gloss on the peaceable intentions of his heart 'void of any provocation' sits uneasily (and typically) with the declared means of *force majeure*: 'such Arguments as would force an assent'. Thus the irresistible violence of logic is married by arrangement to *caritas*; and we are left asking how the union may be happy.

David Martin writes his theology into two genres. The first, academic method, is implicitly built upon post-Enlightenment 'rational' discourse which, in assuming a sceptical reader, usually expects its sceptic not to question certain givens of that method. These are to do with what may loosely be called empirical observation, with more or less consensual rules about how such observation is quantified, processed, made subject to inference and thus to abstract development. The rules of language are above all deemed not only to be reasonably trustworthy in themselves, but to be a more or less transparent (not to say neutral) medium for recording and for considering that which is seen. The second genre, sermon delivery, obeys a primarily homiletic (into which one may read a celebratory) imperative and assumes a highly specific body of reasonably dutiful listeners. We preach to the converted. It on different terms is logocentric too, in that divine utterance, from which our postlapsarian babble finds what force it

---

1.   Izaak Walton, *The Life of Mr Richard Hooker, the Author of Those Learned Books of the Laws of Ecclesiastical Polity*, in *idem*, *Lives* (ed. G. Saintsbury; Oxford: Oxford World's Classics, 1927), pp. 153-249 (208).

may command, is explicitly declared not merely to reflect but in some sense to bring about the being it names. Added to this academic discourse expects a stable textual existence (even if those texts start life as lectures) whereas sermons, though they may find a textual form, expect to be spoken and occasional, co-existing in the circular nature of liturgical time and in the linear time allocated that hour, that day or that year: 11 November 1989; 1 January 2000; or else Easter Day, 1620; Christmas Day, 1624.[2]

These are embedded difficulties largely to do with the valuations of reason, of language and of time in two traditions now distinct in their respective priorities—from which each method is a logical extrapolation. Nor does David Martin miss the point. On the contrary, the teetering balance between the dual persuasions of reason and revelation, of the word which reflects what is and the word which makes it, are where he always works. While in much of that work he chooses to stabilize the point from which he (and thus his readership) must start by a formal privileging either of the academic or of the homiletic mode, he does attempt, not synthesis, but a kind of detente between the positions. This is presented both as a necessary and as a doomed endeavour: the culmination of a life's work (also typically) is seen and offered as heroic failure.

Failure, Martin argues, is where we begin and end. Failure is embedded in the events of the Christian narrative: in the Fall and the subsequent corruption of word and body which followed it; and no less in the narrative of salvation, where the shocking nature and irreparable loss of Christ's innocent death are the only terms upon which salvation and resurrection may be predicated. Failure is no less written into each method: the words we use neither reflect nor transform with any degree of accuracy. If we expect them to we may be sure they will not. If we do not expect them to our defeat is uncontested and so unheroic. David Martin's unhopeful stance is actually contradicted by the sheer frequency and variety with which he explains his reasons for it, even before we consider the times when

---

2.   Easter 1620: cf. Lancelot Andrewes; Christmas 1624: cf. John Donne. Both sermons assume that liturgical time imitates eternity in its reiterated cyclical *now*. See L. Andrewes, *Selected Writings* (ed. P.E. Hewison; Manchester: Carcanet Press, 1995), p. 89; J. Donne, *Complete Poetry and Selected Prose* (ed. J. Hayward; London: Nonesuch Press, 1932), pp. 586-87.

he attempts to find ways to indicate transformation, to slip from under the imprisoning violence of logic.

I want to look at the means he chooses. I am not trained either as a theologian or a sociologist, and my familiarity with my father's work has also been occasional: I have listened to him often, from infancy, reading aloud the latest draft to my mother, giving sermons, delivering lectures. I have read him very seldom, and only recently. My training is literary and textual and my knowledge of my father's work is almost exclusively words spoken in time, and provisionally. Leaving aside those years where the habitual verbal editing process between my parents built for good or ill my model of the tranquilly rational give-and-take, my earliest memory of his work was a sermon he gave in about 1970 at Trinity Methodist Church, Woking. I was seven, and it was a opportunity I seized not to go to Sunday School, which bored me to ill-behaved fury. The sermon, which he gave in his capacity as Methodist local preacher, was about Jerusalem, the holy city. I do not know what he argued, of course, but I was seized by visual images so powerful they are still strong in my mind: of a vista of impossibly tall spires and towers built entirely of golden light; a translucent untouchable version of the teetering Mont St Michels of wet sand he and my big brother would construct with crazy adrenalized speed in the face of the incoming tide.

I want to take this meeting point of the transformatory figure with the contingent, by looking at David Martin's use of the image—the 'sweet language' of metaphor—in his dealings with that ultimate point of glorious defeat for the sociologist (and the Anglican): *civitas*, the city.

In an unpublished sermon on Mt. 13.3, 'Behold a sower went out to sow his seed', given at Guildford Cathedral in the mid-1990s, Martin points out that, unlike Buddha, Confucius or Mohammed, Christ was not a product of the city; that, indeed, his entrance as an adult into the city was his journey to meet his death.

> Everything that happens in history is very unlikely, but nothing is more unlikely than that reminiscences of words cast on the lakeside air should be built into the foundations of the cities of Rome and Byzantium, St. Petersburg and São Paulo. And why? Because no city could for one day take no thought for the morrow or give all its goods to the poor without panicking the Stock Exchange. As the City of London roundly told William Temple: your faith and our money and power don't mix.[3]

---

3.   Unpublished undated typescript.

Martin continues by paraphrasing the then MP Matthew Parris's complaints about Christianity in an article in *The Times*: that 'love thy neighbour' is of absolutely no practical help in negotiating the complex politics of human relationships, and that 'forgiveness' is a word without effective meaning. 'I think he is right about love', Martin adds, 'but exaggerates about forgiveness'. The 'enclosed garden' by which he later characterizes the Church in the secular city is never promised a rose garden; the Word, the flower of peace,[4] grows with difficulty 'in an unpropitious climate'.

At the same time the City stands in the iconography and symbol of Christianity for the perfection of human society. In paradoxical balance to the contingent difficulties of a doctrine of love in a world where every interaction, from the most private to the most public, is based on calculations about power and about who benefits—where every bond is a kind of bargain—divine civics abandons bargain for gift, and the balance of power for a spontaneous social harmony beyond law. The point wantonly (and for precise political reasons) missed by Walton when he has his Hooker ponder the *'blessed obedience and order'*[5] of heaven's holy angels on his deathbed is taken here, but is placed in the regions of hope rather than knowledge. Even the paradox constructed by the author of the epistle to the Hebrews, where faith is characterized as 'the evidence of things not seen' (11.1) is too calculated in its balances to convey (though it might signify) the unconditional conditions of heavenly society.

When Martin, in a sermon on prophecy given in Cambridge in 1999, picks up the phrase from Hebrews 11, he shifts its meaning marginally to make it amenable to a development led by image and by narrative. 'Prophecy', he says,

> projects a frame for the hope of things unseen which brings us through the times of trial until our feet stand again within the gates of Zion. Through prophecy the penury of our contemporary regime is measured against the inclusive scope of a divine generosity. In *that* day, perhaps soon and with our cooperation, there will be a fresh advent embodying truth and love. In that world each and all sit under fig trees and forget the arts of war in emblematic landscapes surrounding

4. H. Vaughan, 'My soul, there is a country', quoted by D. Martin, *Does Christianity Cause War?* (Oxford: Basil Blackwell, 1997), p. 154.

5. Walton, *Lives*, p. 225.

visionary cities. Creation rules, as alien is made citizen, slave made son, and those redeemed from deep estrangement join in one to hymn the sacred name. Jubilate.[6]

This dense passage uses the historic present as its projection vehicle, and acts to underpin the 'emblematic' nature of its narrative made explicit once the word 'perhaps' has heralded and modified a tentative and brief move into the future tense: 'there will be a fresh advent embodying truth and love'. Yet the imminent social harmony it looks towards is one which the emphasized 'that' of 'that day' tells us is distant enough: thinkable perhaps; not practical, not yet. The passage's single imperative 'Jubilate', formalized in being untranslated, is the only truly imminent action this preacher may recommend. The short silence the paragraph's end signifies after his instruction to us is quickly overtaken by the functional side of the prophet's present: 'the presenting edge of crisis and the terrors built into recovery: the depradations and corruptions of power, the expropriation of the weak and disregarded, the expulsion of the stranger'. This too is emblematic narrative, as well as the ordinary stuff of history.

Why does Martin change faith to hope? Why illustrate the hoped-for in such packed drifts of metaphor? What is wrong with dialectic; exegesis; advice? All have served homiletic discourse well (though the former two not, perhaps, that recently). But his precedent is sound. Though paradox is used in the New Testament to stand for divine synthesis of irreconcilables, outside the correspondence of Paul and his contemporaries there are very few attempts to manage God-talk without heavy recourse to images, and the juxtaposition of images (themselves extended into the maxi-narrative of history or the mini-narrative of parable) tends to be preferred to the logical connectives of discursive text. The prescriptive violence of reason drives the epistles, not the Gospels. The epistles are where faith is defined, the mathematics of justification pondered, and—in a different mode—the patterns of elect behaviour suggested; whereas the Gospels are notoriously resistant to the machinery of analytical process, inference and precedent—even, and most frustratingly, to lived imitation. Metaphor is not helpful for a rule of life but it serves to join the corporate—both embodied and social—with the transcendent: it is a

6.   Sermon on Mt. 10.41 given at St Mary the Less, Cambridge, 27 June 1999 (unpublished typescript).

means to startling and unobvious (not to say impossible) reconcilia-tions. That is what metaphor *does*. An image must be sufficiently unlike its subject to illustrate the qualities which make it like,[7] its own synthesis is that delicate balance between distinct and similar called 'recognition' in human love.

In the language of the Church, the juxtaposition of opposing signs is fundamental to Christian discourse. For example, the Lamb on his throne; the Victim-Priest; the kingdom headed by children and the poor—all these attempt to convey in tension an unbounded but unchaotic reality governed neither by time nor space and thus neither by lack nor finitude. In a chapter on Christian semiotics and civil society, 'The Peace Code and Violence', David Martin reads these tensions precisely and is not tempted by the perfect stillness of paradox or oxymoron to assume, within the distorting glass of space and time, either that historical contingency reflects back the vision in its own cities or—at the other end of the scale—that human societies cannot participate in perfection at all. 'The proper strategy of Babylon the Great', he explains,

> is to confiscate the powers of the New Jerusalem by converting them to her own use. The cross might be made the sword of state, in which case the sign of the scapegoat might be expropriated by the sign of the king. *In hoc signo vinces*—in this sign conquer—could then be used for victory in real physical warfare and peace itself would be defeated... The city into which the unarmed man entered, only to be expelled as a scapegoat and killed, can now be forcibly entered by a Christian empire and its faithless infidel inhabitants slaughtered in the name of Christ... The words of Fortunatus' great hymn *Vexilla regis*—'the royal banners advance'—which once accompanied the cross into sixth-century Poitiers, capture precisely this ambiguity: triumphal entry or redemp-tive humiliation. The humble Hebrew maiden is now Our Lady of Victories. When she fails to protect Constantinople many of her ser-vants desert her. There is no icon for Our Lady of defeats. For that one must return to the humble mother by the cross: *Stabat mater dolorosa.*[8]

But he adds later in the same passage: 'it is important to remember that the secular is not *necessarily* Babylon the Great...Christianity itself

---

7. See Aristotle, *The Art of Rhetoric* 3.8-10 (trans. H. Lawson-Tancred; Harmondsworth: Penguin Books, 1991), p. 219; P. Ricoeur, *The Rule of Metaphor* (trans. R. Czerny, K. McCaughlin and J. Costello; London: Routledge & Kegan Paul, 1986), pp. 194-95.

8. Martin, *Does Christianity Cause War?*, pp. 148-49.

inserts into the Christian city the knowledge that its promise is other than its performance'.[9] And, as he is at pains to point out in his recent work on prophecy, promise is not nothing, but something deferred: glimpsed, even touched on. When he gives his congregation the name of the heavenly city for which we wait, 'Philadelphia', his sly wit may be self-aware but it is not ironic.[10] Despair—whatever other costs it may exact—is intellectually a bit easy. On the contrary, points where history is touched by emblem are, to him, perhaps a more truly reconciliatory demonstration of divine carefulness (and in terms of the personal intellect a more consolatory meeting of a sociological with a devotional sensibility) than any paradox or any proof could be. When he illustrates time with eternity he properly and inevitably chooses narrative over argument, because only in narrative, indeed only in the first-person, eye-witness account can the two be seen to touch. In a note identifying the scriptural source for the words 'Ye are come unto Mount Zion' in *The Breaking of the Image*, David Martin writes: 'Perhaps the idea for the present book came when an Australian Jewish guide began to walk over the clear open space of the Dome of the Rock and accidentally "quoted" the Epistle to the Hebrews'.[11] In 1989 narrative was allowed out of the footnotes and became crucial:

> Where then is the unambiguous good and how do we locate Jerusalem which is the mother of us all and not—like Jerusalem today—the hub of hatred? For myself I had almost my first intimation of this alternative citizenship just after the war when I hitch-hiked to an international youth gathering on the Lorelei Rock four hundred feet above the Rhine. After much lecturing on liberty and unity we came together for morning service in an open air amphitheatre once used for Nazi rallies. I remember only the Lord's Prayer which we spoke together in several languages, and the way the sinister word Reich

9.   Martin, *The Breaking of the Image: A Sociology of Christian Theory and Practice* (Oxford: Basil Blackwell, 1980), p. 150.

10.   Sermon on Mt. 10.41 (see n. 6), *passim*; also 'The Nature of Prophecy—and its Relation to Art', an unpublished paper given at a conference in Oxford in July 1999, *passim*; 'Holy Virgin and Holy City', in *The Breaking of the Image*, esp. pp. 45-57.

11.   Martin, *The Breaking of the Image*, pp. 56-57; see also 'Personal Reflections in the Mirror of Halévy and Weber', in R.K. Fenn (ed.), *The Blackwell Companion to the Sociology of Religion* (Oxford: Basil Blackwell, 2001), pp. 23-38.

touched for a moment against the good word 'Kingdom'. That moment initiated me into a universality in which all the walls and partitions were down.[12]

David Martin argues that these fleeting illuminations are what should persuade us that engagement is—in an exact sense—vital. Just because you know you will fail is, he considers, no excuse not to try, any more than the knowledge of mortality implies suicide or inertia. Like Hooker, another academic highly aware that the relationship between the Church visible and invisible had its problems but sure it was (if mysterious) quite real, he does not allow passivity to be any kind of virtuous sign of election but rather the reverse. God is not the only participant in all this, explains Hooker—hedging it as carefully as any theologian in a solfidian climate must:

> His Prayer must not exclude our labour: their thoughts are vain, who think that their watching can preserve the City, which God himself is not willing to keep. And are not theirs as vain, who think that God will keep the City, for which they themselves are not careful to watch? The Husband-man may not therefore burn his Plough, nor the Merchant forsake his Trade, because God hath promised *I will not forsake thee.*[13]

Martin explicitly adds the silent third to the husbandman and the merchant implied in the presence of those who watch for the city's enemies: the soldier, too, may be required—in an act inevitably compromised—to defend the city, and very ugly it will be. My father's impatience with clergy of all denominations who consider apolitical statements in favour of peace to be effective participation (as in a recent paper written for the World Council of Churches) is (or so I guess) partly fuelled by an idealism shaded years ago by disappointment that pure acts of public virtue are not available—and thus by the recognition that both no effective act is costless, and indeed that costs do not always fall only on the speaker.[14]

Martin is equally clear that the diverse problems of scriptural imagery and method are compounded by the historical accretions of the visible Church, its fractured nature and its internal and external

12. D. Martin, 'Remembrance of Times Past, 1914–89' (Guildford Cathedral, 1989), unpublished typescript.

13. R. Hooker, *A Sermon of the Certaintie and Perpetuitie of Faith in the Elect*, in *idem*, *Works* (London, 1676), p. 532.

14. D. Martin, 'Christianity, the Church, War—and the W.C.C.', *Modern Believing* 40.1 (1999), pp. 22-34.

enmities. This is depressingly rare. In current Anglican usage, where sermons are rarely expected to be exegetical and never overtly disputatious, the conventional homily is usually dominated by exemplary but carefully personal private anecdote as a way of sidestepping the whole intractable lumpy package; the practicalities of interpreting prescription or observance carefully avoided; secular contingencies, ecclesiastical as well as secular political alliances and enmities thinly, even scrappily disguised by a refusal to discuss the guerrilla rules of an unacknowledged conflict. One does not need Erastianism to problematize the structures of Christian doing in the world: that is merely one systematization of a universal difficulty. David Martin makes the decision to meet the fearfully mixed nature of religious praxis on its own ground, and chooses narrative to illustrate rather than to avoid.

Thus in his sermon given on Remembrance Day 1989, after the fall of the Berlin Wall and before the fall of Ceaucescu, rejoicing and mourning were seen to touch in a sermon which was anyway already having to be a more-than-usually vertiginous balancing act between religious and secular concerns:

> My text is taken from Mr. Gennady Gerasimov, Russian Foreign Office spokesman, commenting on the collapse of the Berlin Wall: 'Man does not live by bread alone.'
>
> Last Sunday central London lay almost immobile under the November sun. The noble spaces of Whitehall were full of plangent and sombre sounds recollecting the griefs of seventy-five years since 1914. Every year we make the memorial of unnumbered deaths and woundings, and remember that this has been the century of total war. At the same time last Sunday in central Berlin a concrete reminder of grief and waste and division was being finally torn down and resolutely forgotten. People leapt over the Wall shouting 'The Wall is dead'.
>
> ...the things we see are on the margin of miracle... It is almost as if Palm Sunday is enough: crucifixion for the moment suspended.[15]

Preached and intended for a particular day and time, this contextualizes, with the wars I did not experience, a present my daughter does not really remember, and invests it with (uncharacteristic) joy. But even here it is a joy not only clearsighted about its short-lived nature but prophesying war directly out of the conditions of peace it celebrates. The passage's last sentence is wistful, not even conditional;

---

15. Martin 'Remembrance of Times Past, 1914–89'.

its final phrase frames the words 'for the moment' with 'crucifixion' and an ambivalent linked participle. Prediction follows quickly.

> ...we know that what has been lifeblood for one people is easily deadly poison for others. People inherit adjacent lands or even share them whose loyalties, historical memories and foundation myths are worlds apart or even militantly opposed. In places where the great confessional borders run in jagged faults from Londonderry to Lebanon and Kosovo to Azerbaijan it is still possible for the marvellous resources of faith and language and historic memory to be pitted against each other in deadly enmity.

I am told that even before Ceaucescu's death the writing on the wall for nationalism was large enough. As I write, today's *Independent* warns us that the surviving repatriated Kosovan Albanians are already killing the Kosovan Serbs in retaliation for the horrors of this year's war.[16] So much for logic.

But the violence of logic, too, is our necessity. We may not find the theology Paul forged as extra-legal as he hoped, and we may not like (or accept) every aspect of the *adiaphora* he constructed for the early Church, but their existence guaranteed its survival. Man does not live alone by every word that proceeds out of the mouth of God: we need bread too; apply rules; tell stories; make and break love; damage and nurture our own children. Metaphor too (as Christ was given to pointing out),[17] breaks as it makes, depending on which end of the telescope you are looking down. And dialectic, the prose form we use to divine truths of all kind, is the language of bargain and balance, or retaliation and reparation, and although this makes it more controllable and although without it we do not on the whole ascend to freedom but fall into chaos, it still exacts terrible dues.

One could argue that the worst problem of the sermon form is its difficult relation both to contingency and to eternity. I think it is no accident that poets tend to write good ones, and that today's better (and often more diffident) preachers are driven to quoting verse. While Martin most lucidly *explains* the function of Christian images in an academic rather than an homiletic context, within the sermon he is freed to use them without the paralysing apparatus of commentary, as their own internal logic requires. And because his remit is to the faithful this works on the whole. His instinct is to invoke the more

16. Fergal Keane, *The Independent (Weekend Review)*, 14 August 1999, p. 3.
17. E.g. Mt. 10.34.

unbounded balances of the aesthetic as signifiers of a truth beyond evidence or history, and this works for language though (for him as for others) rather less certainly with the ideologically intractable patterns of music.[18] In a fine sermon on John 8, which uses the sentence 'You shall know the truth and the truth shall set you free' to discuss the different ways evidence is understood in the religious and the academic context he defends the aesthetic as a means to the truth that lies beyond proof: 'It invites us', he explains,

> to cross a threshold beyond the rational need to manipulate, dissect, calibrate, or observe. Across that threshold observation gives place to insight, object becomes emblem, and the givens of analysis manifest themselves as pure gift. In such a space a sign language focusses vision, because without focus vision vanishes, though it is not its nature to impose itself the way propositions impose themselves.[19]

When he attempts the same manoeuvre within academic discourse the result is sometimes a little uneasy, an hermetic prose-poem without external anchors, over-reliant on cadence and the arching phrase. Nor is this a difficulty exclusive to him but one which I suspect partly pertains to the form: William Kavanaugh's 'The City: Beyond Secular Parodies' suffers at times the same tendency to self-reference—with the added difficulty in its section 'Extra respublicam nulla salus' that it locates the rape of the civic Eden in about 1530 (before Luther hissed at us about individuality, interdependence was, presumably, a snip[20]). Hooker's deft distinction between 'certainty of evidence' and 'certainty of adherence' is not now part of the consensus of rational discourse, though it is in itself lucidly and conventionally argued via the underlying Pauline point that doubt is a condition of

18. As true for secular as for religious dialecticians. See, e.g., Roland Barthes on Beethoven's *Diabelli Variations*, where the 'inaudible' performance implied by its notation is made the grounds of its purer disengagement from the contaminating historical context in which it was once played live by amateurs (first 'aristocratic', then the drawing room context of 'bourgeois…young ladies' defined, without evidence, as mediocre performers). One suspects the animating principle for his own virtuoso performance to be the shakier ground that it moves him. See Barthes, 'Musica Practica', in *Image-Music-Text* (ed. and trans. Stephen Heath; London: HarperCollins, 1977), pp. 149-54.

19. Unpublished undated typescript on Jn 8.34.

20. W. Kavanaugh, 'The City: Beyond Secular Parodies', in John Milbank, Catherine Pickstock and Graham Ward (eds.), *Radical Orthodoxy: A New Theology* (London: Routledge, 1999), pp. 182-200.

hope and knowledge is its death (1 Cor. 13).[21] Its reclamation would make it a lot easier for both writers to say what they wanted outside the exhortatory genre without sounding landlocked.

Heaven knows how they would adapt Hooker's method to the dominant assumptions of modern methodologies, though. Hooker rests his case by pointing out that if faith were 'not at all mingled with distrust and fear … what need we the Righteousness of Christ? His garment is superfluous: we may be honourably clothed with our own Robes, if it be thus.' This, on its own, is not really going to do—given that fig leaves are uniform. ('But let them beware, who challenge to themselves a strength which they have not, lest they lose the comfortable support of the weakness which indeed they have'.) In a sermon for Quinquagesima, on the nature of hell, Martin incidentally enlarges on the same point:

> [T]he celestial torture chamber operated by the omnipotent sadist to keep us in line and to believe in the proper way is a disease of our imagination and morally monstrous. But viewed in another perspective the abolition of hell dishonours humanity as much as its retention seems to dishonour God. If we live in a moral world where deeds and thoughts have consequences then hell must be a constant possibility: and if we are free beings then God cannot cannot deny our right to deny him, to reject grace and refuse Paradise. After all a God worthy of our worship cannot compel belief nor can he be self-evident. Indeed I suspect that the denial of God's existence is entirely trivial compared with the rejection of grace. Hell then follows from the dignity conferred on human beings by their freedom and from the limitation of God's freedom imposed by his love.[22]

Pursued at any length, and mindful of human interdependence, despair is not so easy after all, but our main sign of humanity, our marker of responsibility. Hope deferred, argues Martin, maketh the heart sick but the sick heart has hope in its regard, and is at least free of ' "the leprosy so perfect it seemed like health"…so wrapped in self that the touch of grace would be too painful to bear… Perhaps in our heart of hearts the Gospel only makes sense at the breaking points of life.'[23] Or, in a different place, embedded in a different conclusion:

---

21. Hooker, *Certaintie and Perpetuitie*, pp. 527-28.
22. 'Quinquagesima: "If I make my bed in hell behold thou art there"', Sermon on Ps. 139.8, unpublished undated typescript.
23. As n. 22 above.

'About the nature of resurrection we barely know anything at all. All we might hope to discover is the gift of a Word of Promise to do with a truthfulness which is able "to set us free".'[24]

David Martin's vision—private and public—is not cheerful. His characterization of the condition of 'chronic anxiety' as hellish but not of hell is itself a kind of act of faith: a reaching towards an edge of light not now seen or easily anticipated. He himself identifies his intellectual position as one of 'sombre Augustinianism' and acknowledges a debt to Niebuhr;[25] but this is only partly a matter of external evidence. As with every subject dealt with here, the questioning spirit, the necessary doubt, and the difficulty even of ordinary mundane hope (for no good reason that he can assign) is part of the freight the intellect bears; the mind which contemplates death cannot lean on resurrection with ease or without self-deception. 'Better it is', wrote Hooker,

> sometimes to go down into the pit with him, who beholding darkness, and bewailing the loss of inward joy and consolation, cryeth from the bottom of the lowest Hell, *My God, my God, why hast thou forsaken me?* than continually to walk arm in arm with Angels. To sit as it were in *Abraham's* bosom, and to have no thought, no cogitation, but *I thank God it is not with me as it is with other men.* No, God will have them that shall walk in light to feel now and then what it is to sit in the shadow of Death.[26]

24. See n. 19.
25. 'Reflections in the Mirror of Halévy and Weber', pp. 31-32.
26. Hooker, *Certaintie and Perpetuitie*, p. 529.

The Sociologist as Liturgical Critic:
David Martin's Witness

Kieran Flanagan

Those now working on the interface between the sociology of religion and theology owe a large debt of gratitude to David Martin. As an ordained Anglican sociologist, attached to the LSE for many years, Martin has given witness to the possibility of believing in God yet belonging to the trade of sociology. Never cultivating the intellectually fashionable, Martin has defied the stereotypes of sociology as a discipline that imperialized religion for the gods of reason. He spoke to and for another God. His sociology is a means of theological reflection and in this pursuit, Martin has laid the trail for many other Christian sociologists to follow, to witness and to seek a knowing of the Divine from within the contours of the discipline. Not all are to be fated to pursue the crippling agnosticism of Weber's science as vocation. There is another, older calling, to faith seeking understanding, and Martin has prepared an analytical way for its pursuit in a sociology seeking theological deliverance.

Unlike his founding father, Weber, Martin's sociological career has been marked by a profound religious musicality, a sensitivity to the Word and to its resonances. This sensibility has lent an unexpected cast of apologetics to his sociology. It has shaped its vision and direction in so many ways. The shape of things to come emerged in the 1960s, when efforts to link sociology to theology were profoundly unfashionable, if not eccentric. Liberal theologians were hardly receptive to Martin-like witnesses. If sociology was part of their deliberations, it was to endorse their efforts to dismantle the cultural apparatus of religious belief designated as largely incredible for deliverance in an existential, scientific age of modernity. In the terms of Sellar and Yeatman, these liberal efforts are likely to receive a 'bad history' and Martin had the courage to say so from the period of their inception.

Times have changed leaving many liberal theologians as orphans of the age, producing no heirs. The modernity they so sought to align with has disintegrated into a culture of postmodernity which has entrapped theology, but in a curious way has released sociology to see the ground of faith better, without the allures of the gods of reason, who made science the belief of the discipline. In his critiques of secularization, Martin fought a heroic battle against a fated capitulation where religion seemed obliged to sell its soul to the fashions of modernity. This need for resistance marks a continuity between modernity and postmodernity. For Martin, religion was never to be reduced to a matter of culture, ethnicity or reason and like his American colleague, Peter Berger, a long battle was fought to hear those signals of transcendence again. It was not so much that signals could not be heard on the field of culture that so perturbed Martin (and also Berger). Rather it was the perverse efforts of liberal theologians of the late 1960s to make these mute, to mark tradition as incredible, boundaries as restrictive, rituals as imprisoning forms of rote and as empty ceremonials unfit for modern man, that so deeply unsettled Martin. Like others engaged on the interface between theology and sociology, Martin has had to fight his battles on two fronts: one against mute, inglorious theologies enslaved in misreadings of the cultural times; and the other, against sociologies riddled with despisers of the sacred, for whom religious belief was the provenance of the analytically challenged. Believing sociologists occupy a peculiar analytical limbo, lodged between both camps and are typical to neither. As Martin elegantly phrased it, within the discipline, 'the sociologist of religion is an academic deviant living by a non-existent subject'.[1]

If Martin felt something of an outsider in sociology, his interests in theology hardly resolved this status. He was puzzled to find himself a decided minority in the fashions of theology, occupying a conservative camp. In a splendid essay, 'Sociologist Fallen Among Secular Theolo-

---

1.   David Martin, *The Religious and the Secular: Studies in Secularization* (London: Routledge & Kegan Paul, 1969), p. 62. See also Kieran Flanagan, 'To Be a Sociologist and a Catholic: A Reflection', *New Blackfriars* 67.792 (June 1986), pp. 256-70.

gians',[2] Martin found himself estranged by the social disembodiment of the existential nature of the modern man theologians invoked in the late 1960s to justify the unravelling of obligation, boundary and tradition to secure credibility in the secular world.[3] Times have not changed. The past five decades have been a history of theologians adjusting belief, in form and content, to meet their perceived notions of what is credible in a contemporary culture not on their side. This has been a disastrous exercise, as sociologists have continually questioned the basis of these cultural perceptions, their context and intended focus of reception. Theologians and liturgists still have an Olympian view of reality, a certainty of tactic that flies in the face of facts, namely that institutional religion is dying and that an unselective modernization effects its extinction.

The effects of the late 1960s still live in many clerical quarters, and their fatal misreadings still shape their view of how to connect to the world. In their fixations on the efficacy of modernization, they are the Bourbons of theology. They violate religious sensibilities with impunity. No aesthetic, no tradition, no settled form of commitment hinders their urge to engage with the world in all its wisdom at any price. But as Berger has argued, often, worldly wisdom has a sociological address and sociologists who inhabit this mansion, if they have any religious sensitivity, are affronted at the letters sent out in their name, supposedly as the governors of modernity. Endeavouring to return the correspondence to the theological senders has always been a problem, mainly because many theologians lack the sociological spectacles to read the reply. Indeed, given the perverseness of what sociologists get agitated about, theologians could afford to give a cold response. Sociological dealings with liturgists can be best described as prickly.

It is given to few sections of theology, which deal with the practice of faith, to be as otiose as liturgists about the sociological implications of what they do. Admittedly, the focal points of complaint of sociological reactions might seem perverse. As the modernization of rite unfolded from Vatican II, sociologists responded with concerns about the abolition of heaven and hell (Luhmann), the anthropological intelligibility of the Tridentine rite (Turner), the unsettlements of

2. David Martin, 'Sociologist Fallen Among Secular Theologians', in *idem*, *The Religious and the Secular*, pp. 70-78.
3. Martin, 'Sociologist Fallen', pp. 72-73.

boundaries of witness of faith with the relaxing of the Friday fast (Douglas), and the fatuity of having female altar servers (Flanagan). Martin's great liturgical cause, however, was a defence of the *Book of Common Prayer*. Unlike Martin, one has to admit to cowardice in the face of the impenetrable sociological ignorance of liturgists. The crassness of two reviews of this sociologist's major work by English Anglican liturgists caused him to flee into other areas of theology and culture.[4] Martin had a longer and more distinguished career battling at the sociological front against liturgical dimwittedness. His sociological interest in liturgy started in 1973[5] and over the course of that decade he fought a brave campaign against the marginalization of the *Book of Common Prayer*, perhaps the last time academic culture took an interest in the activities of liturgists. Such has been the damage that they have effected since, that few now pay any attention to the ritual order of Anglicanism and only sporadic attention to Catholicism, although the times are changing.

Martin has always been sensitive to language. In the best sense of the term, Martin is an English essayist who writes in many literary outlets besides the conventional routes of sociology. Humane, literate and unusually well read, for Martin the shaping of words matters. Always writing in well-hewn sentences, Martin's clear-cut prose carries much sociological conceptual baggage, but lightly borne. Thus, for him, liturgical language matters greatly in its capacities to resonate and to capture the unutterable majesty of God in prose. Efforts of liturgists in the 1970s to modernize the linguistic shape of rite must have been a great shock for Martin.

The *Alternative Service Book, 1980*, marked an attempt to modernize rites, to make their language accessible and to simplify their structures. The purposes seemed self-evident, as were the disastrous consequences which followed. Instead of marking a benchmark—as in Rome, where an order is laid down—this process started a whole process of revision and change that has taken on a life of its own. Liturgists managed to anticipate the basis of postmodernity by fracturing their own rites, by unsettling the faithful and by making commitment an impossible exercise. As Jeanes notes, 'worship is in a state of

---

4.   Kieran Flanagan, *Sociology and Liturgy: Re-presentations of the Holy* (Basingstoke: Macmillan, 1991).

5.   David Martin with G. Rupp, 'The Language of Worship', *Christian* 1.2 (July 1973).

great turmoil'.[6] Many factors have contributed to this destabilization, not least those flowing from the unfortunate decision to ordain women. The effort to engage with all manner of populace according to ethnicity, age and taste has led to a dumbing down of rite in the interests of accessibility. Sanctity, solemnity and the sacred are no longer terms of rite in the present regime of English Anglicanism. Nearly two decades ago, Martin envisaged much of what was to come to pass.

In his editorial to a special issue of the *PN Review* (1979), Martin wrote prophetically, that the ditching of the *Book of Common Prayer* was to abandon the Church of England's most potent resource. ' "Be ye assured" ', he warned that by the year 2000 'generation will have been sundered from generation, the shared devotional inheritance of English-speaking peoples dissipated, and the future handed over to utilitarian disposables'.[7] As a Catholic, the literary cadences of Cranmer might well appeal, providing as they do a hallowed means of utterance to God, but the Word is not the sole sacramental facet of rite. Whatever the deficiencies of the *ASB*, it did centre the Eucharist in Anglican worship. Yet, Martin's comment above has borne the test of time. The efforts of liturgists of the 1970s have not lasted. The *ASB* has been unceremoniously dumped to be replaced by the ironically entitled *Common Worship*, promulgated in December 2000. Seeking to accommodate to all factions in English Anglicanism, the liturgical texts are littered with options and the word 'may' is given a sacerdotal authority of its own. This new form of worship carries forward a matter of sociological puzzlement: an absence of ceremonial instructions and criteria for performance. There is endless concession to contextualization, but in an infinite galaxy of liturgical permutations that only can bewilder the stranger seeking a settled order of rite and estrange the habitual living with settled compass points for finding the Divine in public places. Nobody is likely to be satisfied with the litugical pottage. By the time liturgists recognize and assimilate a cultural fashion, times have changed. More damagingly, they are seen to abdicate authority for the shaping of rite to the cultural

6.   Gordon P. Jeanes, 'Liturgy and Worship', in Robert Hannaford (ed.), *A Church for the 21st Century. The Church of England Today and Tomorrow: An Agenda for the Future* (Leominster: Gracewing, 1998), pp. 243-70 (243).

7.   David Martin, 'Why Spit on our Luck?', in *Crisis for Cranmer & King James* (*PN Review* 13 [1979], pp. 1-5 [5]).

marketplace. Thus, an endemic sociological problem of matching ritual form to cultural shifts has entered Anglicanism. This ambition can only lead to further de-stabilization, fragmentation and anomie, further disabling the witness of liturgies in a culture of postmodernity.

What Martin caught was the wider issue of the disruptive effects of liturgical renewal on memory and tradition, the hallowing efforts of ritual of ordinary people seeking God. These involved processes of engagement, commitment and construction in contextualizations of faith which liturgists still have not grasped.

Liturgists have ended up as the scapegoats for the chaos of rite resulting from their endeavours over the past 30 years or so.[8] Liturgy has become a source of division, disillusion and despair. Church attendance figures are melting. Nobody in Anglicanism seems happy with the present situation, where liturgies are increasingly private arrangements and despite efforts to the contrary, are diminishing in public significance. In liturgical terms, Anglicanism is no longer in communion with itself. As one bishop noted, Anglicanism is in 'liturgical anarchy'. Such is the agnosticism as to which liturgical form 'works', that experimentation was introduced in 1997. Given the tragic outcome of fiddling with postmodernity, such calls for 'liturgical laboratories' from Sheffield by a member of the Church of England liturgical commission can only be described as extraordinary.[9] Endless packaging of rite to all manner of populations generated a minor revolt in the House of Laity, in February 1996, over the prospect of six experimental eucharistic prayers being introduced. Experimentation conceals an agnosticism, a curious belief that involves the testing of God's response to see which form works. It also involves a sort of 'road testing' of the laity, which generated a hostile response from a member of General Synod that he did not regard his church as 'an MOT test station for detecting prayers that should not be on the road'.[10] Commenting on efforts to stem a haemorrhage of youth from the church, *The Times* felt that adjusting to the informal style of its

8.   See the editorial in *Antiphon* 1.2/3 (Fall/Winter 1996). This publication of the Society for Catholic Liturgy reflected on addresses to the Federation of Diocesan Liturgical Commission, in the USA in October 1995.

9.   Jane Sinclair, 'A Precentor's Eye View: Liturgical Laboratories', *Cathedral Music* 1 (1998), pp. 44-46. See also Derrick W. Cooling, 'Picking up the Pieces', *Theology* 99.787 (January–February 1996), pp. 2-6.

10.   *The Church Times*, 29 March 1996.

rivals would not bring them back. Indeed, it noted that 'there is every indication that modernising the Anglican liturgy has had an effect on attendance—it has hastened its decline'.[11]

Martin might have divided feelings about the way Catholicism is changing in his direction. Currently, the Vatican is re-writing its ceremonial manuals and also providing new translations to replace the much discredited ICEL versions. This reflects a realization that something badly *did* go wrong with the liturgical reforms over the past 30 years. A prime mover in this re-appraisal has been Ratzinger. His concerns with permanence reflect a worry about the breach with continuity effected by the reforms, which are now seen as too abrupt.[12] In a passage that reflects significant worries, which sociologists such as Martin might share, Ratzinger wrote:

> I am convinced that the crisis in the Church we are experiencing today is to a large extent due to the disintegration of the liturgy, which at times has even come to be conceived of *esti Deus non daretur* in that it is a matter of indifference whether or not God exists and whether or not he speaks to us and hears us.[13]

To some extent, the sociological critics of the reforms have been vindicated. Thus, in a widely reviewed work, Nichols, possibly the most prolific of English Catholic theologians, turned his attention to liturgy, to supply a critique of the reason and obsession with function that governed traditions of renewal stemming from the eighteenth century. More interestingly, he took on board the significance of ritual and Martin's emphasis on discipline, habit and rule. Indeed, in the same chapter he gave the first kindly Catholic recognition that Flanagan's *Sociology and Liturgy* has achieved.[14] This appreciation forms

---

11. *The Times*, 11 April 1996.

12. See Joseph Cardinal Ratzinger, *Feast of Faith: Approaches to a Theology of Liturgy* (San Francisco: Ignatius Press, 1986), especially pp. 79-95. Ratzinger's brother was choirmaster at Regensberg Cathedral, which is famous for its choir of men and boys. Like Martin, and also the Swiss theologian Hans Urs von Balthasar, Ratzinger has written movingly on the liturgical significance of church music. See his essay 'On the Theological Basis of Church Music', in *idem, Feast of Faith*, pp. 97-126, and *A New Song for the Lord: Faith in Christ and Liturgy Today* (New York: Crossroad, 1996), Chapters 6-8, pp. 94-147.

13. Joseph Ratzinger, *Milestones: Memoirs 1927–1977* (San Francisco: Ignatius Press, 1997), pp. 148-49.

14. Aidan Nichols, *Looking at the Liturgy: A Critical View of its Contemporary Form*

part of a wider movement to restore a sense of the sacred in Catholic worship and also marks a significant parting of the ways from the more evangelically based efforts at liturgical renewal in Anglicanism.[15]

In retrospect, Martin's petition and the publication of the *PN Review* in 1979 has a significance outside the confines of sociology of religion. It invokes a nostalgia for the time when sociology was part of public debate in the 1970s, where theory and practice were interlinked and where Martin (and, Titmuss and Gellner to name a few) could seek to influence decisions about the direction of key institutions of British society. Research assesment and teaching quality exercises have subjected higher education to bureaucratic control in a manner that has squeezed the vision out of the humanities. These exercises have made academic versions of sociology characterless and have accentuated rather than ameliorated their disconnection from debate on culture and social life. This is especially ironic when, as Christie indicates, sociological ideas are making a significant mark on society, and when exceptional and high-profile sociological figures, such as Giddens, are aiding in the construction of the agenda of the Third Way for the Labour party.[16]

Sociological efforts to find a voice on spiritual matters in public life are not helped by the muteness into which much of academic theology has sunk. The professionalization of the study of religion, and the subservience of theology to religious studies, have affected the capacity of academic culture to produce critics of the spiritual state of the nation.[17] Given that academics speak on almost all aspects of public life, ranging from ethics, race relations, education and law, to name a few areas, expectations of their witness in relation to the spiritual state of the nation are hardly misplaced. There are other voices besides those of bishops, who are always urging the laity to give witness, even from an academic culture. The problem sociology faces is finding a theological partnership. The retreat of academic theology into the Milbank territory of the sublime, its current fixations on

(San Francisco: Ignatius Press, 1996), Chapter 2, 'The Importance of Ritual', pp. 49-86.

15. See Stratford Caldecott (ed.), *Beyond the Prosaic: Renewing the Liturgical Movement* (Edinburgh: T. & T. Clark, 1998).

16. Ian Christie, 'Return of Sociology', *Prospect* (January 1999), pp. 34-37.

17. See William Dean, *The Religious Critic in American Culture* (New York: State University of New York Press, 1994), Chapters 1 and 2, pp. 3-39.

postmodernity and on Derrida, deny a point of entry for sociology into dialogue. At present, in academic theology, there is no middle ground for characterizing culture into which sociology could slot. A disembodied academic theology is futile and many theologians feel they have lost their way.

Liturgy might seem to offer a point of connection between sociology and theology. Unfortunately, as a group, liturgists seem uniquely unaffected by the reflexive condition of sociology. Little has been written on the sociology of liturgists, their contexts of operation and the cultural assumptions they make. Because they operate in a sociological vacuum, it is difficult for sociologists to enter their territory, their traditions and argot, to see where they are coming from, never mind where they are going. Rendering the assumptions of liturgical experts to account poses numerous pitfalls.[18]

The issue of liturgical experts poses other sociological problems, which Dinges spotted in the period of the implementation of liturgical renewal immediately after Vatican II. These liturgical changes appeared to emancipate the clergy from imprisonment in the authority of rubrics, but the price was entrapment into conformity with an opaque term know as the 'spirit' of the reforms which only liturgists had the authority to decipher and discern. Liturgical renewal did not remove the issue of authority from the agenda of rite. It simply displaced it to a loosely accountable set of liturgical bureaucrats who exercised a centralizing power, such as in the saga of the ICEL translations, leaving the clergy to cope with an unanswerable theological and sociological question—'which rite is right?'[19] The regulation of liturgy moved from an accountability to rubrics, which gave a degree of independence and expertise to the clergy in local implementation, to deference to forms of interpretation of how the rites should operate. Interpretation was the prerogative of liturgical experts, a profession without equivalent in church history. The vagueness of the liturgical guidelines after Vatican II increased dependence on their power to arbitrate on interpretations at a multiplicity of levels in the church, from Rome itself, to a country and a diocese. Liturgical forms in Catholicism and Anglicanism are floating between

18. Catherine Bell, 'The Authority of Ritual Experts', *Studia Liturgica* 23 (1993), pp. 98-120.
19. William D. Dinges, 'Ritual Conflict as Social Conflict: Liturgical Reforms in the Roman Catholic Church', *Sociological Analysis* 48.2 (1987), pp. 138-57.

an image of regulation that is at odds with a rhetoric of pluralism, inclusivism, in some quarters, and inculturation that denies the need for some defensible contextualization. It is difficult to render forms of liturgy to sociological account, as issues of power, authority and legitimacy are so opaque. This lends an impenetrable property to liturgy that wards off sociological scrutiny. Yet, the issue of liturgy lies at the core of debates on secularization.

It is the focal point of church attendance, of use of sacraments and communal affiliation with ecclesial culture. It is the site of theological enactment and if it becomes incredible, then belief withers and dies. Although issues such as pluralism and differentiation are important in effecting processes of secularization[20] there is a danger of reification, of lending a property of methodological individualism to the term, that places it above critical scrutiny, as if in some way it was part of the climatic condition of modernity. Such is the belief in its basis, despite the divisions and contradictions it embodies, that it can still seem, as Martin suggests, to be a process 'achieved by metaphysical proclamation'.[21] This notion of a fixed belief that is above contextualization would be untenable in other facets of sociology. All beliefs are subject to deciphering, and sociological attachment to secularization can also be subject to critical scrutiny. There is a wish fulfilment in sociology, which reflexivity reveals as a social construction, that somehow endorses the expulsion of religion from the discipline under the argument of the necessary logic of secularization.[22] Like other facets of sociology, however, this is an argument that can be re-thought. As Martin acknowledges, there are hard and soft versions of secularization, those that denote the death of religion and those that mark its marginalization.[23] The former, ultimately, is a matter of theology, but the latter is very much in the elective affinities of sociology itself.

If sociology is to seek its own theology, then analysis takes on a

20. David Martin, 'Sociology, Religion and Secularization: an Orientation', *Religion* 25.4 (1995), pp. 295-303.

21. David Martin, 'Some Utopian Aspects of Secularization', in *idem*, *The Religious and the Secular*, pp. 23-36 (35).

22. Kieran Flanagan, *The Enchantment of Sociology: A Study of Theology and Culture* (Basingstoke: Macmillan, 1996), Chapter 4, 'The Disappearance of God: The Secularisation of Sociology', pp. 100-46.

23. David Martin, 'The Secularization Issue: Prospect and Retrospect', *The British Journal of Sociology* 42.3 (September 1991), pp. 465-74.

redemptive process, one of resistance to secularization realized through sociological understandings. This changes the nature of the game. Instead of looking at ecclesial cultures as passive victims of secularization, fated to be marginalized by the nature of modernity and by apparently irresistible statistics on disconnection from the churches, one has to look at the ingredients for edification that would generate a counterbelief, perhaps a resistance to domain cultural assumptions. This might require a re-writing of theology, with an emphasis on other worldly expectations and duties that is likely to be anathema to liberals and modernizers. Postmodernity seems to suggest to sociology that there is no abiding logic in the world and that any theological strategy failing to recognize this point is doomed to fail, a point which always lay latent in the notion of secularization as a creature of modernity. Ironically, secularization has brought a capacity to fracture to *any* belief system, even sociology, as debate on postmodernity indicates.

The charge of a *trahison de clercs* might be applied to modernizing clerics, a pleasing example of a phrase returning to its original. By assimilating what they perceive to be a credible reading of the face of modernity, liberal theologians and liturgists have effected what Isambert terms an internal secularization. He argued that recent efforts to modernize Catholicism left it dispersing its mechanism of commitment and that in rationalizing its mechanism of beliefs it managed to effect a disenchantment of their basis. The de-ritualization of liturgy exemplified this process of internal secularization.[24] Isambert goes further in his argument. 'Re-magicing' of culture, and ritual in particular, is an issue of enchantment, a point where Weber finished his sociological analysis, but where theological matters begin. These relate to the channelling of grace, a process of rationalization, but without disenchantment and this relates to issues where the relationship of sociology and theology becomes mysteriously intermingled. This points to an interface between ritual and secularization. If those attending Vatican II had only read Weber and Durkheim, how different might have been the recent ill-fated efforts to connect liturgical practice to contemporary culture? If understandings of internal secularization had been different what would be understood?

The most important point to make is that the detail of sociology always comes back to an issue of context and agency. This issue has

---

24. François-André Isambert, 'La sécularisation interne du christianisme', *Revue Français Sociologie* 17 (1976), pp. 573-88 (584-86).

become especially significant in the context of a culture of post-modernity, where matters of self and identity have come to the fore of the present sociological agenda. Secondly, until recently, little attention was given to the issue of transience in processes of secularization, the notion that believers and disbelievers move around and in and out of churches. Biography is a peculiarly neglected facet of debates on secularization and the failure to generate middle-ground theories about its basis has impoverished liturgical understandings of how individual credibility of belief is realized in ritual practice.[25] This is, perhaps, the most central issue sociology can present to theology as worthy of scrutiny. Thirdly, there is a remarkable imbalance in the sociology of religion in favour of chronicling those who exit from religion rather than on those who remain.

The recent growth of interest in the social construction of identity, in sociology as a whole, makes this distortion in the agenda of the sociology of religion all the more apparent. Sexual rather than religious identity has become a consuming interest in sociology, reflecting the pressures of cultural and sexual politics, for instance in the growth of 'queer theory'. Ideal identities, achieved rather than ascribed, fuel its concerns with the politicization of identity. These concerns attenuate a deficiency in the sociology of religion, that its deference to debates on secularization confines it to an implicit concern with the de-construction of identity as against the bias towards construction as in the realm of cultural and sexual politics. Curiously, edification as a form of the managed construction of identity is more likely, with its implicit mistranslations, to be found in the realms of sexual politics than in those of sociology of religion.[26]

In dealing with liturgy and secularization, sociology encounters problems that are beyond its remit to resolve without reference to theology. Many of these problems relate to issues of judgment and authority that are biblical in origin, particularly about accommodating to this world. This reflects a Protestant strategy of adapting to its values but hoping through grace for the faith to ameliorate their

25. See the important study of transience and religious belief by Phillip Richter and Leslie J. Francis, *Gone but not Forgotten: Church Leaving and Returning* (London: Darton, Longman & Todd, 1998).

26. See Kieran Flanagan, 'Religion and Modern Personal Identity', in Anton van Harskamp and Albert W. Musschenga (eds.), *The Many Faces of Individualism* (Leuven: Peeters, 2001), pp. 213-40.

debilitating basis. As Catholicism has modernized recently, its stress on other worldly values has become diluted. This has made life complicated for sociologists happy to leave theology to make distinctions regarding the pursuit of salvation in relation to the world that are beyond its remit. Such difficulties over strategies of investment and commitment to get home are hardly new, either in theology or sociology. One need only think briefly of Weber or St Augustine's *The City of God*. The only remit sociology possesses is to look at the outcomes of arrangements of adaptation and rejection of the world and have the wisdom to invoke theology when it faces limits of understanding.

Martin's stress on the sociological efficacy of rules and regulations, on resistance and contextualization of the Word in reverence, in the sacred and in marked spaces for the holy, might seem arguments liturgists do not wish to know. These violate their most sacred assumptions. Resistance to the wisdom of the world is not so much unfashionable, as to them, incredible, yet in another set of meanings, it forms a continued theme in Bauman's approach to ethics and postmodernity. In his writings, modernity is a mixed blessing. It supplies emancipation through reason, but belief in its power tyrannizes. Eradicating ambiguities and refusing to live with the untidy deposits of history mark reason's gift to modernity, of making things neat and unambiguous. It is this deceiving property that sabotages the quest for authenticity and humanity that underlines Bauman's work. Policing openings is a peculiar task of sociology. This involves preserving ambiguities, marking resistances and keeping the mysterious untidiness of humanity free from the fetishes of tidiness, relevance and the manufacture of culture. Following what Georg Simmel had also argued, and summarizing a long sociological tradition, but this time directed to religion and the issue of secularization, Martin asserted that

> only if we learn to accept the opportunity cost of alternative ideals, and if we accept the need to live with ambiguity, with the ambivalence written into every achievement, and with the elements of determination, limits and sheer arbitrary chaos which enclose and make possible our freedom, order and purpose, only then do we in fact come to terms with the secular. There is nothing so capable of preventing us from seeing what is actually in front of our noses as an over-secularized concept of man.[27]

27. Martin, *The Religious and the Secular*, p. 47.

Similar points can be applied to sociological understandings of liturgy. Making rites too accessible, lowering points of difficulty as estranging barriers to entry, relegates curiosity elsewhere, to the sacralizing powers of a commodified culture. More importantly, it confines those participating to the surface of the rite by denying the need for liturgical labour, for that is what the work of giving worth to God requires. No incentives, no rules of discernment are cultivated that would form habits of affiliation that could cope with profitable and unprofitable ambiguities. Modernizing and packaging rites to the perceived cultural context of clients such as the young is to capitulate to the notion that problems of spiritual seeking can be solved by re-arranging liturgical surfaces, the obvious parts of ritual. The young are clever enough to see through such patronizing efforts, but not clever enough to demand something better, all of which reflects a total failure of leadership in the churches who dilute their rituals for reasons of cultural expedience.

Perhaps through Catholic eyes, Martin's emphasis on the cultural and the theological value of the Word, as in the *Book of Common Prayer*, seems to marginalize emphasis on the performative dimensions of the ritual order, its own sacramental basis. Certainly, in his writing, sacredness of symbols, the interaction of language and silence, pre-suppose ritual contexts of reception, but this is treated in a passive manner that makes little reference to the activities of liturgical actors. The notion of a liturgical career, however, does emerge in his splendid essay on habit in rite.[28]

Habit is an instrument of location, used in a way that complements Bourdieu's approach to habitus, the disposition and capacity to play a game, in this case liturgy. It is the familiarity of the order that makes commitment and trust possible and this pre-supposes a sense of detail, of things in place, that make biographical attachment a securing exercise. Repetition effects a notion of rhythm and stereotypical practice provides a secure framework to secure a ground of faith. As Martin graphically suggests 'boredom is the infrastructure of illumination'.[29] Yet, it is this property of boredom and obscurity that so panics liturgists who assume actors have the attention spans of gnats and that they are incapable of a pious gaze at the settled in the hope of discerning,

28. David Martin, 'Profane Habit and Sacred Usage', *Theology* 82.686 (March 1979), pp. 83-95.
29. Martin, 'Profane Habit', p. 86.

however shadowly, the Divine. This notion of rite and rote has come to be destroyed as liturgists increasingly fiddle and congregations burn away.

It is curious that sociologists have to remind liturgists of what they should already know, that rituals carry a sacramental property, illustrating the notion that beliefs are real in their consequences. If the vehicle of belief, a ritual order, is marked as incredible and therefore continually in need of re-adjustment to 'fit' the cultural times better, it will become so. In seeking to justify continued efforts to enable worshippers to belong, in making access open to all, liturgists have unravelled a necessary tension between rite and culture, that it must contain signs of contradiction if it is to attract the curious. A uniqueness needs to be conveyed if obligation is to elicited. It is the loosening of obligation that has most weakened current liturgies. Beside losing control of the domestic context of rite and the capacity to be definite about boundaries and contours, the churches have also lost their monopoly in areas where minimum obligations could be made. These are in areas of matching and dispatching. These can take place anywhere, without discomforting obligations of doing these rituals in church. As liturgists seek to adjust to that marketplace of the commodification of matching and dispatching, they face a dilemma. The more they reflect contemporary cultures in their rites, the more they can be outmanoeuvred by more professional ritual entrepreneurs, closer to the market, who can package their services more authentically to the needs of their customers. Furthermore, as liturgists dilute what is sacerdotal in their rites, the more clients are likely to shop around for something more spiritually adventurous. This de-contextualization of rites, such as those of hatching and matching—the bread and butter of the Church of England—can only be further undermined in a culture of postmodernity, whose religion is that of the New Age and of self-made spiritualities that are linked to therapy and health. Solutions to holism lie elsewhere and this is also a characteristic of secularization, of dispersal from traditional routes into spirituality, where people make their own multi-faith mixtures.[30] In many respects, liturgists have no option but to dig and form habits of

---

30. See, e.g., Maxine Birch, 'The Goddess/God Within: The Construction of Self-Identity through Alternative Health Practices', in Kieran Flanagan and Peter C. Jupp (eds.), *Postmodernity, Sociology and Religion* (London: Macmillan, 1996), pp. 83-100.

affiliation in relation to the making of ritual attachments. In looking at the collapse of church attendance over the past two decades, in Anglicanism and Catholicism, there is little doubt but that the fault lies within, in an internal secularization, rather than in some endemic propensity to disbelief in culture. Liturgical renewal requires a return to basics, some of which Martin laid out in the 1970s.

This notion of rote in rite is the stuff of the social construction of liturgical biography, and the shaping of a habitus into the seeking of holiness is a process that connects childhood to adulthood. Those young, marginal, mere fledgling actors in ritely enactments are often the victims of liturgical unsettlements, endless changes and the imposition of political correctness on rite. These liminal actors, choristers and altar servers often feel threatened. They have no security of liturgical station, yet, these so marginal are often the most conservative about rite and, as Martin notes, they 'care passionately about minutiae as well as about due reverence and propriety'.[31] Efforts at the pursuit of a political correctness have hit young males badly. They often feel marginalized and excluded from their tradition and from roles they peculiarly embody, such as choirboy. This endless feminization of rite[32] from the ordination of women to the cultic pursuit of inclusive language, means that maleness is excluded in images and representations of rites just at the point when the failure of boys in secondary school examinations is requiring the government to seek role models of imitation and encouragement. Even feminists are revolting against the endless demolition of distinctive male roles. In many areas, male self-confidence has disintegrated, not only in relation to areas such as fathering, but in religion, where it always has been precarious. Again, some liberal theologians and liturgists have

31. David Martin, 'The Stripping of the Words: Conflict over the Eucharist in the Episcopal Church', *Modern Theology* 15.2 (April 1999), pp. 247-61.

32. See Mairi Levitt, 'Sexual Identity and Religious Socialization', *The British Journal of Sociology* 46.3 (September 1995), pp. 529-36. On a personal note, one remembers, with awe, the visit to my office by a former student with his son, a choirboy, who had just left a cathedral where a girls' choir was being implemented by dean's fiat. The boy's indignation, reflecting that of others, he claimed, at the wrecking of a tradition, was memorable. It is the sense of treachery he felt that one remembers. A whole world of awe, reverence for tradition and hierarchy had collapsed for this boy, unlikely ever to return to church again. Spin-doctoring is also the art of deans in cathedrals, who smoothly impose political correctness on their choirs in the teeth of an opposition which is so well suppressed.

clambered on to a cultural trait just as everybody is seeking escape from its consequences.

In seeking to recast rites in ways that match values of gender and lifestyle politics, these theologians and liturgists seem oblivious to more pernicious and destructive trends in culture, not least the misappropriation of the cultural capital of rite, for commodification and profit. This is the ultimate form of secularization of rite, where its stewards permit the disposal of its distinctive resources for representation on an alien scale of values, those of the god of money. The endless and limitless commodification of culture grants a licence to re-appropriate anything for profit not prophecy. If liturgy embodies resources, such as music, and utilizes settings of enormous historical and architectural significance, the issue of use and ownership is highly important. Civic rights of entitlement of appreciation of the cultural capital of rite collide with sacerdotal imperatives to conserve and to regulate the holy, to preserve discipline and fidelity in faith in worshipful appreciation. As pastiches and imitations form the basis of a culture of postmodernity, misappropriations have become all the more manifest as churches display an equivocal attitude to their choral heritage. In an essay, nothing if not honest, Peter Phillips, director of the Tallis Scholars, notes the growth of the secularization of sacred works of arts. This process reflects the demand for rights of appreciation without obligations of faith. For him, sacred art needs to be liberated from the incredible obsessions of faith that restrict its display and performance for art's own sake.[33]

The condition of anomie which has descended on to Anglicanism perhaps reflects an ongoing puzzle as to what are the minimum and maximum obligations surrounding its ritual order and use. There does not seem to be any sensible order of authority governing its rites. For instance, it is difficult to reconcile rulings of ecclesiastical law on the rightness or otherwise of votive candles in churches with the lurid re-decoration of cathedral naves and choir stalls for a rave liturgy. One effort at Bradford was described with the heading 'bubblebath and

---

33. Peter Phillips, 'Material Benefits', *The Spectator*, 19.26 (December 1998), pp. 93-94. The gist of Phillips' complaint arose from an organizational mix-up, where a service was given priority over a rehearsal at the church of Saint Severin in Paris. The complaint has a particular irony as this was the church where J.K. Huysmans, the French writer on modernity and decadence, realized his conversion to Catholicism through hearing sacred music performed within the liturgy.

barbecue as clerics rock cathedral'.[34] A former Archbishop of Canterbury described these events as 'dreadful' and 'dangerous', and was roundly attacked by other bishops, who felt at least they were reaching people—even if figures on church attendance suggested that even more were fleeing.[35] If proprietors of cathedrals manifest an indifference, a lack of commitment to the conservation of their cultural capital, they cannot be surprised if others respond in similar terms. In such circumstances, it is scarcely surprising that cultural entrepreneurs should pilfer liturgical objects for decadent display. Absence of ecclesial stewardship of liturgical symbols and artefacts permits transgression to flourish in a cultural climate where blasphemy has become an instrument of fashion and where 'real' and virtual religion have become confused. Liberal theologians and liturgists end up being the inadvertent suppliers to manufacturers of the culture of postmodernity that so confounds their sense of mission.

Spiritual emptiness carries a price in rising suicide rates but also in the suffering such nihilism effects as it spreads into a mass culture that blindly appropriates the remains, the shell of the sacred, hence the fashion for wearing crucifixes as objects of decoration rather than of belief. Irreverence, the testing of limits, all point to the suffering wrought by emptiness and a futile revolt against a ritual order which liturgists have long dismantled. As Beaudoin elegantly notes, in a fascinating American work on the irreverent quest of Generation X, now 'everything liquefies under the glare of a foundationless commercial culture, a nuclear meltdown, and especially a meltdown of *meaning*—the primary source of Xer suffering'.[36] This is expressed in the current fetish for body piercing, which serves to decorate but also to display a need to feel something of self when living in a spiritually lobotomized state of unquiet desperation.

To mirror these angsts in rites that celebrate postmodernity, as some Anglican liturgists seem to advocate, is to lock the young into an eternal present. It is to seek engagement and belonging at any price, so

34. *The Daily Telegraph*, 26 January 1997. It is noticeable in press reporting that, now, few bother to report such events, which have lost their capacity to shock and which simply confirm that the Church of England is rudderless in its direction of liturgy.

35. See reports in *The Times* and *The Daily Telegraph*, 10 February 1997.

36. Tom Beaudoin, *Virtual Faith: The Irreverent Quest of Generation X* (San Francisco: Jossey-Bass Publishers, 1998), p. 115.

that those evangelicals, who abhorred a ritual order, now ritualize the tasteless in confected rites, banal music, and in raises and praises that evoke deep embarrassment in the liturgically sensitive. Little would matter if they confined their assemblies to fields and halls, but some insist on using gothic buildings. This involves a re-ordering to maximize engagement, so that pews, choirs and anything that smacks of tradition and good taste is ejected, a process that seems to satisfy the management ambitions of the present Lambeth regime. Dumbing down to user friendliness that proffers almost instant access to God, has invaded television's approach to liturgy and, extraordinarily, is presented as a basis for future mission.[37] This rush to remove estranging barriers, to modernize at almost any price of achieving access, seems miles removed from the traditional orders of rite surrounding the *Book of Common Prayer*. Currently, the diversity of forms of rite in Anglicanism defy sociological encapsulation. Indeed, it is doubtful if the range of permutations of rite could be calculated. Being rites of clipboard and committee arrangement, these rites have no enduring significance. Continual re-ordering of liturgical form becomes a form of stewardship, a form of worship in its own rite. Doubt and uncertainty is absolved in liturgical creations. Yet, these give no lasting solace, for new creations are required and it is not long before impoverished imaginations end up imitating the culture of the primary school classroom. The God of surprises cannot but be astonished at what is now on liturgical display. It has no history, no precedent, and as many drift in and out, no securing credibility.

In all this headlong change to mirror a culture, the sense of liturgical past has almost been erased. Choral evensong is an island of liturgical good taste all too ripe for wrecking. Liturgies, with lineages having boundaries to defend and worship habits to protect, present a scandal of discipline to a church increasingly legitimizing the fracture of rite to connect, at almost any price, to the fragmentary characteristics of a culture of postmodernity. In this fall into liturgical pieces, pastiches of past traditions float, mirroring all too well the culture of postmodernity which liturgists seek to emulate so assiduously. Binding, authoritative rites that effect a collective bonding of effort and form belong to the foreign territory of pastness, of eccentric affirm-

---

37. Steve Chalke with Sue Radford, *New Era, New Church? The Millennium Challenge to the Churches* (London: HarperCollins, 1999).

ation of Victorian values of ritual, which seem so peculiarly antique to some, but all too credible to others.

The impoverished reading of culture by liturgists leads them to deny the power of collective memory just as this process is commodified as part of the heritage industry. Producing liturgies with no lineages to the immediate past, lessens the chances of biographical recollection. There is no private memory in these public forms of rite, or of biographical stages realized of advance into appropriation and self-understanding.[38] It might be retorted that such careers betray a seeking of safety, but this is often the pronouncement of the strong, liberal theologians, not those seeking a passage of growth, such as an ex-chorister who has no liturgical ladder to climb to God. It might also be said that stress on collective memory brings out the most conservative reading of liturgy possible, and that in someway it legitimizes a culture of the vestry or sacristy as the ultimate escape from the world. This would be to miss a wider, more significant point. Collective memory might seem undesirable to cultivate because it leads to a false expectation and reading of the world. It effects and secures a liturgical disconnection from reality. But this is to fail to recognize the unique significance of collective memory in a culture of postmodernity. It provides a root of stability, when all else is breaking down. It is an issue that governs questions of identity, is the agenda of nationalism and connects to dangerous traditions which, invoked, provoke profound divisions in contemporary culture. The making of a tradition is a political and a cultural act, but one inconveniently riddled with inescapable theological implications that haunt the present, but which secularization has so deceptively masked. This issue of the divisions of memory in the setting of liturgy and secularization mark a division with Martin from the Catholic side.

The *Book of Common Prayer* symbolizes Martin's notion of collective tradition, of memory that spins cadences of recollection in routinized liturgical engagement. Within the confines of a rejection of the inevitability of secularization and a critique of liberal liturgists who have so unravelled a settled tradition, Martin's defence of the *Book* is sociologically incontestable. Unfortunately, debate on secularization can disguise wider issues reflecting the insularity of the sociology of religion. Other strands of modernity effect differentiations and

---

38. Danièle Hervieu-Léger, *La religion pour mémoire* (Paris: Cerf, 1993).

unsettlements of identity and make its cultural, political and religious agenda contested.

Certainly, the *Book* has a liturgical lineage that binds into collective memory, but it carries a burden of history in events surrounding its promulgation. Translation and memory relate to notions of power and imposition, the marking of differences that effect exclusions. These render collective memory contested, but also the agenda forged within it. One might admire the literary cadences of the *Book*, but as a Catholic one cannot ignore the exercise of civil power to effect this liturgical change, that makes it in some way part of the state apparatus. The *Book* forms part of an unwritten constitution governing the official notion of English identity and its use in ritual order provides a civil and religious means of sustaining the legitimacy of a monarchy. Its use is politicized by the nature of its inception, aiding as it does an affirmation that intertwines Englishness and Protestantism. This interlinkage is naturalized by convention and tradition that it might be divinely ordained. The settlement of identity in a collective memory masks a contested past almost impolite to resurrect for scrutiny. The constructed nature of this past is also veiled, for it bears an oppositional property, that the Protestantism of the identity is set against what is to be excluded—Catholicism. It is cast in a negative estranging identity to embody all that Englishness is not. Thus, patriotism and Protestantism are bound into sound definitions of what is alien, foreign and treacherous and profoundly unEnglish.[39]

This is not to imply in any way that there is a lurking anti-Catholicism in Martin's work, rather it is to point to an inconvenient baggage of cultural and political identity surrounding attachments and defences of the *Book*. It is to ask a wider question, one Martin has also pursued,[40] as to what English religion is and even more importantly, what are the forces that unravel this identity. Other forces besides those of secularization are changing the identity of Englishness and the *Book* in which its collective memory is now being borne.

Three fundamental issues are marking a sea change in the religious and cultural identity of Englishness. First, the process of devolution is stripping away strands of the Celtic fringe that allowed issues of English identity to be subsumed under the term British. As Scotland

39. Linda Colley, *Britons: Forging the Nation 1707–1837* (London: BCA, 1992).
40. See 'The Unknown Gods of the English', in Martin, *The Religious and the Secular*, pp. 103-13.

encounters the collective memory of its nationhood, the issue of its own religious past will also emerge. Secondly, membership of the EC is forcing English identity to think in European terms, which are often cast in Catholic terminology. As this European dimension increases, the place of English identity within it forces a return to past notions of cultural and political allegiance. Thirdly, and perhaps most importantly, re-appraisals of identity have become necessary because the cultural and religious composition of English society has changed. This has generated questions about which religion, if any, should have a monopoly over the use of the ceremonial apparatus that confers and legitimates the power to rule. The politics of culture surrounding identity enter debates on ethnicity but also religion, and it is from these wider sociological concerns that the issue of rights of representation in the ritual apparatus of the state emerge. The fact that these are also part of Anglicanism simply complicates the issue. In this sense, therefore, secular forces seek an appropriation of liturgy to an agenda of civil and ethnic representation. This potential politicization of liturgy, implicit in the regime of an established church, begs questions about religious autonomy in ways that are adjacent to debates on secularization but are not part of them. It is not that religion has been reduced to the margins, to a state of indifference, as certain advocates of secularization assert, but that differentiation in society has *expanded* its significance as a form of political and cultural capital, and of symbolic power well understood in Bourdieu's approach to culture.

Catholicism might well be a 'majestic ruin' for some secularists[41]—and certainly in its numerous architectural manifestations its cultural remains are well fitted for high status in the heritage industry. Yet, the nostalgia it invokes straddles the concerns of secularization and, indeed, precedes them. The destruction of a late mediaeval liturgy, that laid the benchmarks for English identity in so many arenas of cultural life, has left a painful memory[42] and numerous efforts to return again to what was lost. Tractarianism, and indeed the shape of English Anglicanism over the past century, are marked by efforts at resuscitation of this dream. It lies as the great counterfactual of English cultural history. What if it had been otherwise? Some link was broken between

41. 'Utopian Aspects of Secularization', in Martin, *The Religious and the Secular*, p. 26.

42. Eamon Duffy, *The Stripping of the Altars: Traditional Religion in England 1400–1580* (New Haven: Yale University Press, 1992).

ritual and social order that points to wider concerns than those invoked by secularization. These concerns relate to the nature of sociology itself, its capacity to realize social bonds that bind through the power of ritual, for in all this, are Durkheimian questions never resolved, but attenuated in debates on the nature of a culture of postmodernity.

This perception of a link between ritual and the social order being fractured forms a central theme of Ackroyd's recent biography of Thomas More.[43] There is an almost Durkheimian cast to More's insights and his frantic hunting of heretics who bring a cultural, political and ritual ordering crashing down. Iconoclasm destroyed the social bond and ceremonial repairs have been unsuccessful since. The legacy of guilt of what was fractured lies in the symbolic significance of the cathedral in contemporary culture, a place that somehow always exceeds the narrow confinements of the heritage industry.[44] Somehow, these buildings spoil the neatness of secularizing arguments and those sociologists ridden with belief are among the few to see this enigma. Like Hamlet, sociologists suffer from a burden of knowledge difficult to articulate about the basis of the tragedy of culture and its endless acts in the folly of postmodernity.

As cultural expectations shape the packaging of belief and its perception, hermeneutic considerations emerge about what is projected. The gender of God, the credibility of images of heaven and hell and how these are to be understood in a culture of postmodernity, all force theologians into issues of sociological reflexivity, an awareness of the cultural mechanisms of construction that surround and shape discernments of the ground of faith. Sociological questioning of these assumptions of culture, but more importantly, theological and liturgical readings of these, is a peculiar task of often isolated individuals, sociologists by chance struck by providence to give inconvenient witness to theologians and liturgists, however unfruitfully. Working from different and opposite positions—for instance, Martin agrees with the ordination of women and I certainly do not—one is struck by the disparate nature of those who made interventions in the early 1970s, such as Mary Douglas, Victor Turner, Peter Berger and of course

43. Peter Ackroyd, *The Life of Thomas More* (London: Chatto & Windus, 1998).
44. André Vauchez, 'The Cathedral', in Pierre Nora (ed.), *Realms of Memory*, I (trans. Arthur Goldhammer; New York: Columbia University Press, 1997), pp. 37-68.

David Martin. Their anthropology and sociology was markedly different in agenda and analysis, yet they all came to the same perception that the ritual order, its rules and boundaries, denoted a stable and habit-forming means of realizing the sacred. Defeating Durkheim has always been part of the agenda of any sociology seeking to push past issues of religion into matters of theology to affirm the sacred, the majestic and what is beyond its remit to understanding. Is all lost, as this generation of liturgical critics reaches its end, even though some are in long, fruitful Indian summers?

Such sociological witnesses are few and far between. It will take decades to unravel the chaos into which liturgists have thrown their own subject. As liturgical transactions generate more indifference in the face of the multiplication of forms, those with a memory of tradition and habit, such as Martin, might witness no more. If so, theologians and liturgists might rue the past scorning of their few sociological friends. Yet, there are some unexpected consolations and converges afoot that suggest unexpected alliances and forms of theological recognition of sociological scrutinies of liturgy.

Ratzinger and Martin might seem peculiar bedfellows, yet both in recent writings show a remarkable converge of interest in the same question: the direction the priest faces when saying Mass. With user-friendly evangelical assemblies, the issue might seem trivial. For other liturgists, it is just the sort of question that gives sociological interventions into their arena a bad name. Yet, in such apparent trivialities there are significant sociological *and* theological issues abroad.

In his latest essay on liturgy, Martin decries the symbolic and spatial effects of the priest presiding, facing the people. He claims that priests resolve their sense of isolation through eye-to-eye contact and the making of a gathered community. In this essay, Martin wonders about the free-floating notions which follow.[45] Too often, a condition of anomie characterizes liturgical enactments and those so engaged keep amplifying the social, to heighten a sense of communality of worship. The result is that the rite keeps falling into excessive scrutiny of its social mechanism of reproduction and never realizes a distance from it to enable its hidden dimension to be viewed. Monitoring the social rather than the spiritual too often becomes a gauge of liturgical efficacy. Curiously, Ratzinger comes to a similar conclusion in a

---

45. Martin, 'The Stripping of the Words', p. 253.

strongly worded address, part of which is devoted to the same issue: the direction of the presiding priest, east or west?

Ratzinger stated flatly: 'the Constitution on the Liturgy itself does not say a word about celebrating Mass facing the altar or facing the people'. In his address, he goes on to deplore the disappearance of mystery and the sacred in the liturgy 'under the proclaimed imperative of making the liturgy more easily understood'. The fragmentation of liturgy and its reduction to a communal character is also deplored. He goes on to state in terms Martin might applaud, that

> happily, there is also a certain distaste for the rationalism, banality and the pragmatism of certain liturgists, be they theoreticians or practitioners. One can see evidence of a return to mystery, to adoration, to the sacred and to the cosmic and eschatological character of the liturgy, as is witnessed by the 'Oxford Declaration on Liturgy' of 1996.[46]

The issue of liturgy is but a fragment, a significant one perhaps, of Martin's wider interests in the sociology of religion and more particularly its relationship to theology. Martin always writes with integrity, teasing at inconvenient contradictions with a directness and an honesty. Gifted with a capacity to catch the humbug of theologians selling the liturgical silver for a mass of cultural pottage in the name of modernization, Martin has never courted popularity in Anglicanism even though he always speaks loyally for its basis. Always seeking to scrutinize, Martin has sought only to preserve an integrity of witness, a calling that marks the seriousness of sociological analysis, but mixed unexpectedly with pleas for reverence and humility. In his case, the constant theme has been a vigorous defence of the autonomy of religion in sociological affairs and an implacable witness to the belief that it is not a spent force. Looking back over his writings, one cannot but think how incredibly impoverished sociology, and sociology of religion, would have been without his labours. As said earlier, such witnesses come infrequently and Martin has done his prophecy for sociology and liturgy, but more importantly theology, and we can only build on it.

---

46. Joseph Cardinal Ratzinger, speech on liturgy given in French in Rome, 24 October 1998, reproduced in the *Newsletter of the Association for Latin Liturgy* 105 (spring 1999), pp. 19-20. Papers relating to the Oxford Declaration on Liturgy are reproduced in Caldecott (ed.), *Beyond the Prosaic*.

Confirming the Rumour of God:
Why Every Church Needs a Sociologist

Martyn Percy

The joke goes like this. Three rural Anglican clergy meet up at a local inn for a drink. After a few beers, the conversation naturally enough turns to their respective churches.

'My main problem is bats', says one. 'They're in the belfry wreaking havoc, and I can't get rid of them.'

'Amazing', says the second, 'I have the same problem.'

'Me too', adds the third, 'they are a terrible nuisance'.

All agree the bats have to go, and to meet again in one month's time and share solutions to their collective problem. A month later back at the inn, the three clergymen reconvene. The first reports that he used poison; the strategy was initially successful, but the bats soon returned, apparently able to spot the bait. The second had used an air rifle, but his aim had not been good, and the Archdeacon had complained of holes in the roof. The third announced complete success, much to the amazement of the others. 'How did you do it?' they asked.

'Easy', he replied. 'I went up to the ceiling with a bucket of water, baptised and confirmed them all, and I haven't seen them since.'

We know enough about confirmation and baptism rolls within the Church of England during the last 100 years to recognize that the joke contains more than a grain of truth. Yet it is only a grain. The actual 'reading' of these figures is a complex business, as any sociologist knows. And what conclusions are deduced from such statistics can vary widely, usually in accordance with the underlying theological, ecclesiological or sociological presuppositions and interpretations that are brought to bear on the data. This is a commonsensical observation, to be sure; there are no such things as 'plain' statistics—all figures function within a broader narrative that tell a story. Arguably, it is the job of the sociologist not only to have a good imagination to tell that story, but also to be realistic enough to make sure that the narrative corresponds with a social reality that is true to its subject. This may sound simple enough, but in the sociology of religion, it is often very far from being so. The 'story' that statistics might tell about church decline or growth, or perhaps the rise and fall in the number of baptisms or confirmations, is a field often rich with conjecture, con- clusion and counter-argument. The problem, simply stated, is that any reliability attributed to the data can often clash directly with the perceived ecclesial situation, religious imagination or doctrinal outlook. Sociology is an attempt at social realism; religion, though, is about idealism. Let me explain a little more.

A couple of years ago, I chaired a review of an Anglican deanery; the area consisted of 18 parishes, a total of 180,000 parishioners, and a mixture of inner-city, suburban and rural-commuter contexts. Each parish priest was invited to comment on the attendance patterns of their church in recent times, electoral roll figures, and other ministerial aspects. The review was not conducted with a view to making savings or cuts, but it was undertaken with a mind to look at areas where new deployment or redeployment might be considered. In order to obtain a long-term view on the parishes concerned, figures were secured from each parish church (but also from the Church of England Records Office, London) that looked at Easter and Christmas communicants and electoral roll figures stretching back 50 years.

The returns from the clergy and the data from the Record Office produced a remarkable polarity. The clergy were characteristically upbeat about the prospects for their churches and the parish ministry; almost all described their situations in terms of 'growth' or 'potential'. The statistics, conversely, plotted a virtually uniform decline in seasonal church attendance and 'belonging' (electoral roll). Which version of reality was true? The answer from this sociologist was neither and both. A more careful reading of the figures available showed that 'popular' piety had transferred its affection for an annual Eucharist from Easter to Christmas. Electoral roll figures did show an average decline, but there were, in some cases, substantial reasons for this, such as the merging of parishes or the closure of churches. And although baptisms and confirmations were down in number, the

quota of adult confirmees had risen sharply. Furthermore, the
'decline' plotted in the statistics was below average for the diocese,
such that numbers could be deemed to be holding up relatively well.

The story the clergy offered was—as many things are in the Church
of England—based on anecdote, not data or properly commissioned
research. The clergy consulted, in telling a story of growth, were not
engaging in disingenuous spin. However, the statistics did check, and
in some cases critique, the narratives offered, and showed a way
forward that allowed congregations to look at their mission in a more
considered light. The empirical work, hand in hand with the idealism,
produced a good foundation for reviewing the present and imple-
menting changes in the future (Percy 1998).

David Martin's Practical Sociology

Festschrifts are, characteristically, occasions for celebrating the
contribution of a distinguished scholar to a particular discipline. In
appreciating David Martin's work, one is immediately faced with a
problem. Not only does the discipline have something to celebrate,
but also its subjects. Whether it is Pentecostalism, Methodism or
Anglicanism, Martin's work has often brought new insights to those
communities, as much as his writing has illuminated other scholars.
Undoubtedly there are personal reasons why this may be so. David is
a scholar who is critically engaged with his subjects, but also deeply
aware of their own reality and integrity. He is empathetic, kind and
almost generous to the material he works with, mindful that sociology
is about people as much as anything else. Yet this does not subvert his
skill as a reader and interpreter of the world in which he is immersed.
Nor does it obscure the clarity and richness of his method.

A caring attitude to sociology and what it touches is especially
manifest in his work on aspects of ecclesial polity and identity. Two
little-known essays are being considered here, both concerned with
Anglicanism. One prescribes for confirmation, the other for the future
of the parish church. I take these two essays to be representative of
Martin's practical sociology, how his work can begin to build bridges
with theology and ecclesiology, and how this helps the discipline of
the church. This should not surprise readers, who will know that
Martin was raised as a Methodist, but is now an Anglican priest in the
Diocese of Guildford, as well as being a distinguished Emeritus

Professor (LSE). So, the essays, although published 20 years apart (1967 and 1988), demonstrate a cautious and considered approach to the present and future of church life, and how the sociologist can better enable the church to engage in its own critical self-reflection.

Martin was still a Methodist when he wrote 'Interpreting the Figures' for Michael Perry's collection of essays entitled *Crisis for Confirmation* (1967). His fellow contributors include John Robinson, Don Cupitt and Stephen Verney, to name but a few. The book, naturally enough, had arisen out of the perceived crisis that might result from the marked drop in the number of confirmees within the Church of England. Whereas the number of confirmations at the turn of the century was considerable, running at almost 300,000 per year, the number by the late 1960s had dropped to a fraction of that (two-thirds, to be precise). In 1999, at the turn of the millennium, the Church of England confirmed 41,000 people (16,000 men and 25,000 women). Yet the baptized population of the nation (England) is still almost 50 per cent (about 25 million), with around 200,000 people per year being baptized—roughly a quarter of all babies born.

In the late 1960s, as in the late 1990s, these figures show that while the Church of England is hardly disappearing, it has nothing to be complacent about either. This was foreseen by many in the Church of England, and Michael Perry's book is one of only a number that called upon the faithful to reconsider their ministry and mission against a background of increasing secularization. Others in this festschrift will have addressed Martin's work on this, but it is perhaps worth noting that even in the late 1960s, Martin knew that a decline in confirmation could not be read straight off into a secularization thesis. For example, confirmation in Denmark still envelops over 80 per cent of young people there on an annual basis, but no one could say that Denmark was less secular than England. In Finland the confirmation rate is 90 per cent; the same applies. As Perry notes, Martin's comments on our present situation 'may in places be unexpected' (Perry 1967: ix). So what does Martin have to say?

Brief as the essay is, it is no less expansive for the programme it suggests to the churches. Martin begins by describing the role of the sociologist (1967: 107):

> ...at the simplest level he can organise surveys based on sound principles of selection and questionnaire construction to elicit given ranges of fact...the next level could be that of interpreting and collating

> survey results…quite clearly, this level of interest includes an assess-
> ment of all these various kinds of data in historical perspective. There
> remains the level of what may be called institutional analysis: the rela-
> tion between the social structures of the Church and the structures of
> society at large at the national and local level. The task here includes a
> long-term and intimate knowledge of 'geological' shifts in this
> structure…

Lest this presumes too much omnicompetence on the part of any sociologist, Martin is at pains to stress the limits of their discipline. He states that, while on the one hand, 'without such research, comment is useless', the only possible comments after research are in fact 'cautionary': a sociologist can only 'indicate the range of possible interpretations…before any [one] interpretation can become persua-sive'. Thus, '[he] is a man with a set of tools, a training, a group of relevant queries…some accumulated insights which probably bear on the problem in hand… [he] is not a conjuror…' Then, on the other hand, he adds, critically, that a sociologist must have built into their intellectual armoury 'a scepticism about conventional "images" and how the world "works", or explanations of current social phenomena' (1967: 107).

Martin's description of sociology is a verbal cue for the first target in his sights: the culture of well-meaning but amateurish guesswork that guides so much of the church's thinking. Martin points out that the Church of England collects 'just enough statistics to know that it has a variable temperature, but supports no investigation to find out why' (1967: 108). The essay takes a calculated sideswipe at the Church of England for its absence of a real research culture, and calls upon the church to reconsider their 'empirical condition' and the methods of investigation and interpretation that can service the statistics.

All this was written over 30 years ago, and Martin's introduction to his essay must now be regarded as a prophecy that has gone largely unheeded by the churches. Statistics showing decline (or rises) in church attendance are the subject of more intense debate than ever at the turn of the millenium. Alas, the Church of England has yet to sponsor proper research (or a fellowship in a university, as Martin suggested) that can enable the figures to be interpreted and used. If this was true in the 1960s, it is even more so now. The church continues to make decisions based on anecdotes and semi-educated guesses. Because English theology—especially in Oxbridge and theological colleges—has often been snooty about practical or empirical research, it has deprived its own training of clergy of insights that might be gained from sociology. While it has rightly promoted systematic, pastoral or dogmatic theology, this has often been at the total expense of practical theology (by which I mean research work using an empirical base), which is no less worthy. The difference does not concern that many theologians. Those who have realized it often continue to perpetuate it in order to 'protect' Christian theology from the rising star of religious studies, fearing that 'Divinity' will be somehow subsumed under some sort of comparative umbrella.

Yet the difference between proper practical theology and systematic theology can often be as stark as that between an artist and an inventor. At the risk of extending the mechanistic metaphor further, the church largely prefers to commission and collect ornaments; it seldom builds machines. And when it attempts the latter, the design is normally a good decade or so out of date. This is a tendentious remark, granted; but it should be obvious to many sociologists that churches do not normally know how to organize or investigate themselves, are poor at gathering accurate data about their own ecclesial life, and even poorer at interpreting it. In short, they are aesthetically gifted, yet often structurally frayed and dated. Martin's practical sociology (or perhaps his understated ecclesiology) has been on hand to serve here for many years, as has the work of others more schooled in theology, such as Leslie Francis (2000). But so far, there is little sign of the churches waking up to the possibilities of such work in interpreting their present, and helping to shape their future.

As I have pointed out before in other arenas, theological colleges still teach liturgy to their ordinands, as though its boundaries and history were obvious. But what do churches actually *do* in worship these days? For example, hardly anyone examines the phenomenon of new styles of worship such as choruses, which have come to influence, and in some cases dominate, English Christian worship and its hymnals. The Church of England does not know (because it has not asked) how many churches use choruses, when, how and why. The last Church of England report on church music (1988) concentrated on choirs and organs, and barely made mention of the recent revolution in church worship that has seen some congregations abandon hymnals for overhead projectors or television screens, the organ for a band and an electric piano. There is no research on the sociology, musicology, psychology or theology of such songs, in spite of their substantial influence. Yet the last 20 years have arguably been the most productive in terms of new liturgies, where money and resources have been poured in; but there is no proper research on their reception or adaptation.

Equally, one could point to the rise in the number of ordinands over the last seven years (1993–2000), which records a steady increase from 350 to 600 per annum. The Church of England celebrates such figures, but has no account of why numbers fall and rise as they do. More disturbingly, there is no accurate information available on the numbers who leave the ministry, and their reasons why. Yet clearly, it is in the Church's interest to investigate such issues properly, if only for reasons of morale, strategy and finance. As Martin notes, the church is the loser in the end: on its own, 'raw' data only 'gives rise to…depression, which does the clergy no good at all' (1967: 108).

In terms of the sacrament of confirmation, Martin divides his comments on the recorded decline in numbers into three areas: the demographic; the micro-institutional; and the macro-institutional. For reasons that will become apparent, it is the third level that is the most interesting for assessing Martin, for it concerns his feeling and empathy for what he calls 'the relation between the English Church and our society'. It is in this section that one can begin to see an embryonic Anglicanism forming, in spite of the fact that the comments directed towards the Church of England are mostly captious. What begins to emerge is a kind of critically supportive socio-theology, in which a Methodist layman has obviously begun some kind of pilgrimage.

In examining the demographic context of confirmation, Martin notes that conclusions are 'far from self-evident'. One the one hand, the confirmation figures seem to show that the Anglican church is dying 'millimetre by millimetre'. On the other hand, these figures must be read against other demographic trends in the twentieth century, such as migration, mortality and fertility rates. Further-more—and here Martin directs a comment to the church—'the position is even further complicated by those…priests [who] insist on more stringent criteria for both confirmation and baptism and then come [to us] asking why the figures are diminishing' (1967: 110). His conclusion is that the statistics the church has are only part of the picture; more study is needed, but it has not been mooted.

At the micro-institutional level, Martin introduces a range of approaches that can help churches begin to 'read' the trends they think they experience. He speaks of the Church of England as an agent of 'occasional conformity', in which people unite at birth, death, marriage and confirmation. The paradox of confirmation, as he notes, is that 'the process of becoming an adult is roughly collateral with the cessation of religious practice' (1967: 111), such that confirmation, even where it is normal, has its meaning inverted, and becomes, in effect, 'the Leaving Certificate'. Martin's response to this is to appeal for more research. For example, one might do some comparative work on youth groups, their genesis and development, and focus on their style of recruitment and approach to faith. This work could lead to reflection on the formal provision of confirmation. Another approach might be to test causality or efficiency in catechetical methods, which might suggest a 'right' age to confirm. Having said that, Martin is sceptical about the value of this work, believing that it requires too many qualifiers and caveats. 'The Ark of Salvation cannot be run the principles of a motor-works' (1967: 113), he notes.

That final comment in the section is something of an irony for a sociologist. On the one hand, Martin has often stood for preserving the identity of the church, championing, for example, the use of the *Book of Common Prayer*. On the other hand, he advocates a rigour in socio-ecclesial research (presumably leading to change) that would rock the very pillars of the church. The resolving of this paradox is not easy or obvious, but it lies in Martin's deep commitment to the value of an innate English spirituality, and a church that can (partly) give this individual, local, national, social and theological shape and colour. Thus, he writes, to my mind amusingly, that 'to me personally the English Church consists of some beautiful sixteenth and seventeenth century bottles cracked by some rather doubtful Evangelical and Catholic wine' (1967: 115). The point is obvious: the wings or movements within a church should not be allowed to displace the character of its natural socio-historic centre, which is the broadest place of meeting for the nation.

Correspondingly, the macro-institutional section is Martin's most general, but also his most prescient and persuasive. It is here that Martin—who I normally regard as an embodiment of English genteel liberal-conservatism—turns his attention to class. Martin suggests that the real crisis in confirmation is actually concealed: it is a class issue, related to the state of the Church of England. He points out that it is illogical to complain about the falling number of ordinands with university degrees *and* of not appealing to the urban working classes. What the Anglican church must grapple with is not falling numbers of confirmees, or confirmation 'wastage', but rather how to be the church for the nation, and adjusted to the mid-twentieth century. The church, he notes, rather like a university, exists both to adjust and to resist adjustment. And at a time when the population is becoming more mobile and diverse than ever before, the confirmation statistics may indicate not a lack of affection for the rite, but rather a more congregationalist mind-set gaining a grip on the church as a whole.

As one would expect, David Martin's sociology is no less coherent when he comes to address the English parish church, over 20 years later. Again, he notes that 'sociology cannot answer evaluative questions about the social role of the church; it can however clarify thinking by elucidating unacknowledged presuppositions which may be shaping current thinking' (1988: 43). Martin begins his essay by reigning in Leslie Newbigin's theological reflection on the nature of the church, describing it as 'eloquent' but 'tenuous'. As a sociologist considering the apparent increase in 'associational' patterns (i.e. a more congregational-denominational approach to mission) for the church, he prefers to begin with social reality rather than Newbigin's dubious biblical eisegesis.

To do this, Martin narrates a picture of the situation in England of being that somewhere between Northern Europe and Northern America. He is characteristically generous to the American 'associational' model, pointing out (rightly) that some churches that have 'only been put up within ten years [are] riddled with community functions … doing an extraordinary business in putting out tentacles into the wider community' (1988: 46). In Scandinavia, the 'competition is *very* limited', but the service the church offers to the community is 'utterly ecumenical', by which he means socially and theologically comprehensive. This picture describes the broad sociological context. But why has the parish church declined?

Martin is not sure that it has, exactly, and as with his work on confirmation, he presses the church to look a little harder at the material it is offering, and a little longer at the audience it supposes it has lost. That said, there are some remarks made that are sociologically cautious, and are in turn designed to caution the church. For example, he points out, following Hugh McLeod, that between 1880 and 1930 various social and economic factors caused the rich and powerful to lose interest in the church. Labour movements, expanding public services, and consumerism all played their part: England became progressively more a-religious (but note, *not* anti-religious).

Martin then sets about discussing and critiquing various strategies that attempt to address the decline in the status of the parish church. North America and Europe are discussed; but neither offers a viable model for the Church of England. 'Modernizing' or reforming is put up and then pulled down; Martin does not think that 'producing a new book of liturgy…is somehow going to transform the overall situation' (1988: 49). So far, he is proved right. The sudden introduction of the *ASB* for the Church of England has been no panacea, to be sure: but we cannot know (because we have not researched) whether or not modern rites have arrested decline, let alone caused it. Here, Martin asserts rather than argues.

Equally, ecumenism is 'associated with weakness', and as far as Martin is concerned, is unlikely to 'make much difference' (1988: 46). Besides, there is no sociological evidence that competition between denominations impedes the overall mission of the church, even if it is theologically and ecclesiologically undesirable. Martin also rejects the 'less means more' argument: that if churches can lose the alleged drains on their resources (e.g. buildings, clergy, etc.), more could be done. He cites some examples of Finnish churches, which are fantastically equipped and resourced—but otherwise comparatively empty. Only 4 per cent of the population attend church on average, dropping to 0.5 per cent in the inner cities. The other strategies discussed are handled in a more polemical way. Martin rejects liberalizing trends in theology, ranging from left-wing proclamations to process theology. Finally, he also dismisses the recovery of communitarian models of the church as viable strategy, believing that it does not really cut into the problem.

The conclusion of the essay is a most eloquent *apologia* for the parish church as one will ever read from a sociologist. Martin writes out of a deep sociological consciousness when he notes that in spite of so many social trends moving against the parish, it nevertheless retains strengths and virtues. He points out that (1988: 51):

> many of the networks of charity, of voluntary work and of the arts,
> especially music, link up with the social network of the parish…then

there is latent 'folk' religion which....does have some kind of focus in the parish church, notably through rites of passage...the parish church [also] offers some kind of meaning which is embodied architectur-ally...it [is] often the only non-utilitarian building in certain areas. It is *there*...[suggesting that] people are still in some ways located, whatever social or geographical mobility does to them...[enabling] them to retain a sense of place, a sense of origin, a sense of continuity...[this] goes back several hundred years.

One might accuse Martin of preaching at this point, but that would be unfair. Granted, the pilgrimage from Methodism to Anglicanism has evidently flowered by this time; the sociology is now razor-sharp in its critical support for the Church of England and what it can embody. But in terms of the sociology on its own ground, Martin is again ahead of his time here, quite consciously writing into discipline a language of enchantment, imagination and nostalgia. It is this sort of work that makes Martin's sociology so engaging and persuasive. A combination of masterly overview, rigorous research and cautious prescription is always evident. It is a practical sociology for the churches, helping them to meet triumph and tragedy in social trends and statistics, to unmask impostors, and have the wisdom to know the difference. One can only say that that it is a pity that the churches, particularly the Church of England, have failed to make more use of such a sympathetic sociologist, who could have turned the discipline of sociology into something of more regular and central use within empirical and practical theology. What is clear from this survey, on confirmation and on the parish church, is that the churches have need of sociology and sociologists, but have they the courage to commission research that will actually illuminate sociality, rather than a theological construction of ideology?

Theology and the Sociology of Religion

So far I have been exploring how the sociology of religion can work for the church, perhaps producing material that complement or form practical or pastoral theology, or various boundaries for ecclesiology. Sociology tries to offer empiricism married to imagination; forming, exploring and critiquing social reality no less than religious tradition and theology. How strange then, that a new group of theologians—the 'radical orthodox'—have distanced themselves from the social sciences in order to preserve the 'purity' of theology. The political and ecclesial motives for this move need not detain us here; but it is worth rehearsing the argument in outline.

John Milbank's book, *Theology and Social Theory* (1990), remains one of the key rallying posts for the radical orthodoxy camp. It is, in many ways, a brilliant and sharp book. Yet, as I have argued before, it is also a 'hermeneutic of suspicion about hermeneutics of suspicion': strangely anti-liberal and anti-modern; oddly pro-Christendom. While there is plenty to admire from radical orthodoxy—plenty, I say—the trajectory of their work is troubling in places. Subsequent offerings from the radical orthodoxy camp have attacked the 'discipline' of religious studies, or made the point that all social sciences are 'descended' from theology, either as legitimate heirs or as distant bastard children. Such critiques have their merits, maybe; but they lack generosity.

For example, what father or mother tells each of their children, throughout their lives, that all their achievements are really those of their parents? Or that without them, they would not exist, so please, always acknowledge your debt, and know your place? Radical orthodoxy does not argue so much for the restoration of theology as queen of the sciences as it does for the church and theology being the father of us all. Even if this is entirely true—which I doubt—what about some considered praise for other 'disciplines' that can now teach theology, inform it, civilize it, dialogue with it, or even out-narrate it? Is theology so small and shy, or old and grumpy, as to be unable to acknowledge the breadth and depth of other constructions of reality, even if it still wishes to be considered as revealed? So much of David Martin's work is characterized by a gentility and humility, that offers a sociology in the service of the church. It does not threaten, but as we have seen, it does challenge. Theology must take account of such voices if it wishes to be in any way 'practical'.

The sociology of religion is, in part, an attempt at categorization—'establishing normative epoches' for meaning (D'Costa 1996). It concerns itself with describing phenomena in commonsensical ways, creating categories of meaning and knowledge in order to give a 'social' account of what it sees. Thus, 'religion' tends to be treated like a 'thing'—an 'object' of scientific analysis—and deconstructed accordingly. Correspondingly, religion is broken down into its (alleged) constituent parts (e.g. sacred-profane, etc.), or referred to in functional terms (e.g. 'social legitimization', 'projection', etc.). Like many modernist human sciences, however, it often fails to see *itself* as a construction of reality, social or otherwise. As Catherine Bell points out, 'That we construct "religion" and "science" is not the main problem: that we forget we have constructed them in our own image—that is a problem' (1996: 188).

In saying this, Bell is suggesting that a 'pure' description of phenomena is not possible. Both the human sciences and theology are engaged in an interpretative task, and describe what they see according to the prescribed rules of their grammar of assent. In the case of the sociology of religion, this has often tended to assume a humanist-orientated perspective, which has sometimes imagined itself to be 'neutral'. Thus, sociologists describe what they see, while theologians and religious people are said to 'ascribe' meaning to the same phenomena. On the other hand, those who have had religious experiences feel that what they experience is 'real', and the sociological account is therefore deemed to be at best complementary and at worst unrepresentative. Invariably, both approaches forget that 'religion' is something of a complex word with no agreed or specific definition.

The genesis of the problem lies in nineteenth-century approaches to religion. Marx and Feuerbach, among others, distinguished between 'essence' and 'manifestation' in religion. Social, moral and scientific critiques of religion tended to see religion as a 'thing' that could be explained (away) in terms of the applied point of reference. For Durkheim, religion was 'a unified set of beliefs relative to sacred things' (1965: 62). For Marx, it was 'the opium of the people' (1844)—the self-conscious, self-feeling of alienated humanity. For Freud, it was dreams and primal rites that became religious rituals (1939: 160). As Lash points out (1996), these narratives of religion all have their place, but in what way do they correspond to the reality in which people find themselves?

What, though, can theology gain from sociology? Obviously and principally, it is gaining a partner in dialogue that can enrich its self-understanding, and help avoid the narcissism of 'interior enquiries', which are often uncritical and self-serving. Certainly, it cannot afford to assume that sociology is concerned with 'relationality', while theology is only to do with God. Ninian Smart's claim that 'traditional theology has focused, naturally enough, on God as its subject-matter' (1973: 10) misses the point that all theology is to do with that which *relates* to God—there are no 'pure' studies of God. Sociology can come in from the cold.

Thus, when put together, sociology and theology can learn from and enrich each other. Samuel Taylor Coleridge (1840: 39-81) helpfully makes the distinction between *apprehension* (i.e. the rational-empirical) and *comprehension* (i.e. the religious imagination, historically aware and self-conscious) in the study of faith. In the context of late modernity or postmodernity, the journey from apprehension to comprehension in theology and religious studies needs to avoid the polarized dualisms of modernity, and requires (at times) a trusting synthesis of social science and theology (Hardy 1996: 305-327). This is especially the case when evaluating religious experience, ecclesiology, faith-claims and the like (Middlemiss 1996).

It is precisely this kind of practical sociology that David Martin offers in his often sharp and penetrating analyses of church life. The church needs more of this, not less. Theologically minded detractors miss the target when they claim theology will be diluted or compromised when it is placed in dialogue with sociology. David Martin's work does not compete with theology; it complements it. Moreover, used judiciously, such sociology can prevent the costly generalizations or idolizations of the church, by offering observation grounded in social reality, not theology.

Conclusion

The argument in this essay has been simple enough. Aspects of David Martin's sociology offer a practical theoretical ground to churches, through which they can reconsider their mission and ministry. Theology on its own cannot address many of the modern maladies that afflict church life, since these often comprise social and not theological material. In particular, the Church of England, rather than engaging in amateurish educated guesswork based on nostalgia or theological preferences, should look to sociology to help it address its social context and concerns. In particular, I reiterate Martin's call for proper research in the face of complicated and often conflicting social and ecclesial data. The joke about bats is funny, but the social reality of confirmation is more complex, as we have seen.

Because of Martin's own confessional sympathies, his sociology, at times, borders on being practical theology; but it is all the stronger for that. There is no shrinking from the questions posed by 'social reality' to the traditions and practice of the church. Martin, as an Anglican priest and a sociologist, knows as well as anyone that even if the songs of the Lord are now sung in a secular-foreign land, the church must still face the music. Ultimately, Martin's work confirms the rumour of God, alive in the world, through concerned, cautious, conscientious and carefully nuanced sociology. At the turn of the millennium, the Church may well mourn its declining social status and falling attendance patterns. Yet the remedies do not just lie in the laps of a handful of theologians or priests. As many theologians have said in relation to other contexts, particularly mission, the answers may lie beyond the boundaries of the church, in the world, where God's Spirit is already at work. Perhaps here, the church may discover the gift of sociology and its subjects, and treat this not as a late modern trinket, but as treasure. So thank you, David, for sketching a map and marking the spot. All the church and theology now needs to do is have the courage to make the journey, and begin digging. Sociologists? Every church should have one.

BIBLIOGRAPHY

Bell, C.
 1996 'Modernism and Postmodernism in the Study of Religion', *Religious Studies Review* (July): 179-90.

Coleridge, S.T.
 1840 *Confessions of an Inquiring Spirit* (London: Taylor Hennesey).

D'Costa, G.
 1996 'The End of "Theology" and "Religious Studies"?', *Theology* (September/October): 340-52.

Davie, G.
 1995 *Religion in Britain since 1945: Believing without Belonging* (Oxford: Clarendon Press).

Durkeim, E.
 1965 *The Elementary Forms of Religious Life* (New York: Free Press [1915]).

Flanagan, K.
 1996 *The Enchantment of Sociology: A Study of Theology and Culture* (London: Macmillan).

Francis, L. (ed.)
 2000 *Religion: Research Perspectives* (Leominster: Gracewing).

Freud, S.
 1939 *Moses and Monotheism* (New York: Vintage [1937]).

Hardy, D.
   1996   *God's Ways with the World: Thinking and Practising Christian Faith* (Edinburgh: T. & T. Clark).
Lash, N.
   1996   *The Beginning and End of Religion* (Cambridge: Cambridge University Press).
Martin, D.
   1967   'Interpreting the Figures', in Perry 1967: 105-17.
   1988   'A Cross-Bench View of Associational Religion', in Giles Ecclestone (ed.), *The Parish Church?* (London: Mowbray): 43-57.
Marx, K.
   n.d.   *On Religion* (Moscow: Foreign Languages Publishing [1844]).
Middlemiss, D.
   1996   *Interpreting Charismatic Experience* (London: SCM Press).
Milbank, J.
   1990   *Theology and Social Theory: Beyond Secular Reason* (Oxford: Basil Blackwell).
Percy, M.
   1998   *Ecclesall Deanery Survey* (Rotherham: Diocese of Sheffield).
Perry, M.
   1967   *Crisis for Confirmation* (London: SCM Press).
Smart, N.
   1973   *The Science of Religion and the Sociology of Knowledge* (Princeton, NJ: Princeton University Press).
Winch, P.
   1958   *The Idea of a Social Science* (London: Routledge).

David Martin's Reflections on Sociology and Theology

Robin Gill

In 1996 David Martin published his collection *Reflections on Sociology and Theology*,[1] which brings together different aspects of research that he has been doing for over 30 years. In this article I am going to compare this work with some of his earlier writings, mapping in the process some of the continuities to be found in them.

The influence of David Martin on British sociology of religion has been immense. Together with Bryan Wilson he has taught, examined and encouraged a generation of us currently involved in the discipline. However, unlike Wilson, he has maintained an interest in theology. After years of teaching at the London School of Economics, he was finally ordained, continuing an active ministry at Guildford Cathedral since his retirement. For those who know his other writings, the 1996 collection of essays on sociology and theology will come as little surprise. Like most of his works, the predominant mode of the essays here is sociological, yet underlying them are a number of implicit, and sometimes explicit, theological commitments. As always, his essays are multi-layered, creative and, in places, elusive.

Throughout his writings there is an implicit, and sometimes explicit, tension between the different worlds that he inhabits. Writing three decades earlier in the preface and acknowledgments of his highly influential *A Sociology of English Religion*,[2] he notes his own differences from both sociologists such as Wilson and theologians such as John

---

1. David Martin, *Reflections on Sociology and Theology* (Oxford: Clarendon Press, 1996).
2. David Martin, *A Sociology of English Religion* (London: SCM Press, 1967).

Robinson or Harvey Cox writing on the issue of secularization. Yet he concludes:

> ...our perspectives must above all be realistic: to take but one example we need to be realistic when we consider ecumenical aspiration in relation to social fissures of nation, colour and status, and to the fundamental and very varied types of religious organization which had found constricted and creative lodgement within them. Theological discussion (like political discussion) must generally take place on a level of high-flown and self-deluding linguistic camouflage. Nevertheless the key word of recent debates has been honesty, and if we are to have the honesty about the Church—that 'wonderful and sacred mystery' as the prayer book very properly calls it—then sociological perspectives and research are not a marginal luxury but an essential.[3]

What is remarkable about this passage is just how many of its ideas are still present a generation later in *Reflections*: his suspicion of easy sentiments about ecumenism (despite his own long-standing ecumenical friendships); his awareness of social fissures in religious organizations; his comparison of theological and political forms of discourse; his isolation of key signs and metaphors (here it is that of 'honesty'); his love of the language and resonances of the 1662 prayer book (in which he had been nourished even as a Methodist child); and his insistence, albeit against the odds, that sociological perspectives are essential to an adequate theological understanding of the church. There is also another feature which soon follows this quotation, namely his wit in a context of dissonance. It is worth also quoting the following splendid passage in full:

> My major personal debt is to my wife, who has heard it all before and who tried to prevent me from indulging prejudice more than was necessary for my psychological well-being. The liveliness and acerbity of those prejudices may suggest another debt. A pigeon put among the cats is not in a position of maximum security. The London School of Economics is hardly renowned for piety, and a believer working with a noble company of 'cultured despisers' needs frequently to remind himself that faith, in Luther's and Kierkegaard's sense, involves a vigorous scepticism not only about the Church but about all those quasi-religious props that contemporary men (cultured and otherwise) use to maintain their sanity—occasionally with regrettable success.[4]

---

3.   Martin, *A Sociology of English Religion*, pp. 11-12.
4.   Martin, *A Sociology of English Religion*, pp. 13-14.

I suspect that many of us have longed to able to write like that. Like the man himself, the emotions keep switching from one sentence to the next—love for a woman, an awareness of strong and determined beliefs, a concern about health, a gentle humility, a personal piety and scepticism competing with each other, and a strong sense of human foibles. Then there is the unforgettable image of David as the pigeon among all those well-armed Goliath LSE cats. Next there is the curious theological combination of Luther and Kierkegaard—surely intentional and thought-provoking. At their best David Martin's sentences contain paradoxes, binary oppositions (a favourite device of his) and quirky associations which repay reading and re-reading, even after many years.

At the heart of Martin's *Reflections*, as in his earlier work, is a conviction that sociology and theology share a number of characteristics, of which three are particularly important: both disciplines are pattern-seeking forms of enquiry; both return constantly to seminal thinkers; and both depend heavily upon metaphors. The first and third of these characteristics are shared with a number of areas of physical science—notably modern physics at both quantum and cosmological levels—but the second is not. Whereas most forms of physical science keep moving forward, seldom showing much interest, except for historical purposes, in their forebears, sociologists and theologians are profoundly retrospective. Within the sociology of religion the works of Weber and Durkheim (and Marx for more radical forms of sociology) are subject to constant examination and re-examination in a manner very similar to the work of theologians. In both disciplines pattern-seeking and metaphors are constantly tested and re-tested against the ideas of seminal thinkers. Of course the theologian, like the philosopher, draws upon many more seminal thinkers over a much greater length of time than the sociologist. Moreover, the theologian tends to write *sub specie aeternitatis*, whereas the sociologist, if not the philosopher, remains firmly terrestrial. Nevertheless they are, so David Martin argues, involved in parallel forms of undertaking which intersect at points of conflict and change.

Perhaps the place where he expresses this most lyrically is in the early chapters of *The Breaking of the Image*.[5] Before publication they were delivered as the Gore Lectures given, at that time, in the

5.   David Martin, *The Breaking of the Image: A Sociology of Christian Theory and Practice* (Oxford: Basil Blackwell, 1980).

Jerusalem Chamber at Westminster Abbey (today they have become a single, annual lecture given in the less intimate nave of the Abbey to members of the General Synod). Perhaps it was the extraordinary ambience of that location or perhaps just the challenge of the occasion which inspired the lyricism. Whatever social factors lay behind them, I have long considered them the finest of his writings. However, ever the iconoclast, he combines them in the second half of the book with a polemic against liturgical change within the Church of England. The argument is of a piece—namely that the images used within liturgy and worship profoundly shape Christian identity (the first half) and that liturgical changes, which 'are initiated by clerics and defended by them',[6] are in real danger of distorting this identity (the second half). Now, of course, it is perfectly possible to be convinced by the first of these arguments but not the second. Still swimming against the tide, David Martin remains convinced of both, regarding much liturgical change within the Anglican Church as a secularizing factor imposed by the clergy, rather than as a response to popular piety in a context of widespread rejection of traditional liturgical forms. On this we must differ.

Yet, leaving the polemic to one side, liturgical innovators and traditionalists alike can still admire the skilful blend of theological and sociological analysis in the first half of *The Breaking of the Image*. Just to take a single example, he offers an illustration of the way that the cross can become a double entendre within Christianity. He draws, at this point, on his long-standing fascination with the religious symbols and typologies of war and pacifism, which can be found in his earliest and most recent writings.[7] The cross, for him, is at once a symbol of peace and a symbol of war. There is 'a continuous dialectic whereby the sword turns into the cross and the cross into the sword':

> The cross will be carried into the realm of temporal power and will turn into a sword which defends the established order. It will execute the criminals and heretics in the name of God and the King. But temporal kingship will now be defended by reversed arms, that is a sign of reversal and inversion... Another illustration...is provided by the cross which dominates the US Air Force Chapel at Colorado Springs.

6. Martin, *The Breaking of the Image*, p. 100.
7. See David Martin, *Pacifism: An Historical and Sociological Study* (London: Routledge & Kegan Paul, 1965) and *idem*, *Does Christianity Cause War?* (Oxford: Clarendon Press, 1997).

At the centre of the huge arsenal is a chapel built of stained glass spurs like planes at the point of take-off. The cross is also like a sword. Looked at from another angle the combined cross and sword is a plane and a dove. The plane is poised to deliver death rather than to deliver *from* death and the dove signifies the spirit of peace and concord.[8]

This dialectic understanding of sociology and theology is clearly very different from that of John Milbank in his *Theology and Social Theory*.[9] Martin makes remarkably few references in *Reflections* to other authors—indeed, footnotes become scarcer and scarcer in his books the more recent they become—so when he does it is all the more significant. He has an early reference to Milbank's book which he depicts as 'a recent brilliant study',[10] but then seeks to deconstruct it, albeit without any further explicit mention of it. In the mid-1960s he debated with Bryan Wilson in a very similar manner. If Wilson was the leading British proponent of secularization theory at the time— most notably in his *Religion in Secular Society*[11]—Martin was its leading critic—most notably in his *The Religious and the Secular*.[12] They continued this debate well into the 1970s with very few explicit references to each other's works (the reference that has already been noted from the Preface of *A Sociology of English Religion* is rare). Yet it was clear that they *were* responding to each other and disagreeing with each other. In *Reflections* Martin uses the same technique to criticize Milbank, arguing at length that the discipline of sociology of religion (which Milbank believes that he has dismissed entirely, albeit without ever mentioning Martin's own work) does help us to understand religious phenomena without reducing them simply to social phenomena. Taking the example of baptism as it is actually practised, he argues that

> Sociology…identifies structures, makes comparisons, and formulates probes and queries from the special viewpoint of orderly curiosity. In the case of baptism nothing is implied about the validity of the faith

---

8.   Martin, *The Breaking of the Image*, p. 28.

9.   John Milbank, *Theology and Social Theory: Beyond Secular Reason* (Oxford: Basil Blackwell, 1990); see also his *The Word Made Strange: Theology, Language, Culture* (Oxford: Basil Blackwell, 1997).

10.   Martin, *Reflections*, p. 8.

11.   Bryan Wilson, *Religion in Secular Society* (London: C.A. Watts, 1966).

12.   David Martin, *The Religious and the Secular: Studies in Secularization* (London: Routledge & Kegan Paul, 1969).

embodied in baptism. There is simply a widening of interest away from
personal involvement towards curious and controlled observation of
semi-comparable cases.[13]

The last sentence in this quotation accurately depicts Martin's own
role as a sociologist of religion who also happens to be a practising
Christian.

In his recent writings there is one major exception to his general
practice of criticizing the theories of others through indirect rather
than direct means. In his 1997 study *Does Christianity Cause War?* he
devotes a whole chapter and several other direct references to the
views of Richard Dawkins. He is clearly irritated by the latter's
polemic against Christianity and specifically by his contention that
'religion causes wars by generating certainty'.[14] It is not, of course, that
Dawkins is a particularly accomplished or well-informed intellectual
in the area of religion. In contrast to some of the continental atheists
against whom John Milbank contends at great length, Dawkins's
views on religion are generally delivered in rhetorical and populist
forms. They do not appear to represent any sustained scholarly study.
And yet Dawkins is a figure of considerable *social* significance. He is
the author of books on evolution that are more widely read by
university students today than any theological books. It is hardly
surprising, in these circumstances, that David Martin, the believing
sociologist, is especially sensitive to this particular polemic or that he
unusually singles out Dawkins's views for such sustained inspection.

Seeking to exegete Dawkins's claim about war, Martin argues as
follows:

> In one way...the statement is irrefutable because there certainly have
> been wars where religion played a role. In another way it is indefensible
> since there certainly have been wars where religion has played no role
> whatever. Conflicts occur for all kinds of reasons, and hardly ever for
> just a single reason... Not merely does Dawkins regard religious beliefs
> as childish mistakes which we should learn to grow out of. He
> contends that what is scientifically wrong is at the same time morally
> wrong. So clear a moral judgement may seem surprising from the
> author of *The Selfish Gene*, since in that book he indicated a degree of
> programming for survival that might seem to make free will and
> therefore moral judgement otiose.[15]

13. Martin, *Reflections*, p. 10.
14. Martin, *Does Christianity Cause War?*, p. 22.
15. Martin, *Does Christianity Cause War?*, p. 23.

The critique of Dawkins that Martin offers operates at several levels. Much of the book operates at a sociological level; using one example after the next he seeks to demonstrate that war is a multivariate phenomenon, sometimes involving religious institutions and sometimes not. This is probably the easiest of his tasks and the one at which the Dawkins claim is most vulnerable. Alongside this there is also a moral critique, as the final sentence in this quotation indicates. It is indeed one of the surprising features of Dawkins that he makes such a strong, almost 'evangelical', attack upon Christianity. There has been widespread speculation about the sources of his ideological atheism, since it appears so strong and vehement from one who otherwise presents himself as an ideologically free—perhaps even 'value free'—scientist. David Martin has never been able to resist such obvious moral and ideological dissonances in others. The 'cultured despisers' are undoubtedly cultured but they are also still thoroughly biased despisers. Seventeen years earlier he expressed the hope that the sociologist can perform an important task of ethical commentary in society, especially by analysing ethical decision-making independently of those who are actually power holders.[16] In the present critique of Dawkins he observes waspishly at one point that 'Ceausescu would have appreciated at least some of Dawkins's arguments...which in one context are deployed in the cause of liberality can in another context be used to justify persecution'.[17] And in the quotation above he allies the role of ethical commentary with sharp observations about the apparent determinism of his writings on evolution.

Thirdly, his critique of Dawkins operates at a theological level:

> In giving an account of the Christian code I tried to lay out the theo-logic and the socio-logic behind the text 'Thy Kingdom comes not by violence.' The Lord tells his servant Peter to 'put up' his sword and explains that his servants do not fight. At the very least, this suggests that Dawkins's theory of the inherent bellicosity of religion is the reverse of what the Gospels actually teach, and Dawkins would need to explain why this is so. There is, after all, not a ghost of a suggestion that the Gospel should be spread by warfare. There is, of course, God's judgement on those who do not recognize the presence of the Kingdom in the imprisoned, the sick, and the beggars, and who do not

16. David Martin, 'Ethical Commentary and Political Decision', *Theology* 76.640 (October 1973), pp. 525-31.

17. *Does Christianity Cause War?*, p. 75.

repent. But nobody is invited to fit out a military expedition to ensure that judgement is enforced here and now. The powers of restitution are entirely eschatological.[18]

Or is this theology? Much of it might just as readily be classified as sociology. As so often in his writings, David Martin slips from one method to another and back again. Ostensibly he writes at a descriptive level here. In reality he is passionately involved and concerned to refute Dawkins. His end to the work makes this abundantly clear:

> If Dawkins's arguments were correct then the separating out of believers and clergy from the general population ought to reveal them as major proponents of violence towards each other and violence in international affairs. This is far from being the case. The evidence does not bear out the contention. The case falls.[19]

To return to *Reflections*, even though few of its ideas are new, the collection does bring together and summarize many of David Martin's longstanding interests. There are, for example, several essays on ecclesiology and ecumenism, all of which demonstrate his continuing independence of thought. Despite remaining the most ecumenical of people in practice, he continues to voice sociological doubts about the limits and politics of ecumenism. David Martin the sociologist is aware that, however desirable greater ecumenism might seem, 'even as ecumenical unions occur among the older bodies, especially in the diaspora, or in countries where they are minorities, new fissures will open up in response to volcanic social upheavals'.[20] Here too the language and not simply the idea of 'fissures' in this context remains after 30 years.

In *Reflections* he also brings together the grand-scale research he has done, first on European churches in *A General Theory of Secularization* in 1978,[21] and then in his recent work on Pentecostalism in South America, first reported in *Tongues of Fire* in 1990.[22] A particularly useful essay in this respect is 'Religious Vision and Political Reality'. His approach to political intervention by churches is cautious. He is

18. Martin, *Does Christianity Cause War?*, p. 163.

19. Martin, *Does Christianity Cause War?*, p. 220.

20. Martin, *Reflections*, p.146.

21. David Martin, *A General Theory of Secularization* (Oxford: Basil Blackwell, 1978).

22. David Martin, *Tongues of Fire: The Explosion of Protestantism in Latin America* (Oxford: Basil Blackwell, 1990).

convinced that a proper understanding of Christian images should make us suspicious both of political orders *and* of churches as well. Even when Christian beliefs appear to be ambiguously prophetic against particularly egregious political orders, there is a need for some caution. In words that themselves now seem prophetic, he cautions:

> As the Church tangles ambiguously with social processes it will be wise to deploy its weight at the optimum moment, that is, not throw about such weight as it has all the time and explicitly, on one particular side. Even though the circumstances operative at the optimum moment may require an identification with a particular course or side, as in South Africa, pre-independence Rhodesia, and the Philippines, the Church will probably stand back from that identification as circumstances change, fresh divisions appear, and a newly installed regime exercises power more ambiguously and in its own partial interests.[23]

It is important to note that these words were first delivered as a lecture in Australia in 1986. Fifteen years later this warning, especially about Zimbabwe and South Africa today, appears to be remarkably accurate. The theologian nurtured on Cranmer's prayers, and alluding to Luther and Kierkegaard, is never sanguine about the propensities of political orders, even those recently liberated from oppressive political regimes. This is not a critique from the political right but rather from a radically theological perspective. The end of the lecture makes this clear:

> Both compromising Church and rigorist monastery or sect pick up continuing impulses from the sharp angle of eschatological tension set up in the New Testament. If that angle had been less sharp, the warfare of Christian with principalities and powers would have been milder, the tension would have been neither stored nor released, and the continuing irony of the Church would not have been available to create guilt in the Christian or dissatisfaction in the outside critic. Of course, the ideal as embodied in the Sermon on the Mount cannot straightforwardly be realized and, in particular, circumstances can motivate Christians to avoid social responsibilities when they should involve themselves in moral ambiguity. Some will argue that this lack of realism is itself not moral: 'the high that proved too high, the heaven for the earth too hard'. But churches exist to raise spires and aspirations, and sect and monasteries exist to protect the dialectic of hope and spiritual autonomy.[24]

23. Martin, *Reflections*, p. 160.
24. Martin, *Reflections*, p. 161.

That last sentence is characteristically Martin. Even while making a serious and strongly held point, he cannot resist a small piece of word-play. In *The Breaking of the Image* there are numerous examples of such word-play, even at moments of intense seriousness. Here it is achieved through noting the movements of spires and aspirations.

David Martin has always been a writer who responds well when prompted by specific invitations to give papers. One of the most striking papers in this respect is one he gave in 1995 to a series on 'Harmful Religion' at King's College, London. Although published elsewhere,[25] his paper, entitled 'A Socio-Theological Critique of Collective National Guilt', makes a valuable contribution to *Reflections*. Martin is at his most powerful when he has a fashionable concept to deconstruct. He rose to international fame in the 1960s with his essay 'Towards Eliminating the Concept of Secularisation'.[26] Here he channels his energies into deconstructing the concept of 'collective guilt' and has little difficulty showing the illogicality of expecting individuals to feel guilty about issues for which they can have no personal responsibility. However, this is not simply a semantic quibble. He believes that notions of 'collective guilt' can blunt moral seriousness and (once again) distort liturgies. Theologians should also beware of the distorting effect of such misplaced collective notions:

> In sum, the mistake of Christian utopianism is to conceive the polis as…a corporate agent. That mistake represents an abuse of faith because it attempts simple transfers from the sphere of redemption to the sphere of politics. These transfers themselves damage redemption, turning it into a simplistic programme, which mirrors categories and which shifts the last judgement from the realm of eschatology into a historical possibility. It hands justice over to historians and politicians. Christianity then becomes a mode of secular self-righteousness and denunciation, bypassing the careful assessment of different means of amelioration.[27]

Perhaps it is this sharpness, and occasionally acerbity, which makes David Martin such an enduring and thoughtful critic in both theology and sociology. Within both disciplines he remains an individualist. Among sociologists he was instrumental in forcing them to think

25. In Lawrence Osborn and Andrew Walker (eds.), *Harmful Religion: An Exploration of Religious Abuse* (London: SPCK, 1997), pp. 144-62.

26. Published in *The Religious and the Secular*.

27. Martin, *Reflections*, pp. 223-24.

more clearly about secularization, which had seemed such an obvious force to the founders of modern sociology of religion. Among theologians he has been simultaneously a critic of liturgical change and a promoter of a distinctively sociological perspective within theology. I suspect that all of these are areas of debate with much more mileage to come...not least, I hope, from him. Those of us engaged in these interfaces between theology and sociology remain deeply in his debt.

'Restoring Intellectual Day':
Theology and Sociology in the Work of David Martin

Bernice Martin

The argument of this essay is that theology is not an optional extra to David Martin's 'real' work but the indispensible partner to, and completion of, his sociology. The questions which eventually took him to sociology in search of answers were thrown up by theology, and Christianity remains the ground in which his sociology is planted.

Anyone who only knows his sociology will have a one-sided and remarkably sombre-hued picture of the human condition. This picture has power at its centre and in its foreground the inexorable social requirements which systematically and inescapably limit and channel human options and render ambiguous at best all our ideals. In many ways it is a tragic vision, not too far removed from that of Shakespeare's *Troilus and Cressida* and, like that troubling play, a tragedy without catharsis. If the Divine Comedy of Christianity were not there as a counterweight it might well be unbearable.

In a lecture he gave in the induction course for new students at LSE as long ago as 1972, for example, he laid bare certain generic social processes by using the analogy of Greek tragedy to compare the institution of marriage with the then escalating 'troubles' in Ulster. He might as easily have chosen any intimate personal relationship as marriage—between lovers, parent and child, siblings or friends: the point was to use a relationship ostensibly based on love not power in order to highlight the negative spirals of role-playing that such 'private' interactions display in common with 'public' situations of chronic and violent political conflict. The following extract gives something of the tone of voice:

> History both consists of periods, cumulative and different, and of repetitive cycles. The cycles are cycles of hate. Indeed, many marriages are like that: daily recitations of violence against the other person which occur in cycles from which there is no escape... As in marriage so in Ulster every act in the tragic play shows the antagonist to be just what the protagonist always thought him to be. They never change. Each stands posturing in the receding mirrors of all their yesterdays, deriving their judgements from their pre-judgements. Judgement is executed: *people* are executed in accordance with that judgement. The terrible thing about such judgements is that they are often just because the prejudices have made themselves true. The trouble with prejudices is that so often they have become nearly true. Prejudice is error in the process of becoming truth.[1]

This is intentionally discomfiting stuff. In context, it was deliberately provocative, a rhetorical counter to the romantic utiopianism of the naked, authentic person which was sweeping the campuses and the media at the time; but I doubt that he would retract a word of it today, though Kosovo or Rwanda might replace Ulster as the 'worst case scenario'. His technique is to suggest that the processes so starkly demonstrated in the worst case are not aberrations but simply the extreme logic of what goes on under the guise of the absolutely normal in our everyday social performances. He makes the same point very economically in his most recent essay in which he reflects on the development of his thinking.

> Slowly over the years the world as it is forced me to construct an implicit model of social relations which took into account the will-to-power and interested character of international politics as worked out in the partial mutualities of everyday society.[2]

David Martin's model of society and social processes is every bit as bleak as, say, that of Adorno or Foucault for whom power is also at the fulcrum of social reality. In some ways the Martin view is bleaker because it wholly eschews that expectation of utopia-round-the-next-corner which both rationalist and Marxist traditions in sociology project as a palliative to the perceived hell of the present.

A better parallel than these two particular bêtes noires of David can

---

1. 'Parts and Wholes, Objectives and Objectivity', in D.A. Martin, *Tracts against the Times* (London: Lutterworth, 1973), Chapter 13, p. 166.

2. 'Personal Reflections in the Mirror of Halévy and Weber', in R.K. Fenn (ed.), *The Blackwell Companion to the Sociology of Religion* (Oxford: Basil Blackwell, 2001), pp. 23-38.

be drawn from the eighteenth century, for reasons that will unfold below. Jonathan Swift is a better comparison than most modern sociologists. Consider, for example, the last part of *Gulliver's Travels* where Lemuel finds human society so repellent after his experience of the wise and peaceable Houyhnhnms, that he becomes a recluse and only gradually re-acclimatizes himself to life with his own sub-rational species. It is easy to overhear echoes of Swift's caricature of humanity as Yahoos in some of David's cold-eyed, ironic accounts of social reality, particularly his many anatomizations of the underlying self-interest of individuals, groups and institutions (including churches) and the brutalities of power and solidarity. But where Swift's satire shows only tenderness towards the imagined rational utopia of his Houyhnhnms (admittedly, with the object of exposing the unedifying human realities by the comparison) David Martin will have no truck with rosy idealizations which can only work by defining out of existence all those deplorable or chronically ambiguous human qualities and social characteristics which mark our actual lives. In fact, his sociology is an extended explanation and exploration of the *necessity* of self-interest, the *inevitability* of the brutalities of power and solidarity and of what, in a sardonic expropriation of Marxist terminology, he often refers to as the 'sedimented violence' without which a relatively pacified social life would be impossible. Burke rather than Rousseau hovers in the wings alongside Swift.

Swift employed the language of reason, particularly in the *Modest Proposal*, as well as the conceit of imaginary utopias and dystopias, as a technique for counteracting the optimistic rationalism of his age. His view of the human condition is remarkably close to that represented in David Martin's sociology and, indeed, Swift was an earlier influence on David's thinking than any sociologist. The parallels between the two men are compelling. The good Dean's deployment of the blackest irony, his often awkward (thorn-like) relationship with the Anglican Church's hierarchy and, above all, his use of his own marginality as the ground from which to cast an undeceived and unblinking eye on a naughty world, all make Swift a thoroughly sympathetic and suitable comparison. However, my primary reason for conjuring up the shade of Jonathan Swift is to emphasize two points: first, that David Martin's understanding of human society comes, as did Swift's, out of a long *Christian* tradition; and second that like Swift and another of David's great heroes, George Frederick

Handel, David is a cradle Christian, and Protestant to boot, grappling (as if) for the first time with the Enlightenment and all its works.

Whereas most of us 'modern' men and women imbibed the Enlightenment into our taken-for-granted with our mother's (or the welfare state's) milk, David, who was brought up in a fundamentalist household with a street-preacher father, first met the Enlightenment in mid-adolescence—around 14 or 15—initially through biblical criticism and liberal theology. One of the first blows to split open the carapace of his inherited biblical literalism came from Schweitzer's *The Quest of the Historical Jesus*.[3] He spent the next two decades urgently catching up with Western intellectual history (and, in the first few years, single-mindedly ignoring everything in his grammar school curriculum which did not have an immediate bearing on the state of his soul or on his need to resolve the conflict between the faith of his fathers and the works of reason and scholarship which seemed to challenge it or, what was almost worse, reveal it as naive: that was how he finished up in teacher training college instead of university). He arrived at sociology almost by accident towards the end of this long process of passionate but highly selective autodidacticism. He tells the whole story of this out-of-time intellectual history in a recent essay.[4] In that account he underlines the many senses in which he both replicated and mutated the marginality he had originally experienced as part of his parents' insulated world of Dissent, at every subsequent stage of his intellectual development. The skewed and often un-fashionable reading with which he fed his hunger for understanding played an important part in what was, at first, an inadvertent and, later, often a deliberately cussed gravitation to the status of perpetual (semi-) outsider.

The crucial intervening stages between the child of the funda-mentalist household and the mature writer need to be sketched in if we are to appreciate the rationale behind the uncompromising starkness of David Martin's sociological vision. His first, adolescent, refuge from a collapsing biblical literalism was a self-absorbed Romanticism, fed by music and poetry, which, as he has said himself, made him a prime candidate for the 1960s 20 years too soon. (This, of course, is why he was both so perceptive about and so hard on the

---

3.   Albert Schweitzer, *The Quest of the Historical Jesus* (London: Adam & Charles Black, 1948).

4.   'Personal Reflections'.

1960s when they happened.) He was protected from the full excesses of an always seductive antinomian anarchy by the residual demands of discipline, authority, structure and—far from insignificant—respect built into his background. Moreover, as well as the hard-headed Swift, there was enough Christian poetry and mystical prose—Milton, Herbert, Donne, Traherne, Blake, Eliot and Manley Hopkins (he had the good fortune to be taught English at school by Hopkins's first editor)—to hold all this within a Christian frame. At the same time he was ransacking the library shelves for theology from Underhill to Niebuhr, and was also devouring George Bernard Shaw and, largely via GBS, becoming acquainted with a radical political option which had had its hey-day in Edwardian England—and among other things had led to the founding of the LSE.

These interwoven strands drew him inexorably to a Christian utopian position—pacifist, socialist and idealistically aesthetic all at the same time—which, at age 19, resulted in two years of military service as a non-combatant in the toughest and most brutal corners of Britain's peacetime army, the Military Police and the Pioneer Corps.[5] These two years of conscript purgatory gave him a concentrated exposure to the starkest contradictions between his utopian Christian hope and the recalcitrant and wholly surprising world beyond the protected redoubt of his parents' Nonconformist time warp which, as he recalls it, was essentially domestic and utterly non-machismo.[6]

The utopian hope had a bad time of it. In the next few years teaching in rural and tough inner-London primary schools, a failed marriage and a lot of preaching in the Methodist circuits of London and the West country piled up the contradictions. When a Welsh radical teaching colleague enticed him into reading an external London degree in sociology in the mid 1950s, the opportunity to worry at the contradictions in a systematic fashion was irresistible. By the time he had finished his doctorate on pacifism between the wars,[7]

---

5.   An unpublished MSS discussed in the chapter by Christie Davies in this volume was an account of his time in the army. It was commissioned by Radio 3 but never broadcast because the producer regarded the language as unsuitable.

6.   His paternal grandfather, an illiterate farm labourer in Hertfordshire, had been converted from a life of alcoholism and violence: the preciousness of domestic tranquility, guaranteed by evangelical discipline, was a lesson not lost on his gentle father.

7.   This was published in 1965 as *Pacifism: An Historical and Sociological Study*

his dissection of his own position was complete. His pacifism had finally died at Easter 1961 when he heard Frank Cousins address a CND rally. What he recognized on that occasion was his own idealistic rhetoric used as the blunt instrument of ruthless internecine warfare in the Labour Party. From that point onwards he was clear that none of the 'great and good words and signs',[8] from democracy to the Christian cross, can ever be immune to being used in this fashion.

The end-product of this long process of self-formation was a perspective which Rowan Williams recently described as 'deeply Augustinian'.[9] So it is, and that is the point. The Augustinian regards fallen human creation without sentimentality or hopeful illusion and engages all the God-given resources of reason on the task. By the time David Martin stumbled upon sociology he had already cut his intellectual teeth on the contest between faith and reason out of which the discipline emerged. Christianity had, after all, husbanded that long (Greek) tradition of rationality for many centuries before the heirs of the Enlightenment sought its emancipation from religion. He was already attuned to the ways in which the champions of secular reason are prone to mimic many of the things they most deplore in their religious adversaries—*a priori* premises which rest on faith rather than reason, an expectation that the movement of history must culminate in the perfect social order, as well as all those familiar human failures of reason like selective use of evidence and short-cuts in argument. Having met all this in theology it came as no surprise to find it again in sociology.

David Martin was not the first person to have used reason against the idolatry of reason or to savage Enlightenment utopianism with the fruits of Enlightenment knowledge, but it was somewhat unexpected in British sociology at the time.[10] Far from finding sociology the

(London: Routledge & Kegan Paul).

8.　The phrase comes from the essay 'Religious Comment on Politics', in D.A. Martin, *Reflections on Sociology and Theology* (Oxford: Clarendon Press, 1997), Chapter 11.

9.　Rowan Williams, Bishop of Monmouth, and Archbishop of Wales, 'Review of *Does Christianity Cause War?* (Oxford: Oxford University Press, 1997), by David Martin', *Journal of Contemporary Religion* 14.1 (January 1999), p. 150.

10.　Some of his earliest publications on arriving in the Sociology department of the LSE were concerned with the secularist ideology hidden within sociological concepts and ideas, notably his 1965 article 'Towards Eliminating the Concept of Secularisation', in J. Gould (ed.), *Penguin Survey of the Social Sciences* (Harmonds-

knock-down argument for secularism that most British sociologists took to be self-evident, David Martin discovered in his new discipline an intellectual tool-kit for performing more thoroughly that sombre Christian task of understanding the fallen human condition. One of the more often quoted aphorisms that spiced his critique of the 1960s ran: 'Sociology is the documentation of original sin by those who believe in original virtue'.[11] The sociologist who had himself painfully discarded a Christian pacifist utopia simply deleted the second half of the definition.

The thread which connects all the stages of David Martin's development is a personally urgent need to understand 'the world as it is', taking full account, on the one hand, of accumulated formal knowledge of many kinds and on the other, of that less easily defined but deep and pervasive knowledge which arises out of experience refracted through a personal and familial identity indelibly stamped by the culture of the evangelical margin. It is fashionable today to call this 'reflexivity' but I prefer David's own term for it, 'to think with your life'.[12] The view from the margins often makes it easier to see what is obscure at the centre. Further, like so many who come late and unexpectedly from the outer edge to the centre in academic life, he has pursued intellectual enlightenment (I use the words with all deliberation) as a real 'calling' in Weber's sense, where others, whose membership of the university community was less hard-won—natives of the centre—have often been content with a more 'secular' approach to what is for them a mere job like any other. These are some of the reasons which prompted my choice of the phrase 'restoring intellectual day' for my title. There is an intentional perverseness in invoking the supreme Enlightenment virtue which David has consistently used to parry the secularizing thrust of the Enlightenment, just as Swift did. Light, after all, was a key item in the repertoire of Christian signs long before it was secularized and I make no apology

---

worth: Penguin Books), pp. 169-97. This essay has been extensively cited and in most cases that basic objective was either ignored or misunderstood. Perhaps the idea was too far outside the norm to register on the sociological radar of the period.

11. 'The Dissolution of the Monastories' in D.A. Martin (ed.), *Anarchy and Culture: The Problem of the Contemporary University* (London: Routledge, 1969), p. 6 n. 1.

12. 'Personal Reflections', p. 26.

for using my borrowed phrase somewhat counter to the sense it would have had in eighteenth-century England.

My title has a further justification: it comes from a piece of vocal music by Handel, a composer equally at ease with light and enlightenment as Christian or secular metaphor. Handel in particular and music more generally have a place in my argument: they play a not insignificant role in a theology which draws heavily on signs and moments of transcendence and transfiguration which can symbolically invert but never empirically cancel the sociological realities. For David Martin music is one of the great repositories of such signs and moments—a repository which includes but does not wholly coincide with the Christian deposit. For the moment, however, I want to pursue Handel's sociological rather than music's theological significance.

For David, as for so many other Nonconformists, it was Handel above all who opened a golden gate into the whole enchanted realm of classical music. More specifically, he offered an opening on to a tradition of European religious and liturgical music stretching back to plainsong, the Renaissance motet, Mass settings of many periods, sideways to Bach and the Lutheran chorale and forward to Mozart, Beethoven, Howells, Britten, Poulenc, Tavener—all musical resources that make the practice of the Christian faith so much more than cognitive assent to literal propositions of belief. Handel's music formed a bridge which linked the bounded evangelical enclave of David Martin's boyhood to the religious and aesthetic heartlands of European culture.

Methodism and Handel were both creatures of the eighteenth century. We automatically associate the eighteenth century with the decisive moment of secularization in European thought but we often forget that it was also the age of the first evangelical revival. In fact, as David recently remarked, John Wesley's conversion occurred four years before the first performance of *Messiah*. Handel is thus the perfect emblem of the intersection of Enlightenment reason (and baroque artifice) with Christian continuity and revival. Indeed, Handel's music and the evangelical revival have been yoked together, thanks largely to *Messiah* and a few of the other oratorios, in ways that would have astonished the composer, devout believer though he was. Handel's reputation has suffered from this deplorable popularity with the wrong people. It is only in recent years that 'authentic' performances with small, professional forces have redeemed him from guilt-by-association with massed choirs, Nonconformist chapels, Stainer, Stanford and amateur oratorio soloists. Yet it is precisely Handel's ability to straddle the 'low' culture of the evangelical periphery and the high art and high liturgy of the power and status centre that makes him such a potent mediating presence in British culture.

The phrase used in my title comes from one of the most luminous moments in all of Handel's music, the final duet of *Il Moderato*. It is the culminating point of a work which is unashamedly the philosophical credo of the Augustan age.

> As steals the morn upon the night,
> And melts the shades away;
> So truth does fancy's charm dissolve,
> And melts the shades away:
> The fumes that did the mind involve,
> Restoring intellectual day.[13]

The librettist was Charles Jennens, a suspected Jacobite sympathizer, compiler of the prophetic texts of *Messiah* and several other biblical oratorios for Handel. Nowadays Jennens is dismissed as a hack whose attempt to cap Milton's poetry in *L'Allegro* and *Il Penseroso* with his own verses for *Il Moderato* is widely derided—so much so that what Jonathan Keates calls 'the mistaken good taste of hyper-literate England'[14] had made it customary to omit *Il Moderato* from performances altogether, until very recently when passionate Handelians like Keates himself rediscovered the musical value of the third part, of which the duet is the chief glory, and realized its structural importance to the work as a whole. Keates says of the duet that it

> bids fair to be the most beautiful thing Handel ever composed... Of its oboe and bassoon dialogue, the fluid vocal lines and the sinewy grace with which the harmonies evoke the dawning light of reason it is needless to write in praise.[15]

---

13. Charles Jennens, libretto for George Frederick Handel, *Il Moderato*, Part 3 of *L'Allegro, Il Penseroso Ed Il Moderato*, item 16 as published with CD of the work by the Monteverdi Choir and English Baroque Soloists under John Eliot Gardiner (Erato: recorded 1980, republished 1993).

14. Jonathan Keates, *Handel: The Man and his Music* (London: Gollancz, 1985), p. 234.

15. Keates, *Handel*, p. 234.

It is, as he says, very fine. 'The mind's dualism sings as one' is John Eliot Gardiner's verdict.[16] It is, indeed, a moment of translucent calm and glorious serenity; a (secular) evocation of an Eden in which oboe and bassoon, soprano and tenor are in exquisite harmony; an embodied reversal of all those negative spirals which afflict marriage, Ulster, all human life; it is Paradise Regained for six-and-a-half-minutes-out-of-time in the protected bubble of performance; a sign of hope that humans can not only conceive of, but, in concert together, can enact such perfection; one of the things that make it possible to wake up each morning with David Martin's view of 'the world as it is' and still find life worth living. Yet this little miracle is embedded in a piece of special pleading for the virtues of reason and restraint, couched in undistinguished verse.

Both the idea and the title came from Handel himself. He commissioned Jennens to compile a selection of Milton's *Allegro* and *Penseroso* poems which the new material in *Moderato* would unite 'in one Moral Design'.[17] The work was to demonstrate the moral superiority of a middle way between the emotional extremes of mirth and melancholy and call up the power of the human will and the virtues of reason and moderation to subdue excess and bring the mind into equilibrium. It is only one of a number of Handel's works which embody what Ruth Smith terms 'eighteenth-century moral psychology', the object of which was 'to assist listeners to the propitious ordering of their own lives'.[18] The eighteenth century was so convinced of music's special ability to 'lodge ideas in our hearts and minds'[19] that it would not have seemed any odder to Handel and his librettists to employ music as the medium of important philosophical ideas than to use it to convey religious belief. Nor would they have seen any incongruity in working on philosophical as well as religious material. Secularism and Enlightenment may have been identical twins in France but in Britain they were only rather distant cousins.

The Protestant establishment in the eighteenth-century Anglican Church was at its most latitudinarian. Its neglect, almost its

16. Eliot Gardiner, sleevenotes to CD of *L'Allegro*, p. 16.

17. Ruth Smith, *Handel's Oratorios and Eighteenth-Century Thought* (Cambridge: Cambridge University Press, 1995), p. 61. The phrase is Jennens's own from a letter to a friend about Handel's commission for *Il Moderato*.

18. Smith, *Handel's Oratorios*, pp. 61-62.

19. Smith, *Handel's Oratorios*, Chapter 3 'Music Morals and Religion'.

suppression of the doctrines of original sin and redemption through grace, had made room for an optimistic emphasis on ethical improvement through the application of Christian moral teachings. The Church had largely been assimilated to the Augustan vision of harmonious moderation and rational self-governance. The evangelical revival was, of course, a reaction against this complacent slippage at the doctrinal core of the Church. It was a movement of the 'warmed heart' which reasserted the reality of sin and the urgent need for salvation through a repentence which was met by divine grace. The fusion of Christian and Enlightenment ideas was never complete and even the deism which had appeared as the thin end of a secularizing wedge (and which Handel and his librettists quite explicitly combatted in some of the oratorios) failed to hold the fusion stable. Even so, there was a considerable and continuing affinity between Protestantism and the philosophy of reason in Britain. Even the development of an Anglican apologetic against both the secularist and evangelical tendencies was itself couched in the language and rhetoric of reason. Moreover, many of the hymns which found their way into the hymnbooks of both Anglicanism and Dissent at this time have carried forward into the nineteenth and twentieth centuries a layer of metaphors and assumptions which emerged from the eighteenth-century alliance of Enlightenment and religion, for example, all those familiar references to music as 'heavenly harmony' or the 'music of the spheres' which attest the perfect order of a benevolent creator.

It is more than likely that Jennens, and perhaps even Handel, was familiar with the ideas of Boethius, whose *Consolation of Philosophy* had been available in English ever since Chaucer first translated it. Boethius's theme—that the pursuit of wisdom and the love of God together form the true source of human happiness—was part of the deep structure of eighteenth-century thought: Boethius was highly esteemed by Dr Johnson, for example. Michael Prince, in his book on the British Enlightenment, quotes Boethius on the lessons to be drawn from the myth of Orpheus, the figure so often used as a condensed symbol of the power of music: 'This fable applies to all of you who seek to raise your minds to *sovereign day*. For whoever is conquered and turns his eyes to the pit of hell, looking into the inferno, loses all the excellence he has gained.'[20]

20. Michael Prince, *Philosophical Dialogue in the British Enlightenment: Theology, Aesthetics and the Novel* (Cambridge: Cambridge University Press, 1996), p. 9 (my

Although terms such as 'sovereign day', 'sovereign reason' and 'intellectual day' were commonplaces of the time, an echo of Boethius may well sound in Jennens's libretto for *Moderato*. Eighteenth-century optimism and equilibrium were dependent on not looking too hard or long into the abyss: David Martin, in this respect a true child of the original Methodist movement, persists in staring into the inferno, examining the pit of hell, rather than practising the blinkered vision which is the prerequisite of Augustan calm.

Yet the conceit used in *L'Allegro* and *Alexander's Feast*, as well as in the standard formula for baroque opera, involved ranging over extremes of emotion before restoring balance. Even Augustan good taste, which counselled against over-indulgence in these extremes, could not wholly eliminate the danger of finding oneself on the edge of an abyss of feeling. Indeed, it was Handel's capacity to convey deep feeling, especially religious feeling, including a profoundly tragic dimension, which made his music so popular with, and so accessible to, the heirs of the evangelical revival. The Handel/Jennens epigraph-cum-argument on the frontispiece of *Messiah* beginning 'Great is the Mystery of Godliness', as well as the choice of prophetic rather than wisdom sources for that work were, after all, a deliberate riposte to the rational latitudinarianism of the Church.[21] This strain in Handel is not confined to *Messiah* or *Jephtha*: John Eliot Gardiner hears significant traces of it in *Penseroso* and even *Moderato*.

> Both his experience of *the world as it is* and his complete mastery of technique enabled Handel to suggest in *Il Moderato* how precarious the curb of reason is—in the fluctuating chromaticism beneath the elegant exterior…and in the extreme cross rhythms…[22]

Where Jonathan Keates hears only the dawning light of reason in the duet, Eliot Gardiner, despite his description of it as the resolution of the mind's dualism, hears something else as well: 'It is not the victory of Reason but "the fumes that did the mind involve" which are evoked once more now, hinting at the complex of human passions and desires beneath the controlling surface of the will'.[23]

emphasis). I am indebted to my daughter, Jessica Martin, for drawing my attention to this book and to the particular quotation from Boethius.

21. Richard Luckett, *Handel's Messiah: A Celebration* (London: Gollanz, 1992), pp. 73-74.

22. Eliot Gardiner, sleevenotes to CD of *L'Allegro*, p. 16 (my emphasis).

23. Eliot Gardiner, sleevenotes to CD of *L'Allegro*, p. 16.

It is, of course, this double coding, the dangerous intensity and complexity glimpsed within the order and serenity, which makes the duet such a masterpiece, and one which, moreover, can still speak to modern sensibilities more attuned to Romantic intensity than to Augustan equilibrium. It is this doubleness that brings the proverbial lump to the throat, tears to the eyes: it is the reminders of brokenness within wholeness that crack the heart. In this the *Moderato* duet may even be the equal of other breathtaking moments such as the reconciliation of the Count and Countess at the end of Mozart's *Marriage of Figaro*, an exquisite instant which precisely through its delicacy presages all the inevitable further betrayals; or the final movement of Schubert's Piano Sonata in A major Deutsch 959 where the perfection of the simple theme stumbles and falters. The *Moderato* duet is not in the end a paean of praise to what is, sung and played by unflawed Houyhnhnms, but a vision of a state of blessedness that is lost almost as soon as glimpsed by poor wretched Yahoos who, nevertheless, have the grace to long for the transfiguration of their condition that it represents. But then, for all the optimism about the triumph of reason, the Enlightenment also had its Swifts and Voltaires making grim fun of the notion that 'What is, is best'. Rational optimism never had it all its own way even in its heyday.

I have, of course, been playing fast and loose with the hermeneutic problem in my response to this music. But not even Jonathan Keates can hear Handel through authentic eighteenth-century ears, and that is really the point. We hear and interpret this music through the filter of several subsequent artistic and intellectual developments, selectively and partially appropriated according to our knowledge, cultural exposure and experience. But what I have called the 'doubleness' is objectively there in the structure of the composition. Without in the least assuming that the interpretations I offer are David's own (though I know the duet moves him deeply) what I have tried to show is that certain meanings can emerge from it if it is placed in the context of a perspective such as David Martin's view of 'the world as it is' (the phrase also, as you will have noted, used by Eliot Gardiner about Handel's experience) even before any precise theological schema is introduced. (I refer only to secular examples of music for this reason.) The best of Handel always breaks free of the Augustan constraints, which is how he manages to keep one foot in the eighteenth century and the other in our own era.

The Augustan vision which animated *Il Moderato* ran out of plausibility a long while ago as the eighteenth-century ideal of the artist or philosopher as rational sage gave way to later conceptions of the hero, the revolutionary, the tormented genius or, latterly, the fragmented postmodern ironist. Certainly the twentieth century has emphatically rescinded Boethius's strictures about averting our gaze from the pit of hell. Yet the anachronistic values of the eighteenth century still remain as a sedimented deposit in many live cultural forms. They resonate in Handel's music and in the Methodism which partly embodied and partly opposed them, and both Handel and Methodism were important formative influences on David Martin. The structure of feeling associated with and moulded by this music and by the religious language he first experienced in the dissenting cultural ghetto, laid down powerful responses in the soul which confound precise coding as belief or intellectual conviction. What they create is a sensibility which rather like a coin has two equal sides: on the one face is stamped intensity of (religious) feeling (though the boundary between religious and non-religious feeling is highly permeable); and on the other face a delight in form, order and rationality. The *experienced* profundity of music and liturgical language structured around the same duality then becomes a continuing pulse or ground bass which sounds underneath whatever melody the rational mind may be singing at the time. There was a point in David Martin's early adulthood where he briefly managed a high degree of congruence between that almost-Augustan undertone and a Christian pacifism which believed that all that was necessary to bring in the kingdom of peace on earth was for human beings to live by Christian moral teachings. Once he recognized the radical disjunction between the coercive exigencies of 'normal' life and the virtuoso moral reversals of those exigencies in, say, the Sermon on the Mount, the congruence was lost and he was left with a comfortless view of 'the world as it is'. Yet music and the deep structure of feeling in which it was rooted remained an existentially potent reminder that a purely Machiavellian perspective leaves something vital out of the account. Man cannot live by sociology alone.

The doubleness I have discussed in relation to Handel's music and Augustan values teetering on the cusp of religious revival, is also, and not by accident, a persistent feature of David Martin's response to the world. He early learned that powerful ideas and strong feelings pack a double punch when they are expressed through—and just barely contained by—a medium of expression marked by formality, tight structure and elegant order. This combination is the most striking feature of his prose style, even—against the grain of a notably jargon-intoxicated discipline—of his sociological writing. It was one of the bases of his quarrel with the laid-back, antinomian 1960s and of his defence of the *Book of Common Prayer* and the King James Bible against linguistically one-dimensional modernizations. He inherited this double structure—emotionality and formality; religious feeling and rational argument—from the Methodism of his childhood, divided between on the one hand, the untutored emotional outpourings of his father's preaching and prayer, the 'big' emotional, but rhetorically skilful sermons and the massed choral music at Central Hall Westminster and, on the other hand, the high church Anglicanism of the Wesleys themselves and the rational prose of John Wesley's printed sermons (all of which he read) that had their counterparts in the high church Wesleyanism of the local chapel and the scholarly addresses regularly given there by members of London University's theology faculty.[24] This double inheritance gave him a taste for paradox and has been the ground of the creative tension which runs through all his work. It is also the key to understanding the way in which sociology and theology have always been two facets of the same enterprise. In his own account of the development of his thinking he writes:

> Being educated I sought good reasons for what I had already come to believe so that part of the original fascination of sociology arose because my faith was enquiring of my intellect. That in turn pushed me to make sense of Christianity itself, not as a set of propositions but as a repertoire of transforming signs in historic engagement with the deep structures of power and violence.[25]

This makes it clear that he never assumed there was any necessary enmity between faith and reason and that, as a consequence, he always saw sociology and theology as interacting discourses addressing a shared set of problems. A significant number of his published works explicitly weave sociology and theology together, notably *The Breaking*

24. At the beginning of the 1980s, after his parents' deaths, he was ordained deacon then priest in the Anglican Church, a return to a church the Wesleys had never intended to leave.

25. 'Personal Reflections', p. 23.

of the Image,[26] the collection of essays under the title *Reflections on Sociology and Theology* and *Does Christianity Cause War?* But even in the 'straight' sociology it is possible to identify certain themes which are also central to the theologico-social and socio-theological discussions. First, there are exposés of secularist ideology masquerading as disinterested science in so much sociology starting with his first critique of the concept of secularization.[27] Second, there is the reciprocal relationship between religious ideas and institutions and those 'deep structures of power and violence'. His *A General Theory of Secularization*[28] turns around the relations of church and state, centre and periphery, and the same central focus organizes his analysis of Pentecostal growth in Latin America as an instance of the worldwide rise of religious voluntarism and the decline of 'religious monopolies'.[29] The work on Latin America also shows his willingness to take Pentecostals' accounts of their religious ideas and experiences on their own terms rather than employing the implicitly secularizing sociological reductionism which has characterized so much of the sociology of religion.[30]

One of the more intriguing consequences of David Martin's tendency to run sociological and theological argument in tandem is the discomfort it often provokes in religious professionals and theologians, both because of its impertinent violation of the boundaries which are supposed to protect expert theological competence[31] and because of the often very hard sayings it has for religious professionals who attempt some engagement with the world. (It has to be said that the provocation has often been intentional.) Part of the problem lies in the ease with which fashionable nostrums have been

---

26. D.A. Martin, *The Breaking of the Image: A Sociology of Christian Theory and Practice* (Oxford: Basil Blackwell, 1980).

27. D.A. Martin, 'Towards Eliminating the Concept of Secularisation'.

28. D.A. Martin, *A General Theory of Secularization* (Oxford: Basil Blackwell, 1978).

29. D.A. Martin, *Tongues of Fire: The Explosion of Protestantism in Latin America* (Oxford: Basil Blackwell, 1990); *idem*, *Forbidden Revolutions: Pentecostalism in Latin America, Catholicism in Eastern Europe* (London: SPCK, 1996).

30. D.A. Martin and B. Martin, *Betterment from on High: Evangelical Lives in Chile and Brazil* (Oxford: Oxford University Press, forthcoming).

31. He was twice offered prestigious Chairs in Theology in British universities but turned them down on the (tongue in cheek) grounds that his only qualification was as a Methodist local preacher.

taken up out of the 'progressive' sociology of the 1960s and 1970s and more recently out of the postmodern ragbag of ideas, by clergy whose confidence in their function and status has been rattled by the apparently inexorable, creeping process of secularization in the Western (or, at least, the European) world. In its anxiety to demonstrate its cutting edge the church has sometimes used the social sciences disingenuously and David Martin tends to point this out. Partly, too, the trouble comes from his conception of theology not as the analysis of 'a set of propositions' but as a re-presentation of the Christian 'repertoire of transforming signs in historic engagement with the deep structures of power and violence'. Such an approach has an honourable place within theology—Reinhold Niebuhr is, after all, one of the main influences here—but in some theological quarters it is anathema precisely because it discards or by-passes the conception of theology as primarily a proposition-based discipline. Indeed, one of the most fashionable current developments in theology, that associated with the work of John Milbank, takes precisely the reverse position and explicitly rejects the social sciences and their empirical findings as irrelevant to theology proper, which it situates within the abstract territory of philosophical discourse. It is not, however, my object to discuss these disagreements about the nature of theology, or even to offer a theological critique of David Martin's work—I have not the competence to do either—but simply to clarify the relationship of David's particular practice of theology to his sociological work.

I argued at the outset of this essay that the problems to which he eventually sought answers in sociology were initially posed for him by theology as it encountered experience. In particular the agenda was set by his youthful attempt to use Christianity as a vision for transforming the secular city into the City of God where peace and harmony would prevail, a programme which foundered on the stubborn recalcitrance of 'the world'. In the introduction to *Reflections on Sociology and Theology* he sets out the connection between sociology and theology in a passage which shows that the terms of his engagement with sociology, including his focus on the power and violence at the heart of the social, came out of what he calls 'the basic elements of theological discourse'. The passage is also a good illustration of the style and tone of his argument.

Some of the basic elements dealt with by sociology overlap some of the basic elements of theological discourse. They both deal with land, city, exodus, exile, transition, entry, warfare, power, sacrifice and so on, but whereas sociology traces webs of connection theology reassembles these realities as a solid poetry concerned with imperatives of hope and necessary cost. These dramatic poles of hope and cost, vision and sacrifice draw into their scope all the resources of emblem and image, for example, the sacrificial lamb and the visionary lion, crossings through waters of death and waters of life, journeys through wildernesses of testing to delectable mountains, the grass that withers and the rose that never fades. The primary emblems of light and darkness correspond almost exactly to the underlying ground of everything—life and death, provided these are understood as complementary: the gift of life by a passage through death.[32]

Where his sociology systematically exposes the institutionalized, compacted and calculated consequences of power, violence and self-interest and the coercive exigencies of solidarity and generational continuity, David Martin's theology is, as he says, 'a solid poetry' of the Christian 'resources of emblem and image' which reverse these harsh realities—weakness for power, peace for war, unity for division, healing for hurt, life for death. It is the deployment of symbols and images piled up over many centuries and encrusted with accumulated meanings, expressed in a condensed, many-layered, emotionally saturated language which evokes rather than explicates and which operates with concrete imagery rather than abstractions. It turns around paradox or what I earlier called 'doubleness', particularly the fracture which brings wholeness, the powerlessness that becomes a new kind of power, the death that brings life, the Divine with a human face and, above all, the love that 'can only reverse the broken relation by paying the full cost in vulnerability'.[33]

Redemption is recognition: seeing again, noticing that which was always there for the first time. The restoration occurs at the point of deepest breakage. The image of man is redeemed as the image of God is marred: man is reunited to God in the moment of dereliction: 'My God, my God, why has thou forsaken me?' The split and the union are simultaneous.[34]

32. Martin, *Reflections on Sociology and Theology*, p. 14.
33. Martin, *The Breaking of the Image*, p. 75.
34. Martin, *The Breaking of the Image*, p. 76.

This may at first sight seem unassimilable by sociology. Not so. What he then does is to examine the ways in which this complex Christian vision of reversals has been inserted into real social space in historical time both by individuals and groups who have attempted in various ways to make 'the world' conform to the visionary blueprint and by the preservation and development of the images and symbols—in liturgy, architecture, art, music, poetry and so on and even in secular analogues—which then become the storehouse of the vision, ready for activation in those moments of turbulence and change which allow latency to be converted into action. The other half of the analysis perhaps most explicitly developed in *Does Christianity Cause War?* is the examination of how the vision is chronically subject to expropriation by those same structures of power, solidarity and continuity against which it has been raised up, so that the cross becomes the sword and the broken victim of realpolitik in first-century Palestine becomes the legitimating image of the earthly powers-that-be in the centuries after Constantine.

> So the earthly king will place his image on the mosaic next to the King of Kings and the Good Shepherd of Souls, and the humble Eucharist will be assimilated by the courtly cermonies of Constantine's empire... But only *partly*: that is crucial. The return of the old dispensation is not complete.[35]

Although social reality always pulls the Christian hope back to fit the contours of what-is-and-must-be, the precise consequences of these processes cannot be automatically read off from the generalized model of a chronic dynamic tension. As *A General Theory of Secularization* and *Does Christianity Cause War?* demonstrate, exactly how these expropriations operate in different times, places and social contexts needs detailed attention if the variety of patterns of secularization and/or communal warfare and civil strife are to make sociological sense. This particular dual use of theological and sociological insight has proved itself a powerful analytic procedure in strictly sociological terms: it is, in any case, deeply informed by the work of Max Weber, no stranger himself to that disciplinary cross-over and one of the few sociologists with whom David recognizes a close kinship.

The overall tendency of this way of perceiving the place of

---

35. Martin, *Does Christianity Cause War?*, p. 149.

Christianity in the world is somewhat sombre but far short of despairing.

> It is important to remember that the secular is not necessarily Babylon the Great, and not *merely* the arena of violence, power politics, confusion and blood-letting. There is a viable secular city, nurse of the sciences and arts and home of a proper civility. The Christian city is not an impossibility. Christianity itself inserts into the Christian city the knowledge that its promise is other than its performance. That is why the images of the Virgin and the statues of Christ crowning the city are so often clouded in a distinctively Christian irony.[36]

Elsewhere he adds at the end of a notably uncompromising two paragraph summary of 'how "the world" works', a brief coda that shows continuing if modest hope for rational intervention in social life: 'There *are* regulative principles of human reason also at work, except that our Christian accounts of them are often blandly philosophical and abstracted'.[37]

Both the ideals of eighteenth-century civility and the reflections of Max Weber on political engagement resonate here but so also do the arguments of St Augustine and of Richard Hooker. David Martin neither believes that Christians should be simply and without remainder 'conformed to the world', nor that they should withdraw from the world until and unless the full millennial hope is achieved. He believes with Augustine in the possibility of the just war and with Hooker in the church's duty to engage with society as an always flawed but necessary participant in the structures of authority and responsibility. Since the collapse of his pacifist idealism he has given up world-rejecting Christian absolutism in favour of an always precarious compromise with 'the world as it is' which requires the acceptance of that real responsibility for the self and others which is bound to leave the hands somewhat soiled. Christian irony is a very necessary component.

One correlate of this position is the view that those who are theologically and sociologically literate have a particular duty to count the real costs of asserting specific manifestations of the Christian vision. This is where his irritation with many representatives of the church—as well as theirs with him—arises. David has a highly

36. Martin, *Does Christianity Cause War?*, p. 150.
37. D.A. Martin, 'Christianity, the Church, War—and the W.C.C.', *Modern Believing* 40.1 (1999), pp. 22-34 (30).

developed empathy with those who, historically, have been absolutist in pursuit of the millennial hope, especially as so many of them have been sons and daughters of the periphery, but he has also observed the often devastating costs to themselves and others as well as the partial successes of their insertion of the Christian vision into secular history. The paradoxical legacy of cost and hope in these histories moves him deeply. What he finds hard to bear are absolutist gestures which are both costless and impotent. On his own analysis such gestures are to be expected from churches which have been pushed out of the power centre and into the privatized margins of social life where they are freed to say anything at all within the sounding box of their own debating chambers. Perhaps he finds it hard to be forgiving towards those he sees repeating the naivete of his own early self. At all events, some of his most savagely sardonic prose has been reserved for churchmen in comfortable circumstances who play at being prophets or who believe they can make a difference to how the world works by means of virtuous proclamation—proposals for liturgies to expurgate collective national guilt;[38] unrealistic rhetorics of ecumenical unity;[39] the persistent belief that modernized religious language will stem the haemorrhage from the pews;[40] the WCC proposal to declare illegitimate all use or threat of force in international relations.[41] He was even unable to resist a blast against windy ecclesiastical moralizing in the curious end-piece to *A General Theory of Secularization* under the provocative title 'When the Archepiscopal Trumpet Sounds'.[42]

What further fuels a Swiftian ire on many of these issues is the way in which discussions in church circles are so often hedged around by the trappings of piety in a way which makes the intrusion of serious sociological analysis a rude and crude violation of the unspoken norms of 'Christian' discourse. One of the unfortunate consequences of David's involvement in this kind of controversy is that because so

38. Martin, *Reflections on Sociology and Theology*, Chapter 13, 'A Socio-Theological Critique of Collective National Guilt'.

39. Martin, *Reflections on Sociology and Theology*, Chapter 9, 'The Limits and Politics of Ecumenism'.

40. D.A. Martin, *Crisis for Cranmer and King James* (*PN Review* 13 [1979]); David Martin and Peter Mullen (eds.), *No Alternative* (Oxford: Basil Blackwell, 1981).

41. Martin 'Christianity, the Church, War—and the W.C.C.'.

42. Martin, *A General Theory of Secularization*, pp. 306-308.

many of those whom he chides for sociological naivete and/or theological sloppiness are self-defined as radical, progressive or modernizing churchmen, he has been saddled with the wholly inappropriate
label of 'traditionalist'. But, as he would be the first to recognize, that
is how politics works everywhere. I have a sneaking sympathy with
many of his opponents who are, after all, victims of their own
thankless role, well-meaning folk on the side of the angels and the
poor who are simply woefully ignorant of, or wilfully blind to, the
social realities which make it so easy for them to speak out and so hard
for it to make any difference. Occasionally, perhaps, David forgets his
own assertions about the need for the church to keep alive its own
repertoire of signs of reversal, transcendence and transfiguration by
using it, even if the use is 'only' symbolic.

I give the penultimate word to the Archbishop of Wales who ends
his remarkably perceptive and generous review of *Does Christianity
Cause War?* with the following judgment:

> It is a deeply Augustinian perspective—both in its benign scepticism
> about what secular politics can achieve and in its refusal to take the easy
> path of confining Christian concern to the individual sphere.
> Occasionally the benign scepticism threatens to leave the church with
> little to do but shake its head over the radically different standards of
> secular politics…can't we say something about the practices in secular
> politics that tend to undermine the purported goals of such politics?
> that increase cynicism or apathy in a democracy? But the point is well-
> taken. The whole book is haunted, rightly, by the ease with which
> contemporary religiosity and its critics alike slip into a sentimental
> yearning for peace without cost and consciousness without history.
> Martin's alternative is sober, critical, tragic and hopeful; which gives it a
> good claim to be seriously Christian.[43]

And the final word I leave to David himself—all paradox and music
which is where I came in.

> The world upside down is held up before people as a potential (and
> 'held up' in the sense of restrained) by being made complementary to
> the world the right way up i.e. with authorities, boundaries, partitions,
> difference and power. That means we mostly overhear the Kingdom of
> Heaven sotto voce in the condensed poetic images of liturgy and
> scripture, or else in the sound of music and singing.[44]

---

43. Williams, review of *Does Christianity Cause War?*, p. 150.
44. Martin, 'Personal Reflections', p. 38.

Afterword

Andrew Walker and Martyn Percy

This book has been a particular kind of exercise, namely to pay tribute to one of the most significant British scholars in recent times in the field of the sociology of religion. David Martin's work is sociologically imaginative and innovative, and has enabled many to understand the larger historical scene in terms of its meaning for the inner life and the external career of a variety of individuals and groups. David's gentle and cautious liberalism has allowed him to align his sociological thought as part of what Nietzsche called 'the art of mistrust', in which one looks some distance beyond the commonly accepted or denied goals of human actions. In this sense, David Martin's work, in so many fields, provides not only clarity, but also wisdom.

Although we are now at the end of this volume, it is heartening to note that David Martin's work continues. Although we have grouped our contribution into perspectives on secularization and social theory, and then again on theology and sociology, his work is really much more extensive than these categorizations. Through his students and colleagues, and still by himself, David Martin's work will continue to touch many within the field of sociology, the churches and beyond. He has that unusual gift of being able to combine academic rigour with sincere accessibility.

The Editors, on behalf of the other contributors, and doubtless many others besides, would like to thank David again for his scholarship, collegiality, energy, humour and thoroughness. His hugely creative contribution to the sociology of religion and to both the study and practice of religion continues to enrich a vast and diverse field. Knowledge and insight in the social sciences are not uncommon. But wisdom is a far rarer commodity, and it is our evaluation that much of David Martin's work has offered this. In the study of the sociology of religion, it is the case that many who contribute do, in time, become part of the history of the discipline. It is our belief that David will have a special place in such a history. But more than that, his work continues to throw light on the future of the discipline, and offers significant ways forward in scholarship and dialogue.

The study of religion and society has been wonderfully enriched by David Martin, for which we and many others are profoundly grateful. If sociology is partly about a person's life taken out of the value given to them, then it is our hope that this volume has made some estimation of that value in regard to one of its most significant scholars.

David Martin's Life and Selected Publications

Born 1929: London, England
Richmond and East Sheen Grammar School: 1940–47
National Service: 1948–50
Westminster College of Education (Methodist): 1950–52
Diploma in Education, with Distinction: 1952
Primary School Teaching: 1952–59
External Degree London University: 1956–59

1959	BSc Sociology, First Class Honours
	Awarded the Annual University Studentship
1959–61	Postgraduate Studies, London School of Economics
1961–62	Assistant Lecturer, University of Sheffield
1962–67	Assistant Lecturer and Lecturer, London School of Economics
1964	PhD
1967	Reader, London School of Economics
1971–89	Professor, London School of Economics
	Emeritus, 1989–
1971–79	One of the four Academic Governors of London School of Economics
1971–73	Department Chair, London School of Economics
1975–83	President, International Conference of the Sociology of Religion
1983–85	Department Chair, London School of Economics
1986–90	Elizabeth Scurlock Professor of Human Values, Southern Methodist University, Dallas, Texas, USA
1987–	International Research Associate of the Institute for the Study of Economic Culture, Boston University, USA
1988–91	Visiting Professor, Department of Theology and Religious Studies, King's College, University of London
1990	Visiting Professor, Institute for the Study of Economic Culture, Boston University, USA
1992	Fellow, Westminster College, Oxford
1993–	Visiting Professor, Department of Theology and Religious Studies, Lancaster University
1999	Visiting Professor, Institute for the Study of Economic Culture, Boston University, USA
2000	Honorary DTheol, Helsinki University, Finland

Bodies, Memberships, etc.
Committee of Social Responsibility, Methodist Church, 1965–68
British Council Cultural Exchange, Bulgaria/Turkey, March–April 1967
Faith and Order Committee, Methodist Church, 1970–75
Combined Religious Advisory Committee, ITV and BBC, 1973–80
Member, London Society for the Study of Religion, 1975–92
Visiting Fellow, Japan Society for the Promotion of Science, 1978–79
Bloxham Project on Religious Education in Independent Schools, 1980–
United Kingdom Advisory Committee UNESCO, 1981–82
United Kingdom Editorial Advisory Committee of the *Encyclopaedia Britannica*, 1985–99
Co-President (with Conrad Russell), the United Kingdom Committee for University Autonomy, 1988–90
Section Editor, Religious Studies, *New International Encyclopedia of the Social Sciences*, 1998–2001

Church Roles
Lay Preacher, Methodist Church, 1953–79
Ordained Deacon, 1982
Honorary Assistant, Guildford Cathedral, 1982–
Ordained Priest, 1983

Guest Lectureships
St George's House, Windsor (Clergy in-service training), 1968–75
Guest Lecturer, Hebrew Reform Union College, Jerusalem (Centenary Celebration), 1983
Opening Lecturer, Scandinavian Peace Bureau Centenary Meetings, Helsinki, Finland, 1992
Distinguished Visiting Lecturer, University of Manitoba, Canada, Autumn, 1994

Public and Named Lectureships
Cadbury Lecturer, Birmingham University, 1973
Ferguson Lecturer, Manchester University, 1977
Lecturer in Pastoral Theology, Durham University, 1978
Gore Lecturer, Westminster Abbey, 1979
Select Preacher, University of Cambridge, 1979–80
Firth Lecturer, Nottingham University, 1980
Forwood Lecturer, Liverpool University, 1982–83
Bishop Prideaux Lecturer, University of Exeter, 1984
H. Paul Douglass Lecturer, Religious Research Society, Chicago, USA, 1984
Sir Robert Madgwick Lecturer, University of New England, Armidale, NSW, Australia, 1986
F.D. Maurice Lecturer, King's College, University of London, 1991
Sarum Lecturer, University of Oxford, 1994–95
Gunning Lecturer, University of Edinburgh, 1997
Hooker Lecturer, Exeter Cathedral, 1998

Publications

Books

Pacifism: An Historical and Sociological Study (London: Routledge & Kegan Paul, 1965; New York: Schocken Books, 1965).

A Sociology of English Religion (London: SCM Press [Hardback], 1967; Heinemann [Paperback], 1967; New York: Basic Books, 1967).

The Religious and the Secular (London: Routledge & Kegan Paul, 1969; New York: Schocken Books, 1969).

Tracts against the Times (London: Lutterworth Press, 1974).

A General Theory of Secularization (Oxford: Basil Blackwell, 1978).

The Dilemmas of Contemporary Religion (Oxford: Basil Blackwell, 1980).

The Breaking of the Image (Oxford: Basil Blackwell, 1980).

Divinity in a Grain of Bread: Short Studies in Eucharistic Theology (London: Lutterworth Press, 1989).

Tongues of Fire: The Explosion of Protestantism in Latin America (Oxford: Basil Blackwell, 1990).

The Forbidden Revolutions: Pentecostalism in Latin America and Catholicism in Eastern Europe (London: SPCK, 1996).

Reflections on Sociology and Theology (Oxford: Oxford University Press, 1996).

Does Christianity Cause War? (Oxford: Oxford University Press, 1997).

Edited Books or Co-edited Books

A Sociological Yearbook of Religion in Britain, I (London: SCM Press, 1968).

A Sociological Yearbook of Religion in Britain, II (London: SCM Press, 1969).

(with M. Hill) *A Sociological Yearbook of Religion in Britain*, III (London: SCM Press, 1970).

Anarchy and Culture: The Crisis in the Contemporary University (London: Routledge, 1969).

50 Key Words in Sociology (London: Lutterworth Press, 1970).

Crisis for Cranmer and King James (with editorial) *PN Review* 13 (November, 1979).

(with J. Orme Mills OP and W.S.F. Pickering) *Sociology and Theology: Alliance and Conflict* (Brighton: Harvester Press, 1980).

(with P. Mullen), *No Alternative: The Prayer Book Controversy* (Oxford: Basil Blackwell, 1981).

(with P. Mullen), *Unholy Warfare: The Church and the Bomb* (Oxford: Basil Blackwell, 1983).

(with P. Mullen), *Strange Gifts: A Guide to Charismatic Renewal* (Oxford: Basil Blackwell, 1984).

(with P. Heelas and P. Morris) *Religion and Postmodernity* (Oxford: Basil Blackwell, 1998).

Articles and Chapters in Books

The items listed below are mostly selected from some 250 academic articles, and arranged in broad categories of concern. Other items of a journalistic kind, such as regular reviews for the *Times Literary Supplement* over 30 years and a regular column in the *Times Higher Education Supplement* (1975–78) are simply omitted, though one or two pieces of an indeterminate character from *PN Review*, *Theology*, *Encounter* and other journals are included as specially relevant to a particular category. Articles later appearing in books are mostly excluded except where they offer a kind of marker where the earlier date might be significant.

Apart from academic work there is another kind of writing arising out of David Martin's involvement in two major controversies: the student movement of the 1960s with its associated cultural and educational mutations, and the issue of liturgical change. Out of dozens of articles, some in national newspapers, a few have been selected as giving an idea of the drift of the argument.

Secularization

'Towards Eliminating the Concept of Secularisation', in J. Gould (ed.), *Penguin Survey of the Social Sciences* (Harmondsworth: Penguin Books, 1965), pp. 169-82.

'Ends of Religions and the End of Religion', in H. Zinser (ed.), *Der Untergang von Religionen* (Berlin: Dietrich Reimer, 1985), pp. 309-19.

'Religion and Public Values: A Protestant–Catholic Contrast', *Review of Religious Research* 26.4 (1985), pp. 313-31.

'The Secularisation Issue: Prospect and Retrospect', *British Journal of Sociology* 42.3 (September 1991), pp. 465-73.

'Sociology, Religion and Secularisation' *Religion* 25.4 (1995), pp. 295-303.

'Europa und Amerika', in Otto Kallscheuer (ed.), *Das Europa der Religionen* (Frankfurt: S. Fischer, 1996), pp. 161-80.

'Remise en question de la theorie de la sécularisation', in G. Davie and D. Hervieu-Léger (eds), *Identités religieuses en Europe* (Paris: La Decouverte, 1996), pp. 25-42.

'Canada in Comparative Perspective', in D. Lyon and M. Van Die (eds.), *Rethinking Church, State and Modernity: Canada between Europe and America* (Toronto: University of Toronto Press, 2000), pp. 23-33.

War, Peace, Pacifism and Religion

'El Pacifismo y la Intelligentsia durante la "Guerra de Treinta anos" (1914–45)', *Revista Mexicana de Sociologia* 26.2 (1964), pp. 157-82.

'Christianity: Witness for Peace, Motive for Nationalism', *Crucible* (January–March 1995), pp. 5-13.

'Christianity, the Church, War and the W.C.C.', *Modern Believing* 40.1 (January 1999), pp. 22-33.

'Christianity: Converting and Converted', *Modern Believing* 41.1 (January 2000), pp. 13-21.

Evangelicalism, Pentecostalism

'Otro tipo de revolución cultural', *Estudios Publicos* 44 (Spring 1991), pp. 39-62.

'The Economic Fruits of the Spirit', in B. Berger (ed.), *The Culture of Entrepreneurship* (San Francisco: Institute of Contemporary Studies Press, 1991), pp. 73-84.

'The Evangelical Expansion South of the American Border', in E. Barker, J. Beckford and K. Dobbelaere (eds.), *Secularization, Rationalism and Sectarianism: Essays in Honour of B.R. Wilson* (Oxford: Clarendon Press, 1993), pp. 101-24.

'Evangelical and Charismatic Christianity in Latin America', in K. Poewe (ed.), *Charismatic Christianity as a Global Culture* (Columbia: University of South Carolina Press, 1994), pp. 73-86.

'Bedevilled' (Two Brazilian Case Studies), in R.K. Fenn and D. Capps (eds.), *On Losing the Soul* (Albany: State University of New York Press, 1995), pp. 39-68.

'Evangelical Religion and Capitalist Society in Chile', in R. Roberts (ed.), *Religion and the Transformations of Capitalism* (London: Routledge, 1995), pp. 215-27.

'The Global Evangelical Upsurge', in P. Berger (ed.), *The Desecularization of the World's Resurgent Religion and World Politics* (Grand Rapids: Eerdmans, 1999), pp. 37-49.

The Student Movement, the Universities, Education, Cultural Criticism

'Persons and Things: R.D. Laing's Experience of Politics', in M. Cranston (ed.), *The New Left* (London: Bodley Head, 1970), pp. 179-208.

'R.D. Laing's Family', *Encounter* (February 1972), pp. 71-76.

Two Critiques of Spontaneity (Welwyn Garden City: The Broadwater Press, 1973), (2 published lectures)

'Mutations: Religio-Political Crisis and the Collapse of Puritanism and Humanism', in P. Seabury (ed.), *Universities in the Western World* (New York: Free Press, 1975), pp. 85-97.

'Dr Adorno's Bag of Tricks' (A Disscussion of the Minima Moralia), *Encounter* (October 1976), pp. 167-83.

Sociology and Theology: Sociology and the Church

'The Status of the Human Person in the Behavioural Sciences', in R. Preston (ed.), *Technology and Social Justice* (Geneva: World Council of Churches, 1971), pp. 237-65.

'The Sociological Mode and the Theological Vocabulary', in D. Martin, W.S.F. Pickering and J. Orme-Mills OP (eds.), *Sociology and Theology* (Brighton: Harvester Press, 1980).

'Comparing Different Maps of the Same Grounds', in A. Peacocke (ed.), *The Sciences and Theology in the Twentieth Century* (Notre Dame: University of Notre Dame Press, 1981), pp. 229-40.

'Collective National Guilt: A Socio-Theological Critique', in A. Walker and L. Osborn (eds.), *Harmful Religion* (London: SPCK, 1997), pp. 144-62.

'Christian Foundations, Sociological Fundamentals', in L. Francis (ed.), *Sociology, Theology and the Curriculum* (London: Cassell, 1999), pp. 1-49.

'Sociology and the Church of England', in L. Voyé and J. Billiet (eds.), *Sociology and Religions* (Leuven: Leuven University Press, 1999), pp. 131-38.

'The Language of Christianity', *Expository Times* 112.1 (October 2000), pp. 12-15.

Liturgical Issues and Music

'The Sound of England' (A Disscussion of English Music) *PN Review* 5.4 (1978), pp. 7-10.

'Music and Health with a Key to Harmony', in D. Moberg (ed.), *Spiritual Wellbeing: Social Perspectives* (Washington: University Press of America, 1979), pp. 205-14.

'Religion and Music: Ambivalance towards the Aesthetic', *Religion* 14 (July 1984), pp. 269-92.

'The Recovery of the Real Handel', *Times Higher Education Supplement* (21 December 1984), p. 16.

'Marginalization and Restoration', in M. Perham (ed.), *Model and Inspiration: The Prayer Book Tradition Today* (London: SPCK, 1993), pp. 24-28.

(with Grace Davie) 'Liturgy and Music', in T. Walter (ed.), *The Mourning for Diana* (Oxford: Berg, 1999), pp. 187-98.

'The Stripping of the Words: Conflict over the Eucharist in the Episcopal Church', *Modern Theology* 15.2 (1999), pp. 247-62; repr. in S. Beckwith (ed.), *Catholicism and Catholicity* (Oxford: Basil Blackwell, 1999), pp. 135-50.

Religion and Politics

'Ethical Comment and Political Decision', in G. Dunstan (ed.), *Duty and Discernment* (London: SCM Press, 1974), pp. 123-29.

'The Issue of "Revivalism" as it Has Been Articulated in Christian Cultures', in *Culture, religion, politique et la reconstruction du Liban* (Beirut: La Mouvement Culturel Antélias, 1985), pp. 34-44.

'The Warring Peripheries: Lebanon', in R. Cipriani and M.I. Maciotti (eds.), *Omaggio a Ferrarotti* (Rome: Siares, 1988), pp. 413-24.

'The Religious Politics of Two Rival Peripheries: Northern Ireland', in L.V. Greenfeld and Michel Martin (eds.), *Center: Ideas and Institutions* (Festschrift for Edward Shils; Chicago: University of Chicago Press, 1989), pp. 29-42.

'L'Autonomie de la religion à l'égard de la politique', in F. Alvarez-Pereyre and F. Blanchetiére (eds.), *La Politique et le Religieux* (Jerusalem: Peeters, 1995), pp. 343-52.

Sociology of Religion

'The Denomination', *British Journal of Sociology* 13.1 (March 1962), pp. 1-14.

'The Sociology of Religion: A Case of Status Deprivation?', *British Journal of Sociology* 17.4 (December 1966), pp. 353-59.

'England', in H. Mol (ed.), *Western Religion: A Country by Country Sociological Survey* (The Hague: Mouton, 1972), pp. 228-47.

'The Prospects for Non-Scientific Belief and Ideology', in G. Suffert (ed.), *Les Terreurs de L'An 2000* (Paris: Hachette, 1976), pp. 215-16.

'Revived Dogma and New Cult', in M. Douglas and S. Tipton (eds.), *Religion in America* (Boston: Beacon Press, 1983), pp. 111-29.

'Christianity and Secular Modernity', in H. Chadwick and G. Evans (eds.), *Atlas of the Christian Church* (Oxford: Equinox, 1987), pp. 262-69.

'General Theoretical Essay', in T. Gannon SJ (ed.), *Catholicism in Transition* (London: Macmillan, 1988), pp. 3-35.

'The Fall of Rome: Today's Catholic Predicament', *Religion* 24.2 (1994), pp. 95-102.

'Religion in Contemporary Europe', in J. Fulton and P. Gee (eds.), *Religion in Contemporary Europe* (Lewiston, NY: Edwin Mellen Press, 1994), pp. 1-16.

'Unitarianism. A Space in England for Rational Religion and Social Enlightenment', *Social Compass* 44.2 (1997), pp. 207-16.

'Personal Reflections in the Mirror of Halévy and Weber', in R.K. Fenn (ed.), *The Blackwell Companion to the Sociology of Religion* (Oxford: Basil Blackwell, 2001).

Forthcoming (Books)

The World their Parish: Pentecostalism as Cultural Revolution and Global Option (Oxford: Basil Blackwell, 2001).

(with B. Martin), *Betterment from on High: Pentecostal Lives in Chile and Brazil* (Oxford: Oxford University Press, 2002).

Approaches to a Socio-Theology and a Sacred Geography Transformations and Deformations: Meditations on Christian Theology

Forthcoming (Articles, Chapters)

'Peter Berger: An Appreciation', in L. Woodhead and P. Heelas (eds.), *Peter Berger on Religion* (Oxford: Basil Blackwell, 2001).

'On Secularization and its Prediction', in G. Davie and L. Woodhead (eds.), *Predicting Religion* (Aldershot: Ashgate, 2001).

'Changing Your Holy Ground: An Ecology of Sacred and Secular in Cities of the Centre and the Periphery', in S. Barton (ed.), *Holiness Past and Present* (Edinburgh: T. & T. Clark, 2001).

'The Global Expansion of Pentecostalism', in D. Lewis (ed.), *Evangelical Expansion in the Twentieth Century in the Non-Western World* (Grand Rapids: Eerdmanns, 2002).

'Religion, War and Peace', *The International Encyclopedia of the Social Sciences* (Oxford: Elsevier, 2002).

INDEX OF NAMES

Carleton College Library
One North College Street
Northfield, MN 55057-4097